Black
Autobiography
in America

Stephen Butterfield

University of Massachusetts Press

Amherst 1974

Black
Autobiography
in America

Grateful acknowledgment is made to the following publishers for permission to reprint copyrighted material.
Bantam Books, Inc. for excerpts from *Soledad Brother: The Prison Letters of George Jackson*: Copyright © 1970 by World Entertainers Limited. Published by Coward, McCann & Geoghegan, Inc. and Bantam Books, Inc. Reprinted by permission of Bantam Books, Inc. All rights reserved.
Dell Publishing Co., Inc. for excerpts from *Die Nigger Die* by H. Rap Brown, copyright © 1969 by Lynne Brown; and for excerpts from *Search for the New Land* by Julius Lester, copyright © 1969 by Julius Lester; and for excerpts from *Coming of Age in Mississippi* by Anne Moody, copyright © 1968 by Anne Moody.
Grove Press, Inc. for excerpts from *The Autobiography of Malcolm X* by Malcolm X with the assistance of Alex Haley, reprinted by permission of Grove Press, Inc. Copyright © 1964 by Malcolm X, with the assistance of Alex Haley.
Harper & Row, Publishers, Inc. for excerpts (about 1100 words) from pp. 164, 215, 25, 155, 176, 181, 186–87 in *Black Boy* (Perennial Edition) by Richard Wright. Copyright 1937, 1942, 1944, 1945 by Richard Wright. By permission of Harper & Row, Publishers, Inc.
McGraw-Hill Book Company for excerpts from *Soul on Ice* by Eldridge Cleaver. Copyright © 1968 by Eldridge Cleaver. Used with permission of McGraw-Hill Book Company.
Random House, Inc. for excerpts from *I Know Why the Caged Bird Sings* by Maya Angelou, copyright © 1969 by Maya Angelou; and for excerpts from *Seize the Time* by Bobby Seale, copyright © 1968, 1969, 1970 by Bobby Seale.

We have been made the floor mat of the world, but the world has yet to see what can be done by men of our nature, by men who have walked the path of disparity, of regression, of abortion, and yet come out whole. There will be a special page in the book of life for the men who have crawled back from the grave. This page will tell of utter defeat, ruin, passivity, and subjection in one breath, and in the next, over-whelming victory and fulfillment.
—George Jackson

Contents

Introduction

Georgian Orwell's image of the future in *1984* was of a boot stamping on a human face forever. He could have used the same image to represent the Negro past in America, fitting the boot easily to the foot of slave-trader, overseer, master, policeman, soldier, vigilante, capitalist, and politician. But a full portrait of this image drains the terror from his warning; for if the future is to resemble the past at all, then the human face will triumph over the boot. This is the message, the total subjective impression, of black American autobiographical writing. In black autobiography, the wounds on the human face heal to defiant scars; the eyes take on the glint of pride and awareness; the mouth sets in determination; the humanity blooms under the pressure of the boot into a fierce, tough flower, whose blossom tells us that until people are altogether emptied of every quality which distinguishes them from mere implements, there will always be a limit to how many times the foot can strike before it is left behind by a bloody stump.

The genre of autobiography lives in the two worlds of history and literature, objective fact and subjective awareness. It is a dialectic between what you wish to become and what society has determined you are. In response to a particular historical period, the autobiographer examines, interprets, and creates the importance of his life. He may also affect history by leaving the work behind as a model for other lives. Autobiography asserts, therefore, that human life has or can be made to have meaning, that our actions count for something worth being remembered, that we are conscious agents of time, that we not only drift on the current of our circumstances but we fish in the stream and change the direction of its flow.

Any good autobiography does two things for the reader: affirms his potential worth, and calls his realization of that worth into question by telling a true story of someone who has traveled a different path. Black autobiography does these two things for our whole civilization. Black writers offer a model of the self which is different from white models, created in response to a different perception of history and revealing divergent, often completely opposite meanings to human actions. These meanings are accessible to Western man, because they are molded and articulated in response to his society, framed and to a certain extent distorted by his language and culture. They challenge us to consider, among other things, whether a judge has any rights which a defendant is bound to respect.

The Western "self," the concept of identity that dominates most well-known white personal narratives since the Renaissance, is the individual forging a career, a reputation, a business, or a family out of the raw material of his neighbors. Other people are rungs on the ladder of his success or reflections of his greatness. If he makes it to the top, his story, like Benjamin Franklin's, is a kind of manual of how to achieve power, wealth, and fame; or, like Norman Mailer's and Benvenuto Cellini's, a continual affirmation of how much he deserves them. The spiritual journals of white mystics, such as George Fox and Thomas Merton, are exceptions to this rule; and white autobiography since the nineteenth century—notably in the *Diary of Anais Nin*, the journals of Baudelaire, the *Confessions of an English Opium Eater*, and, to a lesser extent, the *Education of Henry Adams*—tends to depict the self as a rebel, an isolated maverick at odds with the direction of his society. Although he may not consume his fellow men as objects to reinforce his ego, he is still driven back on the subjective resources that sustain him as an individual: "pure" aesthetic or religious experience, private imagination, nostalgia for medievalism. That great work has resulted from the concept of the apotheosized private self, and its tragic mask, the alienated rebel, is not denied. It is assumed, rather, that the white West is at a crossroads, that we must learn to "love each other or die," to discover and respect our neighbor, to create mass movements that will dismantle or totally remake all the institutions of society designed for purely private interest groups, and to break the hold of the few over resources desperately needed by the many. At such a time, the Western private self comes to be felt as a hardening skin that must be split and shed.

The "self" of black autobiography, on the whole, taking into

account the effect of Western culture on the Afro-American, is not
an individual with a private career, but a soldier in a long, historic
march toward Canaan. The self is conceived as a member of an
oppressed social group, with ties and responsibilities to the other
members. It is a conscious political identity, drawing sustenance
from the past experience of the group, giving back the iron of
its endurance fashioned into armor and weapons for the use of the
next generation of fighters. The autobiographical form is one of
the ways that black Americans have asserted their right to live and
grow. It is a bid for freedom, a beak of hope cracking the shell of
slavery and exploitation. It is also an attempt to communicate to
the white world what whites have done to them. The appeal of
black autobiographies is in their political awareness, their empathy
for suffering, their ability to break down the division of "I" and
"you," their knowledge of oppression and discovery of ways to cope
with that experience, and their sense of shared life, shared triumph,
and communal responsibility. The self belongs to the people, and
the people find a voice in the self.

There are white American writers who have broken the bonds
of Renaissance individualism, who have realized that the concept
of the isolate self oppresses them too, and who have achieved a more
meaningful humanity in personal narrative; and in early colonial
journals, in the writings of William Bradford and Cotton Mather,
the personal voice is animated by social mission and the dream
of the New Jerusalem. But in black autobiography, the unity of
the personal and the mass voice remains a dominant tradition. It
was never torn apart by the engine of industrialism, or starved by
the long and persistent practice, legalized, institutionalized, and
sanctified, of stealing land and converting other people's lives into
capital. Resistance to the enslaver's boot forced it to grow strong
and supple.

Black autobiographies are also a mirror of white deeds. They fill
in many of the blanks of America's self-knowledge. They help
us to see what has been left out of the picture of our national life
by white writers and critics, how our critical judgment has been
limited, indeed, crippled, by a blind spot toward Afro-American
culture. Most importantly, they are an inspiration and a conscience.
To read closely what they have to say, to allow their message entry
into the bloodstream and vital nerve centers, is to look the monster

of slavery and racism full in the face, to confront it nakedly, without the shield of interpretation by white historians. Knowledge of the sins of the fathers is a terrible burden for the children of pirates, murderers, kidnappers, rapists, for the children of those who received the benefits of stolen labor and genocide and closed their eyes, perhaps with a humanitarian shudder, to its effects. These children must somehow, now, find a way to cast off the fathers' legacy of evil if they dare to dream of a New Land for themselves. The price of ignoring it is to smother the intelligence, with all the consequences this reaction implies: to become divorced from one's humanity, to reduce oneself to a thing, a consumer, a machine for generating or appropriating surplus value, an obstacle to the growth of others. But, as so many black autobiographies demonstrate, one is never required to remain a thing. The humanity won by the slave and his descendants belongs to humanity everywhere. The door of the white prison is opened, not closed, by his story. If the very worst effects of oppression have been unable to wipe out intelligence, compassion, honor, faith, hope, and the courage to resist in the mass of its black victims, then these qualities are preserved for all, including the children of the ruling culture. The slave's victory is the victory of the best in ourselves.

The present work is an exploration of black autobiographical writing in America from the 1830s to 1972. Our purpose is to read the books closely, to evaluate their importance, to trace the development of the genre over a period of time, to discuss the books as embodiments of the black American experience, to relate them where possible to the literature of the white mainstream. We focus specifically on the complex relationships between viewpoint, identity, audience, motive, occasion, and use of language in each book. The analysis of style involves any resource tapped by the writer in his dialogue and prose, such as the arrangement of clauses, phrases, sentences, and larger speech units, levels and types of diction, grammatical usage, cadence, stress and repetition patterns, puns, verbal irony, imagery, metaphor, allegory, and figures of speech. It is essential to relate these works to the overall matrix of Afro-American politics, culture, and history in order to understand the achievement of the literature. A blend of textual, biographical, and sociological critical approaches are used, according to what each work seems to require for the fullest appreciation.

The principle of selection has been to include as many works as possible within the scope of a short study that are powerful in their own right or that reveal an important historical trend. Literary merit has been the chief, but not the only, criterion. Figures who made a large impact on black history are discussed even when their autobiographies have scant appeal as literature. Indeed, the question of "literary merit" itself is reexamined by the method of discussing works in their social and political context; it is argued that the context of a work, especially the values of the author, help to determine its merit. Some autobiographies that would be covered in a comprehensive history have been overlooked here, but enough are included to show the range and depth of the form.

Availability of editions has influenced the choice somewhat; for example, of the hundreds of slave narratives that might have been covered, those actually chosen tend to be from among recent reprints. Availability is of course affected by demand in the market place, and demand is not necessarily an index of merit. The market for a black autobiography expands and contracts according to a combination of political circumstances. Demand is built into American society by the fact that the black writer comes from a minority group, goes through a different kind of social wringer, and has a special story to tell; but the market can be neutralized precisely because the special nature of the story threatens those who benefit from racist institutions. Major publishers usually have shown interest in black stories only when race became a national issue and the political struggles of black people could not be ignored. The autobiographies tend to be clustered around such periods: e.g., the 1840s and '50s, during the height of the abolitionist movement; the 1920s and '30s, during the "Harlem Renaissance," the organization of the CIO, and the zenith of the Communist party; or the 1960s and '70s, during the great urban rebellions and the emergence of Black Power.

Even when social unrest creates the demand, however, political decisions determine which books will go to market and which ones will go in the rejection basket. Other factors being equal, a company's decision to popularize, say, *Yes I Can*, by Sammy Davis Jr., and reject *Here I Stand*, by Paul Robeson, has little to do with either demand or merit. A critic has no choice, therefore, but to rely on his own biases, unless he wants to rely on the biases of others; since the work which has "stood the test of time" may have done so for the wrong reasons. Accordingly, we examine several books that are generally neglected (at one time neglect was the fate of all black literature) but that contribute much to the genre and to our understanding of American history.

The particular bias behind this study is evident in the treatment of the material. Revolutionary narratives are considered more worthwhile than middle-class success stories, not merely because they are revolutionary, but also because they are usually better written and their insight is more profound. In any case, it would not be possible to deal with black autobiography as a sequence of loyal accolades to free enterprise. The main burden of the black writer, regardless of his class origins, has been to repair the damage inflicted on him by white racism, rend the veil of white definitions that misrepresent him to himself and the world, create a new identity, and turn the light of knowledge on the system that holds him down. It takes a certain kind of bias to appreciate such light.

In dealing with some black autobiographies, particularly in the period of slavery, one must take into consideration the hand of the white "ghost writer." A large portion of the slave narratives were directed or actually written by whites, as, for example, the original *Confessions of Nat Turner*, Mattie Griffiths' *Autobiography of a Female Slave*, and Solomon Northup's *Twelve Years a Slave*. The works included here are primarily those subscribed "written by himself" or "written by his own hand" after the name of the author; but it is often difficult, and indeed unimportant, to distinguish between the two categories, due to the fact that the slave narrators generally imitated the popular styles of their time even when they had no assistance. When we come to the *Autobiography of Malcolm X*, which was set down by Alex Haley, we need only consult Malcolm's speeches to see that we are getting his authentic voice in the writing.

The material is divided into three time periods that correspond roughly to stages in the evolution of black political and cultural expression. The slavery period focuses primarily on the last two decades before the Civil War, when the slave narratives came to full maturity and most of their authors were taking prominent roles in the antislavery crusade. The works that fall between 1900 and

1961, the great age of Du Bois and Wright, are covered in a single section. Although it is recognized that this span is a more complex and variegated epoch, the autobiographies do have several features in common which distinguish them as belonging to another period: they are more literary and introspective, the styles are sharply individualized, and the identity more alienated, not only from white America, but from other blacks. After 1961, the form shows a resurgence of political purpose and a trend toward more colloquial language.

Many characteristic black modes of thought, feeling, and expression run through all periods almost unchanged. Taken together, they lend the work a quality of energy, a striving to overcome inward contradictions that is perhaps best described as the tension of reclaiming the human face from the distorted shape of the mask. This tension propels the best works with an incandescent power. We shall look closely at how it is embodied in specific passages.

Part one

The Slave-narrative Period
ca. 1831-1898

Baptism

Into the furnace let me go alone;
Stay you without in terror of the heat.
I will go naked in—for thus 'tis sweet—
Into the weird depths of the hottest zone.
I will not quiver in the frailest bone,
You will not note a flicker of defeat;
My heart shall tremble not its fate to meet,
My mouth give utterance to any moan.
The yawning oven spits forth fiery spears;
Red aspish tongues shout wordlessly my name.
Desire destroys, consumes my mortal fears,
Transforming me into a shape of flame.
I will come out, back to your world of tears,
A stronger soul within a finer frame.
—Claude McKay

Chapter 1 *The stronger soul*
Point of view in the slave narratives

THE slave narrative reached the full peak of its strength during the twenty or so years before the fall of slavery. When the "peculiar institution" was most repressive, seeking to expand into the territories and acquire ever more control over federal policy, is the time when the best of the slave narrators came forth to write stories on paper as vivid as the ones engraved on their backs.

They give us eyewitness accounts of the furnace of misery in the Old South that supplied raw materials for the Industrial Revolution. Taking into consideration the differences between "kind" and "cruel" masters, and between aspects of the system that varied from state to state, these early autobiographies sought to assemble a weight of evidence against slavery that would crush it in every aspect before the court of world opinion. The lives reflected in them were consumed to fuel the factories of capitalism. The used-up bodies could be tossed into the compost of slavery's "bargain basements," where Negroes too old to work in the fields had their hair blacked to make them look younger and were sold at inflated prices to customers unaware of the cheat. Or, if no market existed for them, they might be turned out to starve in the woods, or literally thrown in the garbage can; more than one writer describes seeing a slave murdered in broad daylight before witnesses, and his body left in the gutter to be picked up by the trash collection the next day. The kindly treated slaves were the most pathetic of all if a change in the price of cotton put them suddenly on the auction block. The narrators were among those thousands who resisted, who escaped from the "yawning oven," protected from the heat by the angel of revolutionary purpose. Often they clung to survival under the worst imaginable conditions. They had no rights whatever that could not be violated at any time according to their master's discretion. Their standard of living was sometimes below that of the cows and chickens they were classified with, and a smile at the wrong time or a word of discontent might suddenly escalate into a beating that would leave them crippled for life. Most of them experienced the full range of slavery's horrors: they were torn from their families, underclothed, overworked, whipped, sold, starved, chained, tortured, made to watch atrocities against loved ones, sexually assaulted, hunted by dogs, deceived and betrayed under all kinds of circumstances by whites from every social class. They won their way to freedom past slave catchers and patrol teams, and then wrote as a means of fighting back against their enemies.[1]

More indirect forms of oppression awaited them in the North, forms that could not be shaken off by knocking down an overseer or running away, and that were no less rooted in the whole organization of society. They were frequently barred from practicing skilled trades, not allowed to use hotels, go to museums, travel on public conveyances, attend white churches, and they were denied legal redress for attacks on person and property. The whole repressive energies of the slave system had been devoted to keeping them ignorant and fearful, and they had to discover some means within themselves to free their minds as well as their bodies from this legacy. Even in the antislavery movement, they were often urged into mere support roles for white activists and discouraged from developing their own powers of speech and thought. The slave narratives fight these forms of oppression too, testifying to the mental capacities of the slave, arguing tirelessly for his humanity, answering over and over the same shallow, contemptible rationalizations for slavery, demanding equal treatment for black people in all areas of public life, and wrestling with the mental devils of self-doubt and despair. And little by little, book by book, they construct the framework of black American literature. Autobiography in their hands became so powerful, so convincing a testimony of human resource, intelligence, endurance, and love in the face of tyranny, that, in a sense, it sets the tone for most subsequent black American writing.

The audience of the narratives was largely white. They went through numerous editions in the North, being sold at antislavery meetings, lectures, bookstalls, churches, and by subscription. Often they not only paid for themselves, but provided funds to support the abolitionist cause. We shall see in chapter three that the style and tone are usually managed with the response of the white reader in mind. The fact that many narrators find it necessary to justify incidents in which slaves lie and steal implies that they are defining themselves in terms of how they expect whites to judge them. For as they point out themselves, black people generally stole from their masters whenever they had the opportunity; it would have been superfluous to argue to a black reader that this behavior was morally justified.

The language also assumes a literate audience before whom the writer must prove that slaves have the intelligence and ambition to profit by freedom. The market grew for their testimony as the question of slavery set the nation's political climate on fire. This market may have been exploited by white ghostwriters and some free Negroes who misrepresented themselves as hunted fugitives, but the genuine accounts rose to the demand with missionary fervor. Their object was to condemn the system from a moral standpoint, using—and practicing—the values that sincere patriots and Christians are supposed to esteem. As a true exponent of such values, the slave could therefore claim the rights that attend them.

The narrators develop their values in the process of resisting slavery. Calcined in the heat of its furnace, they were the frame of the "stronger soul" that the authors carried forth into the fight for liberation. On the surface, they are close to the values of white Protestant America. Most of the narratives embrace the work ethic, for example, despite the fact that slaves were stereotyped by whites as lazy and had no reason, given the conditions, to work for their masters any more than was necessary to avoid punishment.

Work is a moral good in the *Narrative* of the Reverend Noah Davis, a former slave who became pastor of the Saratoga Street African Baptist Chapel in Baltimore in the 1850s. His book was sold explicitly to raise funds for his church; and, being located in a slave state, he would not have wanted to alienate very many white readers. But his gratitude to his overseer contains no hint of irony; he thanks the "pious lady" for teaching him precision and competence:

> I have often wished, when I have been seeking homes for
> my children, that I could find one like Mrs. Wright. She
> would spare no pains to teach her servants how she wanted

her work done; and then she would spare no pains to make them do it. I have often looked back, with feelings of gratitude and veneration, to that pious lady, for her untiring perseverance in training me up in the way I should go.[2]

For Josiah Henson, who eventually became manager of his master's plantation, work is a means to compete successfully with his fellow slaves and advance his personal career:

Julius Caesar never aspired and plotted for the imperial crown more ambitiously than did I to out-hoe, out-reap, out-husk, out-dance, out-everything every competitor....[3]

Samuel Ringgold Ward transformed the work ethic into a source of racial pride, a special quality of blackness that will enable the Negro people to throw off their rulers and surpass them in achievement. Ward was pastor of a white church in New York, one of the most prominent speakers in the antislavery movement and advocate of militant resistance to slavery. In his view, blacks are far from being lazy drones on the ambitious white hive; the truth is the other way around. He prophesies that, because whites "are given almost solely to the acquisition of money and the pursuit of pleasure," in the future

they will become less and less active, more and more lethargic, while in their very midst the blacks will become less lethargic and more energetic....[4]

In other slave narratives work is a long, painstaking road to the Promised Land, full of unexpected pitfalls and washouts. Many authors took on extra duties for years in order to buy their freedom, often to be cheated out of it in the end. Moses Grandy bought himself and his wife and son by hiring out his labor on his time off.[5] Frederick Douglass worked long hours in shipyards whenever there was the slightest chance that he could thereby bring himself closer to an independent life, although he was under the immediate threat of beatings from white co-workers.[6]

In all cases, work is seen as a partial solution to the problems slavery creates for the slave. It may advance the narrator within the system or buy his way out of it; it is indispensable for any kind of life he may lead as a free man; it may be a religious value, an act of piety, not so much to advance the toiler on earth as to give him a place in Heaven; or, in the case of Ward, it takes on a kind of proto–black-nationalist importance, coloring in white and black the contrast between the energetic producers of wealth and the effete, pleasure-seeking owners.

Most slave narratives are strongly Christian. Evangelists of freedom, the authors praise God, prayer, good works, and the anti-slavery cause and denounce all forms of sin, especially drinking, swearing, lying, stealing, fornication, and breaking the Sabbath. They are careful to distinguish between "true" Christianity and the religion used by their masters to justify the slave system and teach them obedience. Slavery itself is the most enormous sin, both because it is an intrinsic evil and because it forces a whole range of other sins on the people caught in its coils. It leads the master into the temptation of committing any kind of outrage on his slaves; it tempts the slave to murder and mayhem against the master; it has no respect for the marriage relation and thus en-courages fornication; and the masters do not allow the slaves to practice true religion and meet freely for worship.

According to the *Narrative* of Henry Bibb, a fugitive who re-turned to the South after his escape and liberated his entire family, slaves were deliberately urged on their time off to "gamble, fight, get drunk, and break the Sabbath."[7] Noah Davis describes his training "to bring liquor among the men with such secrecy as to prevent the boss ... from knowing it" as part of the "wickedness" to which he was routinely exposed (N. Davis, p. 15). And Frederick Douglass penetrates incisively to the political motive of the master in being generous with his liquor stores on slave holidays:

> Thus, when the slave asks for virtuous freedom, the
> cunning slaveholder ... cheats him with a dose of vicious
> dissipation, artfully labelled with the name of liberty....
> We felt, and very properly, too, that we had almost
> as well be slaves to man as to rum. So, when the holidays
> ended, we staggered up from the filth of our wallowing,
> took a long breath, and marched to the field,—feeling,
> upon the whole, rather glad to go, from what our master
> had deceived us into a belief was freedom, back to the
> arms of slavery (Douglass, *Narrative*, p. 85).

Typically, Christian doctrine brings coherence into the life of the former slave, so that he may find a new identity he can take pride in. Christianity is a path to salvation from economic and spiritual bondage that has been perverted by slaveholders and can be restored to its original purity by the fugitive. The enormity of the sin of slaveholding explains to the white reader why slaves depart from "Christian" morality in such matters as stealing and telling lies to whites.

Accosted by whites in his flight to freedom, J. W. C. Pennington, the minister who performed Frederick Douglass's first wedding ceremony, concludes that "the facts in this case are my private property. These men have no more right to them than a highway robber has to my purse." He then proceeds to identify himself as an escapee from a coffle stricken by smallpox, a lie worthy of Huckleberry Finn at his best, and he is allowed to go on his way unmolested, with a hasty send-off by the patrol.[8] But unable to escape the sense of sin of having to lie his way to freedom, Pennington turns his action into an argument to condemn slavery because of its responsibility for the sins of the slave:

> The history of that day has never ceased to inspire me
> with a deeper hatred of slavery; I never recur to it but
> with the most intense horror at a system which can put a
> man not only in peril of liberty, limb, and life itself,
> but which may even send him in haste to the bar of
> God with a lie upon his lips (Pennington, p. 30).

Samuel Ward, William and Ellen Craft, Frederick Douglass, and John Thompson, somewhat less squeamish about being found impure at the bar of God, all describe with pride and humor the incidents in which they successfully resisted tyranny by resorting to deceit. William and Ellen Craft were two house servants in Georgia who overheard their master and mistress discussing plans to sell them. They fled all the way to Philadelphia by train and steamer, Ellen passing as a white man and pretending to be her husband's owner. The deceit becomes an occasion for some well-managed irony at the expense of their fellow passengers:

> My master's new friend also gave him his card, and
> requested him the next time he travelled that way to do

him the kindness to call, adding, "I shall be pleased
to see you, and so will my daughters." Mr. Johnson [Ellen
Craft] expressed his gratitude for the proffered hospi-
tality, and said he should feel glad to call on his return.
I have not the slightest doubt that he will fulfill the
promise whenever that return takes place.[9]

To Douglass, the crime of slavery is so unspeakable that anything
the slave does to increase the discomfiture of the slaveholder is a
positive virtue and should be applauded. Henry Bibb offers in
the following passage a more standard justification for stealing from
the master:

But I well knew that I was regarded as property, and
so was the ass; and I thought if one piece of property took
off with another, there could be no law violated in the
act; no more sin committed in this than if one jackass
had rode off another (Bibb, p. 122).

Dishonesty in one's relations with other black people, however,
is considered genuinely immoral. When it occurs, such as on
the two occasions when Henry Bibb was betrayed to slave catchers
by Negroes, it is reported with bitter irony and unequivocally
condemned. Its motive is generally to escape punishment. One
of the few examples in which deceit toward a fellow slave seems to
be regarded on the same moral basis as deceit toward a white
man is in the narrative of William Wells Brown, where he describes
being sent to the local jail to be whipped and tricking a passing
Negro into taking his place.[10]

The moral assumptions of the slave narrative, then, include
temperance, honesty, worship of God and Christ, and respect for
hard work. To the extent that they are shared in the same form by
whites, the black autobiographer uses them to expose the difference
between the white man's precept and his practice. The slave
narrators never tire of pointing out that precisely those masters
who do nothing themselves squeeze the most work out of their
slaves; precisely those who mouth the most Christian platitudes are
likely to underfeed, whip, sell, and otherwise oppress their human
chattel the worst.

What makes these moral assumptions different from those of

white America are the purpose they serve and the way they are practiced. Temperance is a defense against one of the chief means of the master to disillusion the slave with freedom. Honesty is a form of solidarity between members of an oppressed group who are not obliged to be honest toward their oppressors. Hard work is something that has the potential of liberating the slave and building a new life for him, that entitles him to run away from his master, and that may eventually enable his achievements to sur-pass those of the whites. Worship of God and Christ is a means of ideological struggle against the contemptible Christianity of the slaveholder and the guilt feelings incurred by the slave when he disobeys or violates his master's laws. It is also a means of bolstering his own courage to resist by assuring him that God is on his side, and of organizing his new life as a free man after he escapes. In addition, it supplies him with arguments for the abolitionist cause. Each of these moral values serves a direct purpose arising from the experience of being enslaved and black.

The identity of the slave narrator grows around his desire for freedom. The act of resistance is the backbone of his selfhood, and his opinions, goals, politics, dreams, and accomplishments extend from that act like the bones of an embryo, like a new heaven and earth from the words "let there be light." In the literature of the master culture, specifically in the stories of Edgar Allan Poe, characters are given a precise individuality through their class, lineage, address, life-style, or set of tastes. M. Ernest Valdemar is a well-known compiler of the "Bibliotheca Forensica" and resides principally at Harlem, N.Y. since 1839. Roderick Usher, attached to and defined by his house, the last scion of an ancient family, totters under the burden of centuries of heredity. Montresor acts out his coat of arms on Fortunato when his ego is offended. Ligeia triumphs over death through the assertion of her aristocratic husband's individual will. The opposite is true of the slave nar-rator. Again and again we discover in the first few pages of his account that he begins with nothing: he is uncertain of his exact age, he has no name of his own or his name changes whenever he is sold, he cannot trace his family much further back than his mother, and he is punished whenever he shows the slightest aspira-tion to become more than a piece of property.

To estimate the sad state of a slave child, you must look
at it as a helpless human being thrown upon the world
without the benefit of its natural guardians. It is thrown
into the world without a social circle to flee to for hope,
shelter, comfort, or instruction. (Pennington, p. 2).

"Your name is Platt—you answer my description. Why
don't you come forward?" he demanded of me, in an
angry tone.

I informed him that was not my name; that I had
never been called by it, but that I had no objection to it
as I knew of.

"Well, I will learn you your name," said he; "and so
you won't forget it either, by ———," he added.[11]

I don't know where any of my other four children are,
nor whether they be dead or alive. It will be very difficult
to find them out: for the names of slaves are commonly
changed with every change of master: they usually bear
the name of the master to whom they belong at the
time: they have no family name of their own by which
they can be traced (Grandy, p. 1).

I do not remember to have ever met a slave who could
tell of his birthday. . . . I was not allowed to make any
inquiries of my master concerning it. He deemed all such
inquiries on the part of a slave improper and impertinent,
and evidence of a restless spirit (Douglass, *Narrative*,
p. 21).

Richard Wright, in *Black Boy*, had wondered if "clean, positive
tenderness, love, honor, loyalty, and the capacity to remember
were native with man," or if they "were not fostered, won, struggled and suffered for, preserved in ritual from one generation to
another."[12] The slave narratives had not only to foster and preserve
these human qualities, but prove that black people were capable
of them. The movement of the narrative itself is away from the
limbo of anonymity, toward definite goals and values other than
those of the slaveholder. What the writer struggles to achieve is
self-definition and self-respect, a life where clean, positive tender-

ness, love, honor, loyalty, and coherent tradition are possible, life as a free and equal human being belonging to a free social group, and the destruction of the system of society that prevents him from realizing his dream. His identity consists of all these things together. In constructing that identity, he must overcome the obstacles which slavery puts in his way, the most elemental of which is physical force.

The most common method of dealing with force is by means of guile. William and Ellen Craft's account indicates the relationship between guile and identity. To avoid punishment, the slave has to learn to wear a mask, to seem as if he fits the owner's concept of "the nigger." At the same time he has an identity of his own that must be hidden, because it is a threat to the slave system. In effect, he maintains a double identity and shifts between the two according to the occasion. The pretense kept up by the Crafts during their journey, one partner passing for white and the other attempting to play the role of "his" faithful servant, while both have a life entirely invisible to the passengers around them, is a perfect metaphor to convey the psychology of double identity found in a large number of black autobiographies. Poe, Melville, Gogol, Conrad, and many others have explored the symbolism of the mask, but here it is real; the symbol is contained in the reality rather than the other way around. If the mask slips, the author does not suffer an existential crisis, but arrest, capture, whipping, and possibly death. The influence of the split identity experience continues far beyond this period, offering a partial explanation for the predilection toward irony and satire in black writing.

When guile and double identity were not sufficient, the slave could resort to violent resistance. Meeting force with force, striking down the oppressor and refusing to succumb to beatings, is a persistent motif in the outlook of the slave narrators. It is as much a standard pattern of their stories as the punishments and forced sales which provoke it. Often it is the crisis that impels them to escape and the crucial turning point in their quest for an identity. The difference in the way resistance is treated from book to book is primarily in the extent to which the author approves of it in print. The more pacifistic authors, such as Pennington, use the violence of the slave merely as evidence to condemn slavery, whereas the more militant ones, such as Ward and Douglass, advocate violent resistance as a virtue because it earns the respect of the oppressor and forces him to back down.

William Wells Brown, a fugitive who later became the first Negro American novelist, reports sympathetically an incident in which a slave who had never allowed anyone to whip him beat his overseer and several companions in an effort to resist punishment. The slave was later subdued (W. W. Brown, pp. 18–20). A similar incident appears in the *Life of John Thompson*, where a slave named Ben, struck by his overseer's whip handle,

> sprang from the ground, seized his antagonist by the throat with one hand, while he felled him to the ground with the other; then jumping upon his breast, he commenced choking and beating him at the same time, until he had nearly killed him. . . . For a while the discomfited man was senseless, his face became of the blackness of his hat, while the blood streamed down his face.[13]

Unlike the slave in Brown's account, however, Ben, although he was later lashed "until his entrails could be seen moving within his body," keeps his spirit and remains obdurate. After his recovery he is never bothered a third time. The submerged pun on the "blackness" of the overseer's choked face springs from the narrator's awareness of the irony in his material: to be black is to be beaten, but in this case the tables are turned, and to be beaten is to become black. Thompson makes this pun a second time in a passage where he is the subject:

> I tried to explain the reason of my delay, but he would not listen, and continued beating me. At last I caught hold of the stick, wrenched it from his hands, struck him over the head, and knocked him down, after which I choked him until he was as black as I am (ibid., p. 54).

The resistance in the narrative of Solomon Northup is carried out by himself, more than once, against an overseer who finally forces him to hide in a swamp. After refusing an order to strip, Northup takes the lash away from his adversary, throws him to the ground, and beats him "until my right arm ached." Again, acting out successfully the urge to turn the tables on the oppressor is an occasion for irony:

> At length he screamed—cried murder—and at last the
> blasphemous tyrant called on God for mercy. But he who
> had never shown mercy did not receive it (Northup,
> pp. 110–11).

The beauty of the irony in this passage is the reversal, not only of
the oppressor's role, but of his use of religion to support that role.
The context of Northup's enslavement would make this resistance
seem long overdue and thoroughly justified to all but a firm
proslavery audience. Northup was a free Negro in New York who
was kidnapped, smuggled South to New Orleans, renamed "Platt,"
and sold to a Louisiana plantation. He spent twelve years in the
deep South before he could be traced.

In the *Narrative* of Moses Grandy, the refusing to bow to the
excessive work demands of the master and the complaining of the
food allowance—actions which are charged with the possibility of
violence—result in better conditions for all the slaves (Grandy, p.
19). Samuel Ward states that

> he who would have enslaved me would have "caught a
> Tartar": for my peace principles never extended so
> far as to *either seek or accept peace at the expense of
> liberty*—if, indeed, a state of slavery can by any possibility
> be a state of peace (Ward, p. 12).

But it is Frederick Douglass who most fully expresses the moral
and psychological importance to the slave of violent resistance. His
ability to articulate what is only an undercurrent in the other
works is essentially a literary skill, and it will be dealt with in the
chapter devoted to Douglass as a literary artist. Here it may be
noted that the beating he gave to his worst overseer "revived . . . a
sense of my own manhood. It recalled the departed self-confidence,
and inspired me again with a determination to be free" (Douglass,
Narrative, p. 82). He adds that it was nothing less than a resurrection of his spirit, a discovery that he was not afraid to die; and once
having made that discovery, he had achieved his identity as a
free man; that is, he had developed goals that could never be reconciled with those of the master and was determined to act on them
regardless of the price.

The militance of the slave narrator is related to what he expects and desires from his white audience. Noah Davis conceives of freedom as something to be earned from the whites by convincing them through his actions that he does not conform to their stereotype of the Negro: he is ambitious, honest, trustworthy, religious, and competent. Therefore he deserves the freedom and respect which is theirs to award as a merit badge. Samuel Ward, on the other hand, has no faith that the equality of black people will ever come through American whites; it must be fought for and taken by blacks, with the assistance of God and Europe. His attitude toward the white world, therefore, is not to ask for sympathy, but to demand his rights:

> What the Negro needs is, what belongs to him—what has been ruthlessly torn from him—and what is, by consent of a despotic democracy and a Christless religion, withholden from him, guiltily, perseveringly. When he shall have that restored, he can acquire *pity* enough, and all the sympathy he needs, cheap wares as they are; but to ask for them instead of his rights was never my calling (ibid., pp. 86–87).

Ward's basic outlook and identity are racial. He is an early advocate of black entrepreneurship as a defense of the dignity and freedom of black people. He has no confidence in the will of American whites to achieve racial justice, so his solution is for blacks to build an economic power base of their own.

> Then I saw, that the *chief*, almost the *only* business of the Negro, is to be a man of business. Let him be planter, merchant, anything by which he may make his impressions as a business man. . . . Then, when such devoted men of business as Mr. Cunard have before them the question of treading under foot some Negro, they will conclude differently (ibid., p. 233).

The class values which he assumes are essentially bourgeois. The whites whom he respects are educated, refined, wealthy. Racial discrimination, or "Negro-hate," he explains by reference to the class background of the racists:

> The early settlers in many parts of America were the very
> lowest of the English population: the same class will
> abuse a Negro in England or Ireland now.... Also, the
> best friends the Negro has in America are persons gen-
> erally of the superior classes, and of the best origin
> (ibid., p. 40).

For the Irish, who have a history of oppression comparable to the
record of the Negro, and who, at the time Ward wrote, had not
recovered from the abject desperation of the potato famine, he has
only sentiments of profound contempt. Confronted with a situation
in which the white poor of Ireland could arrive in New York and
New England, shoulder aside the black poor of America, and steal
the black man's opportunities because they were white,[14] Ward's
defense is to apply the moral assumptions of capitalism to the
immigrants: class exploitation through the system of wage labor
permits the ambitious and energetic to rise to a better class by their
own efforts; therefore poverty among "free" people is the fault
of the poor.

Many narratives do make blatant and melodramatic appeals to
white pity, and piety, but they usually appear side by side with
images of defiance. The political purpose of the author is to portray
the misery of slavery's victims while at the same time humanizing
and dignifying them. Pity without respect reduces the slave to the
level of mistreated cows and dogs, with the implication that a
reform movement such as the SPCA, to soften the worst "abuses" of
the system, would be more to the point than abolition.

Douglass has faith in those whites who are engaged in antislavery
politics, and, like Wells Brown and Thompson, in Quakers and
other groups who shelter fugitive slaves; but he appeals to their
sense of justice and revolutionary indignation rather than their
pity. Freedom in his view is still something which should be taken
by blacks, if necessary through force. Defiance reminds white
America of its own revolutionary traditions and of the common
yearning for liberty in both white and black. Defiance makes it
difficult even for the slaveholder to cling to the myth of Negro
inferiority.

> The doctrine that submission to violence is the best cure
> for violence did not hold good as between slaves and

overseers. He was whipped oftener who was whipped easiest. That slave who had the courage to stand up for himself against the overseer, although he might have many hard stripes at first, became while legally a slave virtually a free man. "You can shoot me," said a slave to Rigby Hopkins, "but you can't whip me," and the result was he was neither whipped nor shot.[15]

Physical resistance is a movement away from brutalization toward freedom of the spirit. The moment that he resists, the slave is free from the master's definition of him.

Education is an equally important movement toward an image of the self and the world different from that given by the master, and toward the possibilities offered by life as a free man. But because any kind of education except work instructions, as Douglass points out, makes a man unfit to be a slave, it is something which also has to be struggled for at every step along the way.

> I have already said that it is forbidden by law to teach colored persons to read or write (Grandy, p. 36).

> As my friend poured light into my mind, I saw the darkness; it amazed and grieved me beyond description. Sometimes I sank down under the load, and became discouraged, and dared not hope that I could ever succeed in acquiring knowledge enough to make me happy, or useful to my fellow-beings (Pennington, p. 44).

> One day in the year 1830, I picked up a piece of old newspaper containing the speech of J. Q. Adams, in the U. S. Senate, upon a petition of the ladies of Massachusetts, praying for the abolition of slavery in the District of Columbia. . . . While reading this speech, my heart leaped with joy. I spent many Sabbaths alone in the woods, meditating upon it. I then found out that there was a place where the negro was regarded as a man, and not as a brute . . . (Thompson, pp. 37–38).

> The work of instructing my dear fellow slaves was the sweetest engagement with which I was ever blessed. . . . Every moment they spent in that school, they were liable

> to be taken up, and given thirty-nine lashes. . . . They
> had been shut up in mental darkness. I taught them,
> because it was the delight of my soul to be doing something
> that looked like bettering the condition of my race
> (Douglass, *Narrative*, p. 90).

Learning to read and write, in these passages, is a revolutionary act, for which one may be whipped or perhaps killed. For Thompson, Pennington, Davis, and Bibb, it is part of the process of achieving an identity as a devout Christian; for all of them, it opens doors that lead away from the plantation and introduces them to the abolitionist movement. Every step toward education gives the lie to the white world's concept of Negro inferiority and helps to safeguard the freedom of each fugitive by advancing the progress of black people as a whole.

Moreover, it is usually the slave himself, or one of his parents, who is the teacher; sometimes it is a Quaker, abolitionist, or renegade white; very seldom does the slave's first introduction to letters come through the master or any member of his household. Literacy, like every other step toward freedom, is not something which is given by "kind" or "enlightened" masters, but seized as a battle prize by rebellious slaves.[16] The initial fruits of knowledge are profound bitterness and discontent; but these feelings are wind to the flame of creation, waking a fierce glint of humanity in the eyes of the chattel.

Other militant black political literature of the time juxtaposes the same two themes: the threat of violent resistance and the necessity for black people to get an education so that they can take their place in American society on the same footing as whites. Violent resistance is defended ideologically by reference to the traditions of the American Revolution. David Walker, for example, in his *Appeal* of 1829, which antedates Ward by a generation, argues that

> It is no more harm for you to kill a man, who is trying to
> kill you, than it is for you to take a drink of water when
> thirsty; in fact, the man who will stand still and let another
> murder him, is worse than an infidel.[17]

On the subject of education, Walker writes that he would

> . . . crawl on my hands and knees through mud and mire,
> to the feet of a learned man, where I would sit and
> humbly supplicate him to instil into me, that which
> neither devils nor tyrants could remove, only with my
> life—for colored people to acquire learning in this coun-
> try, makes tyrants quake and tremble on their sandy
> foundation (ibid., p. 44).

The sense of restless movement toward clearly defined goals is a
pattern that characterizes this whole period in black literature.
The geographical movement of the fugitive from South to North
is the structural spine, the definitive feature of the slave narrative
as a genre. It involves ruse, pursuit, suspense, confrontation,
disguise and double identity, retreat and attack, escape, capture,
and renewed escape. On this level the problems are basic: finding
food and shelter, eluding pursuers, deceiving strangers, and cover-
ing distance in the shortest possible time. The goal is immediate
and simple: to get to a free state. Afterward both problems and
goals become more complex, but are clarified by using the flight as
a conscious metaphor for the fugitive's personal and social movement from anonymity to identity, from self-contempt to self-
respect, from ignorance to enlightment, and from sin to salvation.

> For freedom, like eternal life, is precious, and a true man
> will risk every power of body or mind to escape the
> snares of satan, and secure an everlasting rest at the
> right hand of God (Thompson, p. 143).

> . . . my attention was seriously drawn to the fact that I
> was a lost sinner, and a slave to Satan; and soon I saw that
> I must make another escape from another tyrant
> (Pennington, p. 52).

> To my father, mother, brothers, and sisters. . . .
> Dearly Beloved in Bonds:
> About seventeen long years have now rolled away,
> since in the Providence of Almighty God, I left your em-
> braces, and set out upon a daring adventure in search of

freedom. Since that time, I have felt most severely the
loss of the sun and moon and eleven stars from my social
sky. . . . And you have doubtless had your troubles and
anxious seasons also about your fugitive star (ibid., p. 74).

In describing himself to his family as a "fugitive star," Pennington implies an association with the North Star, the night guide
of the runaway slave. The image suggests that he is offering himself
as a guide to bring the rest of his family out of bondage. In view
of his role as a minister and teacher, bringing the gospel to his
brethren, the kind of "guiding" he had in mind was probably
educational and spiritual; but he would never have thought of these
as separated from more tangible kinds.

Both Pennington and Thompson relate winning their moral
identities in images of movement and flight, which are drawn from
their experience as real fugitives. Like the other slave narrators,
they are aware that they are not moving alone. Their goals must
be won on three levels: freedom of the body, freedom of the mind
and spirit, and freedom for the whole Negro people. The metaphor
of flight applied to the quest for identity helps to tie these levels
together.

Because the narrators identify and are identified with the Negro
people, the struggle for abolition and equal rights is an extension
of the quest for personal freedom. The three levels merge easily
into one. We have already seen how an advance in learning by a
single Negro helps to combat the racist ideology which rationalizes
the oppression of the entire group. Aside from the fact that many
of these writers, like Douglass, Ward, and Pennington, became
teachers in turn and passed on their knowledge to other black
people, even the private success of one slave breaks laws that applied
to all. The slave narrators are therefore conscious of speaking for
"all" to the white world. They are black abolitionist former slaves,
articulating the experience of slavery in order to hasten its down-
fall. In addition, they fight the slavery principle in the North by
doing battle against racial discrimination in any form. This is a
fundamental aspect of their identity. What it means in terms of how
they construct their autobiographies is that they become historians
and polemicists. They feel free to range over the whole subject
of race relations and antislavery politics. Their personal careers

merge so closely with the political movement that relating the story of their lives is a political act.

> These men [abolitionists] have the right view of the subject. They see that in every case where the relation between master and slave is broken, slavery is weakened, and that every coloured man elevated, becomes a step in the ladder upon which his whole people are to ascend (ibid., p. xv).

> I shall be understood, I hope, then, if I include the chief facts of my life, whether in the editorial chair, in the pulpit, on the platform, pleading for this cause or that, in my anti-slavery labours. God helping me wherever I shall be, at home, abroad, on land or sea, in public or private walks, as a man, a Christian, especially as a *black man*, my labours must be anti-slavery labours, because mine must be an anti-slavery life (Ward, p. 43).

There is no sharp distinction of form, content, or general purpose between the agitational pamphlet, of which Walker's is an example, and the autobiography. William and Ellen Craft quote extensively from the laws of Louisiana, South Carolina, and Georgia in order to give the reader a better idea of what they were running away from, thus relating their personal story to the history of law (Craft and Craft, pp. 277–78).

The slave narrator does not always construct his political identity on the basis of race alone. Class loyalty and perspective often cut across racial lines. Because slavery was a form of class, as well as racial, oppression, the struggle of black people for freedom was both racial and class in character. Consequently, slave narrators and black leaders generally were also sympathetic toward the feminist movement, the European working class, and poor American whites. Pennington makes a connection between abolitionism and the European revolutions of 1848:

> During the last year or two, we have heard of nothing but revolutions and the enlargements of the eras of freedom, on both sides of the Atlantic. Our white brethren everywhere are reaching out their hands to grasp more freedom (Pennington, p. xi).

William Wells Brown becomes a profeminist when a white woman persuades her husband to give him shelter on his journey to the North:

> She asked him [the husband] two or three times to get out
> of the way, and let me in. But as he did not move, she
> pushed him on one side, bidding me walk in! I was never
> before so glad to see a woman push a man aside! Ever
> since that act, I have been in favor of "woman's rights!"
> (W. W. Brown, p. 108)

And Henry Bibb, distinguishing between social classes among whites in the South, implies a common interest between black people and nonslaveholding whites who are themselves impoverished by the system:

> It is true, that the slaveholder, and non-slaveholder, are
> living under the same laws in the same State. But the
> one is rich, the other is poor; one is educated, the other is
> uneducated; one has houses, land, and influence, the
> other has none. This being the case, that class of the
> non-slaveholders would be glad to see slavery abolished,
> but they dare not speak it aloud (Bibb, p. 25).

Class loyalties on the part of black writers and political activists could lead in a bourgeois direction too, as we have seen in the *Autobiography* of Ward; but the antislavery stance is the starting point in every case.

The identities of the slave narrators, then, like their values, are constructed in response to the needs forced on them by class and racial oppression. These needs are both personal and political: to throw off the ideology of the oppressor, neutralize the guilt incurred by resistance, acquire enough knowledge and skills to live as a free man, build pride and self-confidence, and escape from the master's reach; to further the cause of abolition, defend the gains made by other fugitive slaves, increase the economic power of black people, and sway white public opinion against slavery and racial discrimination. The fact that they are writing for white audiences may explain in part why their values are similar to those of the white cultural mainstream; but, unlike the "native" of Fanon's analysis in *The Wretched of the Earth* and *Studies in a*

Dying Colonialism, the Afro-American was a transportee, a forced immigrant on a foreign soil with a shattered tribal culture, living within the colonizing power as a minority group. It would have been almost impossible, given these differences, for the slaves to maintain wholly separate selves, even after the catharsis and resurrection of total life-or-death resistance to the master. What they did was reinterpret the mainstream culture to fit black needs. Education is part of the struggle against slavery; violent resistance is a defense against being "well broken," or psychologically emasculated; restless, energetic movement carries the fugitive on toward freedom.

All these autobiographies share a sense of purpose and direction which is not found again in black literature until the 1960s. The problems of the writer's life are gigantic in sheer criminal brutality, but they are clear and immediate, and their solutions obvious. Until the slave's arrival in the North, the only mask hiding the face of the oppressor is the flimsy Christianity put on to indoctrinate the slaves. Abolitionism is the obvious direction for continued resistance once the narrator arrives on free soil; his reasons for writing and his confidence in what he has to say are never subjects of uncertainty or doubt. As time passed, his faith in the ultimate destruction of the slave system was only strengthened by the sharpening division of the country.

Chapter 2 *The shape of flame*
Language and the slave experience

SLAVE-NARRATIVE rhetoric stems largely from the writer's Christian perspective and involvement in abolitionist politics. Sermons, direct contact with the facts of slavery, and the religious culture of Afro-America compose the main black influences on the choice of language. The white influences came from the Bible and other Christian literature, editorials in abolitionist newspapers, Websterian and Garrisonian oratory, the expectations of the white reading public, and the antithetical prose style inherited from eighteenth-century England. Some of the stylistic devices of this period have all but disappeared; others have ripened into modes of expression that are now characteristic of black political writing. The concrete diction, ironic humor, understatement, polemics, and epithet that we recognize in contemporary black essayists all appear first in the slave narrative. Although black writers in the slavery period wrote according to the standards of English and American whites and imitated the style of their white models, at the same time they initiated traditions that were developed and refined by their descendants into something distinctly "black."

There are some exceptions to the rule that diction and syntax were derived from white models. Occasionally we find idioms that sound as if they might be derived from the speech of the narrator's own background:

> I got into a fair way of buying myself again (Grandy, p. 16).

> ... when he was present, it was cut and slash—knock down and drag out (W. W. Brown, p. 21).

Henry Bibb, who at one point was sold to Indians, describes an Indian dance as though he were speaking aloud:

Their dress for the dance was most generally a great
bunch of bird feathers, coon tails, or something of the
kind stuck in their heads, and a great many shells tied
about their legs to rattle while dancing. Their manner of
dancing is taking hold of each others hands and forming
a ring around the large fire in the centre, and go stomp-
ing around it until they would get drunk or their
heads would get to swimming, and then they would go
off and drink, and another set come on (Bibb, p. 154).

And Thompson includes idioms from his experience as a sailor on a
whaling vessel:

He ordered me back, but I, being homeward bound, and
under full sail, thought best not to 'bout ship . . .
(Thompson, p. 44).

Some authors also go out of their way to imitate dialect when they
reconstruct the speech of their characters:

Say, brudder, way you come from, and which side you
goin day wid dat ar little don up buckra? (Craft and Craft,
p. 300)

Jake, I is gwine to wip you today, as I did dem toder boys.[1]

Although the syntax of slave narratives is usually formal and
periodic, it is possible to find paragraphs of loose, rhythmic prose,
where the order of clauses approximates modern usage. We are
most likely to encounter them in minor works which are otherwise
uninteresting as literature, such as the autobiography of James
Mars:

They hitched up the parson's team, put on board what
few things he had and his family, in the still of a dark
night, for it was very dark, and started for Norfolk, and
on the way we run afoul of a man's wood-pile, for it was
so dark he could not see the road.
. . . The beguilers were both, I do not say preachers, but
they were both deceivers, and he talked so smooth to
mother that he beguiled her.[2]

Here the clauses, arranged in simple order of subject and verb, are linked together by "and" and "for"; the tense of "run" in the first quotation is colloquial; there is very little subordination and no attempt to build expectation through the use of antitheses or items arranged in a progressive series. Key words in the narrative are repeated to create mood ("in the still of a dark night . . . for it was very dark . . . so dark, etc."). Just as in oral dialogue, the author interrupts himself in midsentence to qualify the thought and relies on repetition and emphasis to amplify material rather than additional images or complexity of phrasing.

What helps to account for this simplicity and looseness of syntax is that the *Life of James Mars* appeared several years after the peak of the slave narrative period, and was written for his own family; it was not part of a political movement, and the writer therefore was under no sense of obligation to impress white readers or sway public opinion.

The language of more typical slave narratives, though far from idiomatic and colloquial, is close to the material facts of experience. The slave narrator's political role requires the use of description, detail, and concrete language. He is called upon, as part of his activity in the antislavery movement, to supply first-hand information about slavery from the victim's point of view. What it was like to pick cotton and tobacco, how often and for what offenses the slaves were whipped, their standard of living, the duties expected of them, what took place during a slave auction—these and others were questions which might be in the mind of a reader unfamiliar with the slave system, and to which the slave narrative gave specific answers.

> At noon the cart appeared with our breakfast. It was in large trays, and was set on the ground. There was bread, of which a piece was cut off for each person; then there was small hominy boiled, that is, Indian-corn, ground in the hand-mill, and besides this two herrings for each of the men and women, and one for each of the children. Our drink was the water in the ditches, whatever might be its state . . . (Grandy, p. 17).

> When the tobacco is ripe, or nearly so, there are frequently worms in it, about two inches long, and as large as

one's thumb. They have horns, and are called tobacco worms. They are very destructive to the tobacco crop, and must be carefully picked off by the hands, so as not to break the leaves, which are very easily broken. But careful as the slaves may be, they cannot well avoid leaving some of these worms on the plants. It was a custom of Mr. Wager to follow after the slaves, to see if he could find any left, and if so, to compel the person in whose row they were found, to eat them. This was done to render them more careful (Thompson, p. 18).

There is in many narratives a preoccupation, amounting at times almost to an obsession, with the whips, paddles, spiked collars, chains, gags, cowhides, and cages used to control the slaves. We see the South as a vast torture chamber, the memories of the instruments of torture seared indelibly into the narrator's brain, as though this tireless enumeration of the objects of horror were a rite of exorcism.

> The whip had a short wooden stock, braided over with leather, and was loaded at the butt. The lash was three feet long, or thereabouts, and made of raw-hide strands.
> ... Winding the lash around his hand, and taking hold of the small end of the stock, he walked up to me, and with a malignant look, ordered me to strip (Northup, p. 110).

> He tied Sarah up and whipped her, until the flesh so cleaved from the bone, that it might easily have been scraped off with the hand; while the blood stood in puddles under her feet (Thompson, p. 39).

> We had an overseer, named Blackstone. . . . He always carried a long hickory whip, a kind of pole. He kept three or four of these in order, that he might not at any time be without one.
> I once found one of these hickories lying in the yard, and supposing that he had thrown it away, I picked it up, and boy-like, was using it for a horse; he came along from the field, and seeing me with it, fell upon me with

the one he then had in his hand, and flogged me most
cruelly (Pennington, p. 3).

The effect is to drive home to the reader what kind of social system
he supports every time he pays taxes, goes to the polls, and sings
the national anthem; but perhaps, too, by thus confronting his
memories, the writer lays them to rest with the realization that,
having endured everything, there is nothing further to be feared,
nothing to lose but his chains, and that he can never be intimidated
by white power again.

The concrete detail of men familiar with specific work is also
used for purposes other than giving information about slavery.
Thompson describes his experiences aboard a whaling vessel in the
same manner:

> The harpoon is sharp, and barbed at one end, so that
> when it has once entered the animal, it is difficult to draw
> it out again, and has attached to its other end a pole,
> two inches thick and five feet long. Attached to this is a
> line 75 or 100 fathoms in length, which is coiled into the
> bow of the boat (Thompson, p. 113).

Passages such as these are not notably more concrete than white
writing of the same period, as one can easily demonstrate by
opening to any page in *Moby Dick*. But there is a difference of
emphasis and context that distinguishes the white from the black.
Compare Melville and Thompson on the same subject:

> Thus the whale-line folds the whole boat in its compli-
> cated coils, twisting and writhing around it in almost
> every direction. All the oarsmen are involved in its
> perilous contortions; so that to the timid eye of the lands-
> men they seem as Indian jugglers, with the deadliest
> snakes sportively festooning their limbs.[3]

Melville's language is symbolic and weighted with ambiguous
moral meanings: the rope is a snake, a traditional Christian symbol
of evil, but "complicated . . . twisting and writhing around . . . in
almost every direction." It involves "all the oarsmen," including
those who had nothing to do with coiling it in the tub. And the
crew live with it and by it as a necessary tool of their livelihood,

only peripherally aware that it can kill them. Indeed, more than
peripheral awareness of this fact would make them less efficient as
oarsmen and increase the danger.

Thompson also makes the imagery of a whaling voyage carry
moral and allegorical meanings, as is evident from the sermon at
the end of his narrative. But in his and most of the other slave
narratives, the language is a direct consequence of a political purpose. It is the political objective, the role of the book as a weapon
in a class, race, and cultural struggle, that more than anything
else distinguishes the concreteness of these black writers from that
of Melville. For them there can be nothing morally ambiguous
about the need to resist and abolish slavery, and there is little
ambiguity about the reason for their suffering. Although they look
at the issues from a Christian perspective, they do not see oppression in terms of a symbol structure that transforms evil into a
metaphysical necessity. For to do so would be to locate the source
of evil outside the master-slave relationship and thus cut the ideological ground from under the abolitionist movement.

It is true that the literary disadvantage of such a heavy concentration on political involvement may be to reduce experience to a
single dimension, to iron the complexity out of language and
turn it into a vehicle for reporting data that will be of service to the
cause. But the best writers in the history of black autobiography
are able to share the same political involvement of the mediocre
ones without being noticeably crippled by a monotonous style or a
one-dimensional outlook. Their close grasp of the material facts
of human social relationships, their ability to bring power and
clarity of thought to political issues and to connect personal conflict,
frustration, and quest for identity with the large streams of mass
movements in human history, are precisely the greatest strengths
of Frederick Douglass, W. E. B. Du Bois, J. Saunders Redding,
Richard Wright, and George Jackson as authors. These qualities
are what we miss in all but a few white Americans; they appear first
in black literature with the attempt of the slave narrative to describe the master-slave relationship in the most persuasive and
explicit of terms.

In addition, the slave narrator's rendering of concrete experience
leads naturally to the use of understatement. The facts which he
gives are so overwhelming in their barbarity and so convincing as

a case against slavery that his political conclusion is an anticlimax. Anything he can say is bound to understate the point; it is an inevitable rhetorical method. This, for example, is Wells Brown's description of the taming of Randall, a slave who had laid his overseer's posse "prostrate on the ground" rather than allow himself to be whipped, but who was finally captured with the aid of pistols and clubs:

> He was then taken to the barn, and tied to a beam. Cook gave him over one hundred lashes with a heavy cowhide, had him washed with salt and water, and left him tied during the day. The next day he was untied and taken to a blacksmith's shop, and had a ball and chain attached to his leg. He was compelled to labor in the field, and perform the same amount of work that the other hands did (W. W. Brown, p. 70).

The account concludes: "When his master returned home, he was much pleased to find that Randall had been subdued in his absence" (W. W. Brown, p. 20).

Wells Brown is one of the best sources, other than Douglass, for examples of understatement and the use of experience alone to state the antislavery case. Elsewhere in his narrative he tells of seeing a slave jump into the water from a steamboat to avoid being punished for stealing meat. Despite his cries and pleadings, the pursuers strike him with pike-poles until he drowns. After hauling the corpse on board with a hook, they accuse him of "playing possum" and kick the body to make him get up. The men leave when there is no response, and the captain says after them, "you have killed this nigger; now take him off my boat." The body is then dragged ashore, left for the night, and picked up by the trash cart the next morning. Brown's only comment is: "During the whole time, I did not see more than six or seven persons around it, who, from their manner, evidently regarded it as no uncommon occurrence" (ibid., pp. 59–61).

The most effective understatement by Wells Brown concludes his description of a case where a woman had jumped off his boat. The large room on the lower deck contained "men and women, promiscuously—all chained two and two," and a "strict watch" kept

on them; for, he continues, echoing the cautionary language that
might be used by a trader toward the sentries, "cases have occurred
in which slaves have got off their chains, and made their escape
at landing-places, while the boats were taking in wood." It is not
until the final line that the true restraint of his tone is revealed:

> with all our care, we lost one women who had been taken
> from her husband and children, and having no desire
> to live without them, in the agony of her soul jumped
> overboard, and drowned herself. She was not chained
> (ibid., p. 40).

In the image of release from chains, Brown is making use of a
grimly ironic motif that is common in slave literature: death brings
freedom. When a slave dies he is "free at last." But the cautionary
echoes add an especially subtle undertone: the trader would see
her death as a loss of capital, a consequence of failing to make sure
the woman was properly chained like the others. Brown returns to
this simpleminded, yet coldly factual explanation, after having
shown her jump to be the last resort of a free human spirit. In
effect, he mimics the slaveholder's attitude ("see what happens
when you don't keep chains on them") and then leaves it stripped
for exposure by a significant silence.

Irony and shifts in tone between satire and rage are more explicit. As might be expected, these methods suit especially well the
temperament of the more militant authors, such as Ward and
Douglass, but one also finds examples in the narratives of Grandy,
Thompson, Northup, Wells Brown, and William and Ellen Craft.

> While we were lying there by the jail, two vessels came
> from Eastern Shore, Virginia, laden with cattle and
> colored people. The cattle were lowing for their calves,
> and the men and women were crying for their husbands,
> wives, and children (Grandy, p. 28).

> But when I thought of slavery with its Democratic whips
> —its Republican chains—its evangelical blood-hounds,
> and its religious slaveholders—when I thought of all this
> paraphernalia of American Democracy and Religion
> behind me . . . I was encouraged to press forward . . .
> (ibid.).

The very amiable, pious-hearted Mr. Theophilus Freeman, partner or consignee of James H. Burch, and keeper
of the slave pen in New-Orleans, was out among his
animals early in the morning. With an occasional kick
of the older men and women, and many a sharp crack of
the whip about the ears of the younger slaves, it was not
long before they were all astir, and wide awake
(Northup, p. 78).

The irony in these three passages indicates the major sources of
ironic and satirical perception in the slave narrative: the contradictions between the official rhetoric of the American Promise and
the actual treatment of black people, and between the theory that
slaves were chattel goods and the fact that they were human beings.
Underlying both contradictions are the larger ones between master
and slave, pro- and antislavery religion, and the economic systems
of North and South. The slave's location in society where the
contradictions were sharpest naturally inclines him toward the
use of a literary method whose essence is contradiction.

INDICTMENT

| Commonwealth of Virginia, ⎫ | In the Circuit Court, the |
| Norfolk County, ss.   ⎭ | Grand Jurors impannelled |

and sworn to inquire of offences committed in the body
of the said County on their oath present, that Margaret
Douglass, being an evil disposed person, not having the
fear of God before her eyes, but moved and instigated
by the devil, wickedly, maliciously, and feloniously, on
the fourth day of July, in the year of our Lord one
thousand eight hundred and fifty-four, at Norfolk, in said
County, did teach a certain black girl named Kate to
read in the Bible, to the great displeasure of Almighty
God, to the pernicious example of others in like case
offending, contrary to the form of the statute in such case
made and provided, and against the peace and dignity
of the Commonwealth of Virginia.

        Victor Vagabond, Prosecuting Attorney
(Craft and Craft, p. 288. The passage is probably based

on an actual conviction of a white woman in Virginia for this crime.)

In this parody of legal language and institutions by William and Ellen Craft, the irony is based on four contradictions: (1) between the religious ideals given lip service by whites and those permitted to blacks; (2) between the theoretical purpose of law, which is "the peace and dignity of the Commonwealth of Virginia," and the actual purpose of the Indictment, which is the forcible suppression of a subject class; (3) between the traditions of the American Revolution invoked by the date of the "crime" and supposedly represented by the state, and the way that institution reacts when a black person behaves in the same traditions; and (4) between the subject and the pompous officialisms of the language.

The Crafts in fact are extremely good at parody. At one point in their journey, on board a steamer from Savannah to Charleston, the captain advises Ellen, who is disguised as William's master, to watch her "boy" like a hawk when they get to the North.

> Before my master could speak, a rough slave dealer, who
> was sitting opposite, with both elbows on the table, and
> with a large piece of broiled fowl in his fingers, shook
> his head with emphasis, and in a deep Yankee tone,
> forced through his crowded mouth the words, "Sound
> doctrine, captain, very sound." He then dropped the
> chicken into the plate, leant back, placed his thumbs in
> the armholes of his fancy waistcoat, and continued, "I
> would not take a nigger to the North under no considera-
> tion. I have had a deal to do with niggers in my time,
> but I never saw one who ever had his heel upon free soil
> that was worth a d———n. Now stranger," addressing
> my master, "if you have made up your mind to sell that
> ere nigger, I am your man; just mention your price, and
> if it isn't out of the way, I will pay for him on this board
> with hard silver dollars" (Craft and Craft, p. 296).

The details of the slave trader's mannerisms are close in spirit to the quasi-surrealist caricatures of Ralph Ellison. He speaks with his mouth full of chicken, in a deep *Yankee* tone; the involvement of Yankees in the slave trade, and the fact that they often made the most brutal, savage, despicable racists in the business, is an irony remarked in several of the slave narratives, as well as in *Uncle Tom's Cabin*. The trader puts his elbows on the table, shaking his head, placing his presumably greasy thumbs in his waistcoat, showing off his expertise on the subject of "niggers" to a fugitive slave, and offering to buy her husband in "hard silver dollars" as evidence, we suppose, of his honesty, plain dealing, and sterling dependability in business affairs. The perception that sees the world in terms of irony and caricature is shaped by having to live with oppression, hypocrisy, contradiction, and double identity as daily conditions of existence.

The hypocrisy of maintaining one set of politics and religion for whites and another for blacks is brought out again in the following caricature of the mother of a white proslavery minister. The woman boards the train, and, unable to "tell niggers apart," mistakes William Craft for her "runaway nigger Ned." A discussion ensues in which she relates having changed her husband's will in order to keep all her slaves from being manumitted; for "it always seems to me such a cruel thing to turn niggers loose to shift for themselves when there are so many good masters to take care of them." After accusing the "niggers" of being "ungrateful wretches" because they are always running away, she continues:

> If my son and myself had the money for those valuable
> niggers, just see what a great deal of good we could do for
> the poor, and in sending missionaries abroad to the
> poor heathen, who have never heard the name of our
> blessed Redeemer. My dear son who is a good Christian
> minister has advised me not to worry and send my soul to
> hell for the sake of niggers; but to sell every blessed one
> of them for what they will fetch and go and live in peace
> with him in New York (ibid., pp. 305–6).

The irony of the "good Christian minister" advising his mother to sell her slaves is given an added dimension by her comment that the money could be used to send missionaries abroad to the heathens. The immediate intention is to mock them for thinking they could be of any use to the "heathens" when they are incapable of common justice and mercy toward the "niggers." But the passage also contains overtones of anticolonialism and Pan-Africanism: that is, the purpose of Christian missionaries in Africa was more or less the same as that of the proslavery minister: to provide an ideological mask for the colonialist exploitation of black people. The author's perception of the link between the two roles is less than one step away from seeing a common interest between himself and those lucky "heathens" who were getting to hear the name of the blessed Redeemer through the market value of their Afro-American cousins.

Samuel Ward parodies the ideology of slavery, not by means of caricature, but by pretending to argue the slaveholder's point of view. His comments on the sale of his mother, which synthesize the tones of irony and outrage, must be quoted at length to reflect their roots in abolitionist oratory. Just prior to this passage, his father has been whipped, and his mother is to be punished somehow for defending him.

> Besides, if so trifling a thing as the *mere marriage relation* were to interfere with the supreme proprietor's right of a master over his slave, next we should hear that slavery must give way before marriage! Moreover, if a negress may be allowed free speech, touching the flogging of a negro, simply because that negro happened to be her husband, how long would it be before some such claim would be urged in behalf of some other member of a negro family, in unpleasant circumstances? Would this be endurable in a republican civilized community, A.D. 1819? By no means. It would sap the very foundation of slavery—it would be like "the letting out of water": for let the principle be once established that the negress Anne Ward may speak as she pleases about the flagellation of her husband, the negro William Ward, as a matter of right, and like some alarming and death-dealing infection it would spread from plantation to plantation, until property in husbands and wives would not be worth the having. No, no: marriage must succumb to slavery, slavery must reign supreme over every right and every institution, however venerable or sacred; *ergo*, this free-speaking Anne Ward must be made

to feel the greater rigors of the domestic institution.
Should she be flogged? That was questionable. She
never had been whipped, except, perhaps, by her parents;
she was now three-and-thirty years old—rather late for
the commencement of training; she weighed 184 lbs.
avoir-dupoise; she was strong enough to whip an ordinary-
sized man; she had as much strength of *will* as of mind;
and what did not diminish the awkwardness of the case
was, she gave most unmistakeable evidence of "rather tall
resistance," in case of an attack. Well, then, it were wise
not to risk this; but one most convenient course was left
to them, and that course they could take with perfect
safety to themselves, without yielding one hair's breadth
of the rights and powers of slavery, but establishing
them—they could sell her, and sell her they would: she
was their property, and like any other stock she *could* be
sold, and like any other unruly stock she *should* be
brought to the market. . . .

However, this [her] sickly boy, if practicable, must be
raised for the auction mart. Now, to sell his mother
immediately, depriving him of her tender care, might
endanger his life, and, what was all-important in his life,
his saleability. Were it not better to risk a little from
the freedom of this woman's tongue, than to jeopardize
the sale of this *article*? Who knows but, judging from
the pedigree, it may prove to be a prime lot—rising six
feet in length, and weighing two hundred and twenty
pounds, more or less, some day? To ask these questions
was to answer them; there was no resisting the force of
such valuable and logical consideration. Therefore the
sale was delayed; the young animal was to run awhile
longer with his—(I accommodate myself to the ideas and
facts of slavery, and use a corresponding nomenclature)—
dam (Ward, pp. 15–17).

Ward's use of animal nomenclature and age and weight statistics
to parody the idea that slaves were chattel goods recalls Swift's
method in *A Modest Proposal*:

It is true, a child just dropped from its dam may be supported by her milk for a solar year, with little other nourishment. . . .[4]

The best feature of Ward's irony is that every single reason he pretends to espouse in defense of selling his mother is, from the slaveholder's point of view, valid. It would indeed "sap the very foundation of slavery" if Anne Ward were allowed to assert her identity as a human being with family loyalties in place of her legal definition as an article of property. The contradiction between master and slave is completely antagonistic; the interests of one cannot be asserted without suppressing the interests of the other. The effect of the ironic mask is consequently to denounce the whole institution rather than any single injustice. It is made clear in the content, as well as the tone, that slavery is the chief target, for the woman is sold in order to defend the rights and powers of the system.

The tone of the passage is that of the impassioned orator, speaking directly to an audience of whom he asks rhetorical questions and then gives answers. Certain words and phrases seem intended to carry the weight of the additional anger, sarcasm, pause, and innuendo that could be supplied by a speaker's voice: for example, the underscoring of *"could," "should," "article," "immediately," "mere marriage relation,"* the repetition of "no, no," "slavery," "sell her," and the name "Anne Ward," and the understatement of "rather tall resistance." Ward builds up expectations in the reader, too, by means of progressive clauses: "Well then, it were wise not to risk this; but one most convenient course was left to them, and that course they could take with perfect safety to themselves. . . ." The expectations are then satisfied by concluding with the crowning injustice, contradiction, or irony of the incident. The writer demonstrates by his ability to parody the oppressor that he is the real master of the situation; he comprehends the oppressor's ideas, and exposes their flimsiness and hypocrisy to the ridicule of his audience; he is utterly free of the oppressor's image of himself, and throws it back in his face with a sardonic laugh. The response which this tone demands from the reader is not pity, but respect.

The slave experience affects the style of the narrative, then, by impelling it in the direction of precise description, detailed rendering of work gangs, plantation conditions, and atrocities, understatement, irony, parody, and indignation. The use of parody provides still another analogue to the response of the colonialized "native," who parodies the mannerisms, ideology, culture, and self-righteous ignorance of the white colonizer. The slave narrator may be different from the "native" in that his parody appropriates the best traditions of the master culture for his own use; Ward, for example, upholds the Western concepts of marriage, republicanism, free speech, government by the consent of the governed, and the right of revolution. His appeal is for full acceptance as a Westerner and American.

Chapter 3 *The White influence*

W HEN he came to set his story down on paper, the slave narrator had little choice but to adapt the literary forms and traditions of white American culture. What African literature had orally survived the trip to America may have served the black writer as a cultural defense against the deliberate effort of the slave system to wipe out his identity and as a means of communicating with his own people. But what he most wanted to do in his writing was to move white public opinion against slavery, to undermine racism by affording proof of the ability of Negroes to master the literary material of white culture, to open the door for the entry of black people into the mainstream of American society, and to strike off his mental chains, to become a whole human being in the sight of Western civilization. African forms and motifs were seldom useful for any of these ends except striking off the mental chains, unless transmuted almost beyond recognition.

In speaking of the "white influence" on the slave narratives, however, we must qualify repeatedly the nature and source of the influence. Some of it came directly from the slave's reading of white literature or exposure to white speeches and sermons; much more came from white materials *as assimilated* by Afro-American social life: Christian imagery drawn from black church and revival meetings, language rhythms from the speech of Negro preachers, religious and political symbols and slogans that had special meanings in a black context. As in the case of white American values, the slave narrator refits white styles to a purpose and identity derived from black experience.

The Christian impact on slave narrative language was conveyed through the prose of the King James Bible, John Bunyan's *Pilgrim's Progress*, the *Journal* of John Woolman and perhaps other Quaker writing, the traditional Christian symbols of cross, lance, cup, ark, flood, chariot, golden city, wounds of Christ, etc., interpreted anew by black history and eloquence, and the oratorical cadences of revivals and sermons. It is common in most of the narratives to run across passages like these:

> Little did Mr. Adams know, when he was uttering that speech, that he was "opening the eyes of the blind"; that he was breaking the iron bands from the limbs of one poor slave, and setting the captive free. But bread cast upon the waters, will be found and gathered after many days (Thompson, p. 38).

> Malinda was to me an affectionate wife. She was with me in the darkest hours of adversity. She was with me in sorrow, and joy, in fasting and feasting, in trial and persecution, in sickness and health, in sunshine and in shade (Bibb, p. 41).

> I was a starving fugitive, without home or friends—a reward offered for my person in the public papers—pursued by cruel manhunters, and no claim upon him to whose door I went . . . he took me in, and gave me of his food, and shared with me his own garments (Pennington, p. 41).

> My cup of sorrow was full to overflowing. Then I lifted up my hands to God, and in the still watches of the night, surrounded by the sleeping forms of my companions, begged for mercy on the poor, forsaken captive (Northup, p. 77).

These passages echo the rhetoric of Bible and preachment. In the quotation from Henry Bibb, paraphrasing a marriage service to describe his wife would serve to remind the reader indirectly of the sacredness of the marriage relation, whether black or white, and thus help to move the emotions in condemnation of the master's disregard for slave marriages.

Other passages use both this rhetoric and the tradition of the sermon to build carefully, by means of an architecture of periodic and parallel clauses, toward effects that approximate the African song of praise:

> For about three weeks the storm raged most furiously,
> the wind became a hurricane, the waves rolled and
> dashed mountain high, sweeping our boats from their
> hangings, and dashing them in pieces; while the sun was
> hid by dark and portentious clouds.
>
> All hands looked upon the captain as their deliverer,
> while he stood looking at the clouds, seemingly with
> deprecating vengeance. But it was the work of our God,
> whom the winds obey, and to whom the sea does
> homage. Well might the Scripture say, "He has his ways
> in the whirlwinds, and his paths are known to the
> mighty deep." He looks, and the fearfully threatening
> clouds hide their deformed faces; He speaks, and the
> winds are hushed in profound silence; He commands,
> and the lofty billows lowly bow their heads (Thompson,
> p. 117).

The Scriptural allusions dominate the atmosphere of the writing,
but the final sentence, in which each clause repeats and amplifies
the form of the previous, may be a lingering breath of Africa. God
has an African immediacy and presence in nature; his attributes are
listed as parts of the storm. He walks before the eyes of the listener,
like the God of James Weldon Johnson's poem, "The Creation."
The parallel lines, a method extending all the way up to the
speeches of Martin Luther King, occur also in the work of many
contemporary African poets.

In their use of Christian rhetoric, the slave narratives parallel
the development of colonial and early federal autobiographies,
journals, and diaries by William Bradford, Samuel Sewall, Cotton
Mather, Jonathan Edwards, John Woolman, and many other
whites less well known. There is a similar alternation between
lofty cadence and ordinary detail, and the same tendency in each
group to slip into the language of Scripture and read religious
significance into any casual incident. The *Narrative* of Noah Davis,
for example, occasionally gives us something of the flavor of "Sinners in the Hands of an Angry God":

> As I sat on the shoe-bench, I picked up a bunch of
> bristles, and selecting one of the smallest, I began to
> wonder, if God could see an object so small as that. No

sooner had this inquiry arose in my heart, than it appeared
to me, that the Lord could not only see the bristle, but
that He beheld me, as plainly as I saw the little object in
my hand; and not only so, but that God was then
looking through me, just as I would hold up a tumbler
of clear water to the sun and look through it (Davis, p. 20).

Elsewhere we find strains of the religious mysticism of Edwards'
Personal Narratives and Woolman's *Journal*:

I felt such a love and peace flowing in my soul, that I
could not sit longer; I sprang to my feet, and cried out,
"Glory to God!" (Ibid., p. 22).

About two rods from Uncle Harry's house I fell upon my
knees . . . with hands uplifted to high heaven. . . . I received a spiritual answer of approval; a voice like thunder
seeming to enter my soul, saying, I am your God and
am with you; though the whole world be against you,
I am more than the world; though wicked men hunt you,
trust in me, for I am the Rock of your Defence (Thompson, p. 81).

The influence of Woolman, in fact, was probably direct. The
Journal, first published in 1794, enjoyed wide circulation as both
a spiritual odyssey and an antislavery tract. Woolman himself was
instrumental in persuading the Quakers to take a stand against
slavery and his essays, particularly "Some Considerations on the
Keeping of Negroes," were part of the arsenal of abolitionist
literature (if one may use so military a term for the gentle and
pacifistic Woolman) which many of the slave narrators would have
encountered in their efforts to get an education. Woolman was
well known to the prominent abolitionists of the early nineteenth
century, among them Channing, Whittier, and Phillips. Woolman's mystical experiences are unmistakeably like Thompson's,
and, again like Thompson, he ends his *Journal* with a sea voyage
that supplies metaphors and context for a sermon. Pennington,
who was sheltered and taught by Quakers as a hungry, illiterate
fugitive, would certainly have been given the *Journal* to whet his
appetite for learning; and, as a final note of evidence for a direct
relationship between the white narrative and the black, both Pen-

nington and Thompson seem to have structured their autobiographies like Woolman's. There were scores of less renowned Quaker spiritual journals that followed the same pattern: the subject feels divine intimations in childhood, passes through a phase of youthful frivolities, repents of them in a series of acute spiritual conflicts, is converted to Quakerism, surrenders his will to the inner light, and experiences a call to the ministry.[1] Thompson, though far from saintly and pacifistic in tone, was clearly affected by this pattern, and Pennington differs from it only in the overlay of another, equally standard pattern—the flight to freedom.

One other parallel with the slave narratives, and possible source of influence on them, were the narratives of white prisoners of war held by the British during the Revolution. These included, among quite a large number, *A Narrative of the Capture and Treatment of John Dodge, by the English at Detroit; The Old Jersey Captive, or, a Narrative of the Captivity of Thomas Andros*; and *A Narrative of Colonel Ethan Allen's Captivity*. The accounts of Allen and Andros were popular: first appearing in 1779 and 1781, respectively, they had been widely distributed and were still on the scene when the slave narrators began arriving with empty stomachs, hungry minds, and determined purpose in the major cities of the North. Ethan Allen's narrative came out again in 1846, though it had gone through several previous editions, and Andros' *Old Jersey Captive* was reprinted in Boston in 1833. The Revolutionary War prison narratives are full of descriptions of tortures, misery, and oppression no less compelling than the whippings and maimings related by the slaves. Like the slave narrators, Andros appeals to Christian piety and makes ironic references to the enemy's institutions. One might well speculate that some of the slave narrators were inspired in their accounts by the discovery of a prison narrative; their appeals to the ideas of the Revolution as just cause for the rebellion of slaves certainly attempt to include themselves under the same blanket of public sympathy that covered the resistance of the colonials to the British. If prison narratives were enlisting a patriotic response from the white readership, the fugitive slaves would have every reason, and impulsion, to demand a hearing for their suffering on the same terms.

The parallel between the white autobiographies and the slave narratives shows yet again that the values of the black writers not

only mirror, but magnify and intensify those of the white cultural
mainstream. The slave narratives speak like a conscience to the
ghosts of Mather, Edwards, Andros, and Allen, in their own
language. They are echoing the same religion, the same Biblical
texts, the same spirit of freedom, even the same experiences, but
in a way that, by implication, mocks and denounces the dismal
failure of white America's Christianity to live up to the hopes and
ideals of those early autobiographies. For it is to defend them
against this Christianity that the slaves are calling on the Christian
God. Only in the *Journal* of Woolman does the religion of the
white culture seem whole and clean enough to merit the respect
and acceptance of the blacks. A Biblical allusion in Cotton Mather
might refer to the struggle of the Puritans to found their New
Jerusalem in the wilderness. A Biblical allusion in Henry Bibb,
like historical counterpoint, cries out to the God of the Hebrew
slave to deliver the black man from the bondage created by this same
New Jerusalem:

> Yet I was in a far worse state than Egyptian bondage; for
> [the Israelites] had houses and land; I had none; they had
> oxen and sheep; I had none; they had a wise counsel, to
> tell them what to do, and where to go, and even to go
> with them; I had none . . . and I thought of the fishes of
> the water, the fowls of the air, the wild beasts of the
> forest, all appeared to be free, to go just where they
> pleased, and I was an unhappy slave! (Bibb, pp. 29–30).

In Pennington, the imagery in the description of whipping scenes
depicts the black man as Christ, and the civilization of the white
slaveholder as his persecutor and crucifier:

> The next morning, my master . . . led the poor old man
> away into the stable; tied him up, and ordered the son to
> lay on thirty-nine lashes, which he did, making the
> keen end of the cowhide lap around and strike him in
> the tenderest part of his side, till the blood sped out, as
> if a lance had been used (Pennington, p. 10).

The thirty-nine lashes perhaps invert and parody the thirty-nine
articles of the Anglican Church. If so, the irony was not the inven-

tion of Pennington, for thirty-nine lashes is referred to in Douglass'
Narrative as a standard legal penalty for learning how to read
the Bible: "these dear souls came not to Sabbath school because it
was popular to do so, nor did I teach them because it was reputable
to be thus engaged. Every moment they spent in that school, they
were liable to be taken up, and given thirty-nine lashes."[2]

The Crafts twice allude to *Pilgrim's Progress* as a source of
metaphor to express their flight from slavery. The South is their
"City of Destruction," the free states, and finally England, the
"Great City" (Craft and Craft, pp. 309, 313). Hawthorne, in "The
Celestial Railroad" and the chapter, "The Flight of Two Owls"
in *The House of Seven Gables,* parodies Bunyan but with no
connection to slavery. By applying Bunyan's work to a contemporary context with life-and-death issues, the Crafts were breathing
new life into it, giving it an unexpected range and dimension that
Hawthorne did not know it could possess. The image of a journey
through suffering and trial, surrounded by devil-inspired obstacles,
to the "Great City," expresses succinctly how the slave narrators
generally conceived of their escapes. In this they were building
on Negro Christian folk motives as well as on Bunyan, for there
were any number of songs with Biblical images ("Twelve Gates to
the City," "Crossing Over Jordan," "Let My People Go") that
expressed the same theme to black listeners. It was a supremely
ironic commentary on the white Protestant culture for which *Pilgrim's Progress* was bedside and fireside reading that this literary
badge of their righteousness should have inspired faith, hope, and
the courage to resist in their black victims. It was the courage to
resist that Bunyan gave to the religious dissenters of England who
migrated to America to escape persecution, and two centuries later
he was being used as a weapon against their descendants.

In the Christianity of the early black writer one finds total
rejection of proslavery religion and total certainty that God is on
the side of the oppressed. A day of reckoning will come, when God,
the same God who holds Edwards' sinners over the pit as one
holds a spider or some loathsome insect over the fire, will deal with
the sins of the slaveholder in the same manner. There is often
the suggestion that the instrument God has chosen for this task is
the rebellious black slave.

> But how will the case stand with those reckless traffickers
> in human flesh and blood, who plunged the poisonous
> dagger of separation into those loving hearts which God
> had for so many years closely joined together. . . . It is
> not for me to say what will become of those heartless
> tyrants. I must leave them in the hands of an all-wise and
> just God, who will, in his own good time, and in his own
> way, avenge the wrongs of his oppressed people (Craft
> and Craft, p. 275).

> You may do your best to keep us in wretchedness and
> misery, to enrich you and your children, but God will
> deliver us from under you—and wo, wo, will be to you
> if we have to obtain our freedom by fighting (Walker,
> p. 80).

The most fascinating, and, in a way, most terrible parallel between the Puritan autobiography and the slave narrative—terrible
because of what it reveals about American culture and because
of the way in which it strips the distractions of civilization from the
man and throws him back entirely on his own spiritual resources
—is the religious mysticism inspired in each by the wilderness
and by the loneliness and introspection man feels while confronting it. To Mather, the wilderness was a catalyst for all the complex
attitudes that made up the intellectual superstructure of Puritan-
ism: the interpretation of the struggle to found their society as a
dramatic battle between God and the Devil, their hatred for the
heathen Indian, contempt, fear, and racism toward black people,
sexual repression, the sense of God's direct presence and intervention in human affairs, belief in witchcraft, and the search for
signs of God's will in the phenomena of nature. In New England
folk traditions, the "black man" wandered freely through the
heathen forest, presiding over the black mass, bedevilling churches
and settlements with Indian attacks and spectral visitations, and
organizing covens of witches. By the time of Edwards, the forest
has been Christianized enough to inspire visions of the Son of God,
and in Bryant is a microcosm of God Himself.

The historical and literary counterpoint of this tradition is to be
found in the apocalyptic visions of Nat Turner in the back woods
of Virginia:

... and shortly afterwards, while laboring in the field, I
discovered drops of blood on the corn as though it were
dew from heaven ... and I then found on the leaves in
the woods hieroglyphic characters, and numbers, with the
forms of men in different attitudes, portrayed in blood.
... I heard a loud noise in the heavens, and the Spirit
instantly appeared to me and said the Serpent was
loosened, and Christ had laid down the yoke he had borne
for the sins of men, and that I should take it on and fight
against the Serpent, for the time was fast approaching
when the first should be last and the last should be first.
... And on the appearance of the sign ... I should
arise and prepare myself, and slay my enemies with their
own weapons.[3]

Here is the most explicit example of any of the slave narratives of
Christian rhetoric and imagery which is adapted to the needs of
the slave. The materials of the white master's culture have been
mobilized to strike him down. When this passage is juxtaposed with
Cotton Mather's *Wonders of the Invisible World*, the effect is
something like insight into the crazy wheels of America's race
history. Both works superimpose religion on nature, both reinforce
their values with signs and symbols from the wilderness, which
they have no difficulty finding once the need for them has created
the mental set. It should be granted that both works, too, may
have as their basis the experience of being "touched" by the Holy
Spirit, plunged directly into unmitigated confrontation with the
self and its true relationship to other people and things—a confrontation which proves unendurable to Mather and from which he
must shield himself by making the wilderness into an object of
terror. For Mather, "heathen," "black man," "devil," "serpent,"
libido, the "inner light," and any evidence of Puritan mendacity
are all in the same category, to be suppressed with the assistance
of God and the gallows. For Nat Turner, the wilderness remains a
source of inspiration. Turner may also be acting in the African
tradition of the direct, personal relationship with God which we
have already seen in Thompson's praise song to the storm at
sea. Nat's bloody deeds are no more appealing than Mather's, in
themselves, but this very fact lends them a tragic/triumphant

grandeur; he has been chosen to focus the evil of slavery and send it boiling back onto the slaveholder's head, and as the bearer of a yoke of evil, he cannot remain untainted. But it is the white man who is the serpent; the blood of Christ is transposed into a symbol and a call for insurrection. Asked by Gray if he felt that he was wrong, Turner replies "Was not Christ crucified?" The wilderness has returned him to society as a messenger of war, the state of war being the essence of the slave system, the bitter truth which he publishes with axe and gun. As the black man is last, so shall he be first.

It must be considered that the white man Thomas Gray was the ghost writer of Nat Turner's *Confessions,* but in this case there does not seem to have been much difference between white influence and actual white authorship. The rhetoric and imagery seems to differ from that of other Christian-influenced slave writing only in its degree of militancy and intensity of purpose. What gives power to the imagery is the living culture of prayer meeting and revival from which it is derived.

The best instance of sermon rhetoric used for artistic purposes occurs in the *Life of John Thompson.* Chapter nineteen of that book is an extended allegorical comparison between the voyage of a whaling ship, from which Thompson had recently returned, and "the passage of a Christian from earth to glory." In the exactness of image, the management of sound and cadence, and the control of the overall narrative and metaphor, it is a piece that compares with Father Mapple's Sermon in *Moby Dick.*

Thompson expands the imagery of a flight or journey to encompass his struggle to build a Christian identity. In doing so, he is wholly consistent with the approach of the other Christian slave narrators, in particular Ward, Davis, Pennington, and the Crafts. What makes Thompson's work unusual is the elaborate care he has taken to explore all of its aesthetic dimensions.

> While at sea and learning the uses of the various nautical
> instruments, I also studied their spiritual application
> (Thompson, chap. 19).

He has placed the chapter at the climax of his autobiography; it opens with the phrase, "while at sea," which, in context, should be read as a description of his spiritual state, and closes with the words,

"secure an everlasting rest at the right hand of God." In between
is the voyage of the Christian from sin to salvation.

The helm of the ship is conscience, the rudder is understanding,
the masts are judgment and reason; the sails are the affections,
and "education stands in the place of carving and gilding." If the
sails are overloaded, there is danger of foundering. "Pride represents too taut rigging," and falsehood or "assumed professions" are
false colors. At its first launching, the ship was "dashed on the
rocks of presumption" but repaired by the Owner at the cost of
His "only begotten and well beloved son." The planks and timbers,
on the conversion of the individual, are cemented, bolted, and
caulked by Faith, Love, and eternal Truth. The soul "receives
sailing orders from the inspired oracles" and is wafted toward the
port of endless rest by the Holy Ghost. There are similar spiritual
equivalents for storms, clear and rocky coasts, sunlight, and calm.
The whole complex performance is given life by the music of the
language:

> Every piece is hewn by the law in the work of convic-
> tion; every faculty purged from sin and guilt by the great
> atonement, received by faith in Christ Jesus; every
> plank bent by the fire of divine love, all fitted to their
> places by the invincible energy of sovereign grace, and the
> structure is completed according to the model prepared
> in the council of peace, and published in the gospel, which
> divine illumination is made visible to the mental eye,
> through which it is received into the heart, and leaves its
> impress there. . . .
>
> If faith is not genuine and enduring; if those principles
> typified by the planks and timbers of a ship, be rotten or
> unsound at heart, not consistent with each other, and
> not shaped so as to lie compactly; or if each is not well
> secured by bolts of the endurable metal of eternal truth
> from the mine of divine revelation; if all is not carefully
> caulked with the powerful cement of unfailing love
> and redeeming blood; in a word, if Christ is not the
> sole foundation, and his righteousness the grand security,
> then on the slightest trial, the seams open, the vessel
> bilges, and every soul on board is lost. . . .

> How carefully then should we accompany our
> prayers with watching, heedfully marking every change-
> ful appearance of the sky. How eagerly should we seize
> the first favorable moment, when the long wished for
> opportunity of sailing was in our power. . . . Nor must the
> fairest gale entice us to sea without the heavenly pilot;
> for without thee, blessed Jesus, we can do nothing; to
> thee we must turn in every difficulty, and upon thee call
> in every time of danger. We dare trust no other at the
> helm, because no other can safely steer us past the
> rocks and quicksands. How kind thy promise, to be with
> us when passing through deep and dangerous waters.
> How gracious thy word which engages never to leave nor
> forsake us . . . (Thompson, chap. 19).

Assigning specific allegorical equivalents to all the details of the metaphor is a method very much in the general tradition of Christian writing, where the intention is to teach an attitude toward life. The structure of the sermon is an elaborate conceit. Within that structure, the language creates its effects in the manner of a free-form poem: by the repetition of words and syntax, the use of parallel clauses, the rhythm of stressed syllables, and the shifts between moral meaning and image.

The first half of the first sentence, for example, has three parallel subjects, each beginning with the word "every" ("Évery piéce is héwn by the láw . . . évery fáculty púrged from sín and guílt . . . évery plánk bént by the fíre of divíne lóve. . . ."). Each clause ends on a stressed syllable, like the stop at the end of a line of poetry; the cadence varies between iambic and anapestic, like that of speech, with the images receiving the heavier stress. The second half of that sentence, following the conjunction "and," links the three parallel clauses under a single governing idea: the "módel prepáred in the coúncil of peáce, and públished in the góspel, whích divíne illūmináton is máde vísible to the méntal éye. . . ." Here again, the cadence tends to be metrical (the phrase up to the first comma has four anapestic feet, with a weak syllable missing from the first), and the consonants are strongly alliterative.

The second paragraph is a well-executed, periodic *tour de force*, with a conclusion powerful enough to satisfy the expectations

built up by the five parallel "if" clauses that precede it. The second
and third clauses translate the first into images; the fourth trans-
lates the image into an additional concept, that is, redemption
through the love of Christ; and the fifth summarizes and climaxes
the first four by juxtaposing the Christian's ultimate hope (salvation through Christ) and his ultimate fear (the loss of the soul). The
image of the ship is maintained throughout, with the thought
shuttling back and forth between the two terms of the metaphor
to reinforce each term with the other. The "ship of death" arche-
type, submerged but always present, takes on the insistent force of
deep ocean swell; coming as it does at the end of a factual account
of whaling, during which the reader familiar with Milton, Melville,
and Lawrence gazes out the porthole of Thompson's journalism
and wonders if the author knew he was floating on a sea of symbolism, the effect when the poem begins is like being led suddenly
for a walk on the waves.

There may be a third term for the metaphor, a trade wind of
antislavery meaning that would make Thompson's sermon a
magnificent compression of politics, religion, and poetry. He would
not have found a more knowledgeable, sophisticated, or responsive
audience than the congregations of New Bedford's three or four
black churches, for whom the use of whaling images to convey
antislavery material was probably a time-honored tradition. In
1859, of the 25,000 native American seamen, more than half were
Negroes, and 2,900 of them served in the whale fishery.[4] New Bedford was also a haven for fugitive slaves. One new arrival was
shipped North in a box by sea; and, according to a brother in his
church, "the first time he came into church I thought he would
set it on fire. I tell you he *blowed* there!"[5] Whales were also compared to slavery itself in the *Abolitionist*, a journal of the New
England Anti-Slavery Society: "We found the Leviathan weltering
in the sea of popularity. . . . We have fixed the harpoon, and the
monster begins to blow and bellow. We are now pulling upon
the line, and we shall soon, we trust, come to lancing."[6] And by
1863 the metaphor had become popular enough for Lincoln to use
it as he signed the Emancipation Proclamation.[7] Thompson's
voyage of the soul toward everlasting rest, then, may also imply a
symbolic hunt for the Leviathan of slavery and a flight on the sea
from the slave-catching hunters. He may be inspiring his listeners

with the theme that flight from the master is worthless unless the fugitive is also running *toward* something, i.e. submission to the eternal God. A relationship this intimate between poetry, reality, and audience is coveted in vain by most contemporary poets.

After sounding the maximum danger of the journey ("the seams open, the vessel bilges, and every soul on board is lost"), the sermon moves smoothly into a reference to prayer as a safeguard, and then, with no break in continuity, becomes itself a prayer. The last paragraph has the same structure as the first two: parallel clauses and repeated words and syntax patterns, the content of which builds steadily toward some sort of climax: "How carefully. . . . How eagerly. . . . How kind. . . . How gracious." The climax in this case is the prayer to Christ. The handling of words within sentences also shows an accomplished control over language: "we dare trust no other at the helm, because no other can safely steer us. . . ." "No other" is used the first time as an object, the second as a subject, giving a sense of variety within a rhythmic pattern. And the repetitions of "every" as part of a prepositional phrase are echoes of the repeated "everys" of the first paragraph, where they were part of the subject.

All in all, this chapter is the highest level of art touched by Christian rhetoric anywhere in the slave narratives, although Thompson's autobiography taken as a whole is not the best work. The sermon is an example of a black writer taking traditional Christian forms and giving them a blood transfusion through his own experience as a fugitive and wanderer.

In Pennington there is a good description of an abandoned and dilapidated plantation which does essentially the same thing: it realizes a traditional Christian theme through black experience, and constructs a response to and defense against the cultural oppression of slavery.

> To see the once fine smooth gravel walks, overgrown
> with grass—the redundances of the shrubbery neglected—
> the once finely painted pricket fences, rusted and fallen
> down—a fine garden in splendid ruins—the lofty ceiling
> of the mansion thickly curtained with cobwebs—the spa-
> cious apartments abandoned, while the only music heard
> within as a substitute for the voices of family glee that

once filled it, was the crying cricket and cockroaches!
Ignorant slave as I was at that time, I could but pause for
a moment, and recur in silent horror to the fact that, a
strange reverse of fortune, had lately driven from that
proud mansion, a large and once opulent family. What
advantage was it now to the members of that family,
that the father and head had for near half a century stood
high in the counsels of the state, and had the benefit
of the unrequited toil of hundreds of his fellowmen,
when they were already grappling with the annoyances
of that poverty, which he had entailed upon others
(Pennington, pp. 70–71).

Pennington's message is the vanity of earthly things, and the
house itself a *memento mori* which reminds the reader to lay up his
treasures in heaven; but it is specifically slavery that the writer
attacks as an earthly vanity; the Christian point of view has been
adapted to the needs of political struggle against a specific object,
and, as in the case of Thompson, affects the language by transforming it into sermon oratory. The first sentence is a series of parallel
clauses with repetition of key words, and the subordination of the
final clauses in the last sentence brings out the irony in the material: the first has become last, the despoiler of others is himself
despoiled.

A brief comparison with the house of Usher illustrates that we are
dealing with a characteristic "black" way of handling material.
For all its cracked face, dank tarn, and brilliantly rendered miasma
of decay, Usher's house is deliberately removed from history and
society, a separate world in itself.[8] The house of Pennington's
description has connections to the past and present; it is both a
product and an object lesson of time, a lesson that applies in the
world beyond the author's private imagination. The language is
rooted in the soil of the politics and religion practiced by black
abolitionists.

The features of style we have noted appear in many varied contexts wherever elevation of tone is called for, and sometimes where
it is inappropriate: parallel clauses, repeated words placed in
different positions in the sentence, rolling periods with a metrical
cadence that build to a climax, antithesis, formal and sometimes

pompous and melodramatic diction in the manner of the time, and images designed to play on the emotions; all these methods are used also for non-Christian content, or occur almost as a matter of habit or mannerism. In the following sentence by Henry Bibb, the main appeal is in the sound. The oratorical tone is not applied to any specific object and so seems inept and merely sentimental:

> I was struggling against a thousand obstacles which had clustered around my mind to bind my wounded spirit still in the dark prison of mental degradation (Bibb, p. 47).

Elsewhere he plans his effects with more skill:

> I have often suffered from the sting of the cruel slave driver's lash on my quivering flesh—I have suffered from corporeal punishment in its various forms—I have mingled my sorrows with those that were bereaved by the ungodly soul drivers—and I also know what it is to shed the sympathetic tear at the grave of a departed friend; but all this is but a mere trifle compared with my sufferings from then to the end of six months subsequent (ibid., p. 88).

Here the parallel clauses are cumulative in their effect, arranged in order of ascending importance.

The same style and method of arrangement occurs in this passage from Solomon Northup:

> He fears he will be caught lagging through the day; he fears to approach the gin-house with his basketload of cotton at night; he fears, when he lies down, that he will oversleep himself in the morning. Such is a true, faithful, unexaggerated picture and description of the slave's daily life . . . on the shores of Bayou Boeuf (Northup, p. 171).

The styles of Webster and Garrison were among the immediate literary models from which this rhetoric is derived. Turning to Webster's *Plymouth Oration*, for example, we find similar techniques and cadences:

> No sculptured marble, no enduring monument, no honorable inscription, no ever-burning taper that would

drive away the darkness of the tomb, can soften our
sense of the reality of death, and hallow to our feelings the
ground that is to cover us, like the consciousness that
we shall sleep, dust to dust, with the objects of our
affections.[9]

Indeed, as F. O. Matthiessen points out, oratory was the dominant
literary tradition of the period.[10] Emerson, Thoreau, and Whitman
all show the influence of the oration, and the most popular medium
of political communication was public address. The slave narratives, as instruments in a political struggle, would be especially
open to this influence and would receive it from a vast number of
immediate sources. Webster's cadences can be heard in Garrison
and Thoreau as well as in Thompson and Pennington; and
Garrison most directly affects the style of Frederick Douglass, as
the latter's mentor and first exposure to abolitionist literature
in the years following his escape.

The dignity achieved by an elevated tone can also be accounted
among the many reasons why slaves would take Webster, Garrison,
and John Q. Adams as stylistic models. In the popular white fiction
of the period, the black writer was perpetually confronted with
assaults on that dignity in the form of the Jupiters, Dinahs, Pom-
peys, Sambos, Catos, Mingos, and other stereotypes ranging in
character from loyal dogs to libidinous black savages, who clown,
simper, drink, steal, and gabble their way through the pages of
William Gilmore Simms, A. J. Knott, and John S. Robb. Some
of the most vicious anti-Negro portraits, although he was not popular, appear in the stories of Edgar Allan Poe. The "negro" of white
fiction usually spoke a dialect that was intended to demean his
intelligence.[11] The slave writer's choice of formal diction and
polished periods was a key element in the construction of his human
identity, for it countered these parodies with the most effective
weapon available: the ability to command, and parody, the master's voice. The best slave narrators, in fact, beat the Negrophobic
writers at their own game, by alternating at will between parody
and credible representation, whereas the master's blindness
placed credible representation of anything black beyond his reach.

The greatest problem of the slave narrative, solved in Thompson and Douglass, was how to assimilate the magic of the enemy's

language into a new identity entirely under the slave's control. Thompson achieves a solution, as we have seen, by synthesizing religious rhetoric, African poetic survivals, and his personal background in the whaling industry, using as a catalyst for these diverse elements the great historical movement of black life in the nineteenth century—the flight to freedom.

It is Frederick Douglass, among all the slave narrators, who made the best use of his materials, who mastered and assimilated the rhetoric of the literary mainstream, stamped it with his personality and experience, and most ably turned it to whatever purpose he chose: persuasion, propaganda, passion, rational argument, narrative, and drama. In Douglass, the "white influence" and the black experience make one continuous grain of accomplished artistry. He was able to dominate his influences where most of the narrators, in style at least, were dominated by them. We turn to Douglass for the finest example of the slave autobiography as a literary art form.

Chapter 4 *Frederick Douglass*
Language as a weapon

THE literary career of Frederick Douglass spans over half the century in which he lived. He was able to observe and participate in all the most crucial events of that period in America: the growth of the anti-slavery movement, the Civil War, Reconstruction, the rise of industrial capitalism, and the expulsion of the freedmen from political power. His personal career, ironically, reached its apogee duing the very years that black people were being driven from legislatures, offices, polling places, schools, trades, business, and public facilities in state after state all over the South. He became more and more like the North Star he had once used as a name for his newspaper: a distant guide, a remote symbol of hope for the fugitive trapped in the wilderness of racism.

Like W. E. B. Du Bois, Douglass produced three autobiographies: the *Narrative* of his life, published in 1845 shortly after his escape from slavery; *My Bondage and My Freedom*, published ten years later; and *The Life and Times of Frederick Douglass*, completed in 1892, three years before his death. The two later editions include most of the material from the early *Narrative,* with some rewriting, plus the experiences and development that occurred after 1845. Both the *Narrative* and *My Bondage and My Freedom* were written as contributions to the antislavery struggle, the latter gaining in urgency and militance with the approach of the Civil War. *The Life and Times*, while still very much involved in the defense of Negro civil rights following the period of Reconstruction, takes on a more reflective tone. The writer is reviewing and commenting on the past, rather than waging the struggles of the present; his audience is posterity; he must speak to a whole new generation of Americans, to whom the Civil War was only a childhood memory. His portraits of John Brown and Harriet Beecher Stowe, for example, are meant to stand as history, whereas the

sketches of his overseers in the *Narrative* are intended as part of
the immediate polemics of a living movement.

Point of view and style are blended so well in Douglass that it is
difficult to discuss them separately. In his outlook and identity,
Douglass represents most of the characteristic themes we have
already seen in the other slave narratives: he believes in the positive
values of hard work, forceful resistance, and education as tools to
win freedom, both for the individual slave and the entire slave
class. Education is a revolutionary act subversive to the slave system.
Hard work is not something which any slave is morally required
to hand over to his master; slaveholders, as plunderers and pirates,
have placed themselves outside the pale of morality, and the slave
is therefore justified in withholding work, truth, or cooperation
from the master whenever the opportunity presents itself.

Douglass's attitude toward Christianity is similar to that of
Ward, Thompson, Pennington, Wells Brown, and Bibb in that he
distinguishes between the false Christianity of the slaveholder
and the true Christianity of Christ; he rejects the former as a vicious
mask for oppression, which, in his view, is worn by the entire
country and not just by the South; and he embraces the latter as a
means for exposing the full moral horror of slavery. But unlike
Thompson and Pennington, his identity is not formed primarily
in Christian terms. Where Pennington or Noah Davis, for example,
will oppose alcoholism as a sin and condemn slavery for encourag-
ing the sin of intemperance, Douglass, penetrating directly to
the political motive of the master in giving his slaves alcohol, ad-
vocates temperance as a political defense. Where Pennington
considers lying and violence to be sinful in themselves and condemns slavery because it forces these things on the slave, Douglass
supports them as positive forms of struggle when they are directed
toward the master class.

Douglass in fact felt obliged to add an appendix to the *Narrative*,
lest his vigorous assault on the social role of Christianity in America be misconstrued as an assault on religion. Here we can observe
at the same time the viewpoint on this subject that he shared in
common with his contemporaries, together with the attitude, tone,
and rhetoric that distinguished him as an individual:

> . . . between the Christianity of this land, and the
> Christianity of Christ, I recognize the widest possible

difference—so wide, that to receive the one as good, pure, and holy, is of necessity to reject the other as bad, corrupt, and wicked. To be the friend of the one, is of necessity to be the enemy of the other. I love the pure, peaceable, and impartial Christianity of Christ: I therefore hate the corrupt, slaveholding, women-whipping, cradle-plundering, partial and hypocritical Christianity of this land. . . . The slave auctioneer's bell and the church-going bell chime in with each other, and the bitter cries of the heart-broken slave are drowned in the religious shouts of his pious master. Revivals of religion and revivals in the slave-trade go hand in hand together. The slave prison and the church stand near each other. The clanking of fetters and the rattling of chains in the prison, and the pious psalm and solemn prayer in the church, may be heard at the same time. . . . The dealer gives his blood-stained gold to support the pulpit, and the pulpit, in return, covers his infernal business with the garb of Christianity. Here we have religion and robbery the allies of each other—devils dressed in angels' robes, and hell presenting the semblance of paradise (Douglass, *Narrative*, pp. 120–21).

The primary concern in this passage is not so much to represent the experience of the "true" Christianity, but to expose the social role of the false; to unmask the contradiction between the preachment of slaveholding America and the practice. The preachment in fact not only contradicts the practice, but supports it. "The dealer gives his blood-stained gold to support the pulpit, and the pulpit, in return, covers his infernal business with the garb of Christianity." The rhetoric expresses this twin relationship perfectly through the antithetical and parallel balance of clauses, where images of slavery are juxtaposed with images of religion, in a series leading toward the theme of the mask. Like the clauses that describe them, the two institutions complement and parallel each other. At the end, the mask is taken away to disclose the devil behind it.

Douglass's ability to sustain this complex level of style is what raises him above the level of the other slave narrators as a literary artist. His way of accumulating denunciatory adjectives ("I therefore hate the corrupt, slave-holding, women-whipping, cradle-plundering, partial and hypocritical Christianity of this land") is a device learned and tempered at public meetings and speeches and suggests a direct verbal relationship with the audience. The tone is of a man who is not afraid to unmask enemies, who is concerned to be understood but determined to assault and offend frontally the allies of oppression. He expects resistance and is prepared to deal with it; he brings, not peace, but a sword. The themes of force and violent struggle, which are felt through the language even when the subject is Christianity, distinguish Douglass's religion from Pennington's.

The identity of Douglass, like the identities of his contemporaries, evolves in the process of fighting slavery; but his words give off the fiery glow of righteous power in action; he emphasizes the necessity for the slave to defend himself with fists and guns; and, in contrast to Samuel Ward, he has a sense of common interest with oppressed whites. In his feelings toward America, Douglass is caught in the dilemma that persists throughout the history of black writing: he cannot reject being "American," yet he must attack America as the enemy of freedom and justice for the black man; he is in the country, but not of it. He assumes the identity of a "loyal American" when, breaking with Garrison's views, he decides to support the Constitution as an antislavery document,[1] and again when he supports Lincoln and the Republican party during the War and the Reconstruction period (Douglass, *Life and Times*, pp. 351–72). But his perception that racial oppression is a national problem, together with his experiences of discrimination in the North, often lead him to reject that identity, as in the following excerpt from a letter to Garrison:

> In thinking of America, I sometimes find myself admiring her bright blue sky, her grand old woods, her fertile fields, her beautiful rivers, her mighty lakes, and star-crowned mountains. But my rapture is soon checked—my joy is soon turned to mourning. When I remember that all is cursed with the infernal spirit of slaveholding, robbery, and wrong, when I remember that with the waters of her noblest rivers the tears of my brethren are borne to the ocean, disregarded and forgotten, and that her most

fertile fields drink daily of the warm blood of my outraged
sisters, I am filled with unutterable loathing, and led to
reproach myself that anything could fall from my lips
in praise of such a land. America will not allow her
children to love her (ibid., pp. 242–43).

We have seen in the autobiographies by Wells Brown, Henry
Bibb, and the Crafts, that slave narrators sometimes consciously
took a class perspective toward racial oppression, linked the existence of slavery with property relations, experienced oppression
specifically in terms of the expropriation of their labor, and were
willing to reach out and join hands with poor white farmers and
workers. There are also examples of this perspective in the writings
of Douglass. He bestowed great praise on John Brown and was
in danger of being arrested as Brown's coconspirator after the raid
on Harper's Ferry. His views on the government of Virginia, and,
for a time, on the federal government, were that they represented
"an organized conspiracy by one part of the people against another
and weaker" (ibid., pp. 310–11). Such a view implies clearly that
the government is an instrument of class domination. It was the
ownership of property that first brought home to his mind, as a
child, the condition of slaves in relation to masters:

> It was not long, however, before I began to learn the sad
> fact that this house of my childhood belonged not to my
> dear old grandmother, but to some one I had never seen.
> ... I learned, too, the sadder fact, that not only the
> home and lot, but that grandmother herself and all the
> little children around her belonged to a mysterious
> personage ... (ibid., p. 30).

And it was the exploitation of labor and the use of racism by slaveholders to divide whites against blacks that imposed a common
class interest between white and black workers:

> The slaveholders, with a craftiness peculiar to themselves,
> by encouraging the enmity of the poor laboring white
> man against the blacks, succeeded in making the said
> white man almost as much a slave as the black slave him-
> self ... the latter belonged to one slaveholder, while
> the former belonged to the slaveholders collectively.

> The white slave had taken from him by indirection what
> the black slave had taken from him directly and without
> ceremony. . . . The slave was robbed by his master of
> all his earnings, above what was required for his bare
> physical necessities, and the white laboring man was
> robbed by the slave system of the just results of his labor,
> because he was flung into competition with a class of
> laborers who worked without wages (ibid., pp. 177–80).

Here and elsewhere, Douglass anticipated the Communist viewpoint of twentieth-century autobiographies by Angelo Herndon,
Benjamin J. Davis, Hosea Hudson, and W. E. B. Du Bois; but
Douglass never actually attacked wage labor itself as a system of
exploitation; what he attacked was the effect of slavery on wage
laborers. In the later sections of *The Life and Times*, he called on
the Negroes of the Reconstructed South to make themselves indispensable to their former masters through the power of their labor
(Douglass, *Life and Times*, pp. 430–32).

In his use of language, Douglass did most of the things his
contemporaries were doing but did them more consistently and
skillfully and with a more careful blending of content and form.
His style and rhetoric, too, were conditioned by the fact that he was
addressing a largely white audience, but he never made concessions
to their racism, rarely sank into melodrama and sentimentality,
and never relied on their pity. His tone and syntax, typically, were
agitational and oratorical. The most characteristic features of
Douglass's rhetoric are antithesis, periodic syntax, irony and satire,
alternation between long and short sentences, occasional wordplay, parallel clauses arranged in a cumulative series, repetition,
and well-aimed, well-calculated invective. *My Bondage and My
Freedom* and the *Life and Times* reveal maturity and development
in the handling of these features over the *Narrative*.

The following quotations from his description of the overseer
Austin Gore show the manner in which Douglass manipulated
antithesis in the *Narrative*.

> To be accused was to be convicted, and to be convicted
> was to be punished; the one always following the other
> with immutable certainty. To escape punishment was to
> escape accusation; and few slaves had the fortune to do

either, under the overseership of Mr. Gore. He was just
proud enough to demand the most debasing homage
of the slave, and quite servile enough to crouch, himself,
at the feet of the master. . . . His words were in perfect
keeping with his looks, and his looks were in perfect
keeping with his words. . . . He spoke but to command,
and commanded but to be obeyed; he dealt sparingly with
his words, and bountifully with his whip, never using
the former where the latter would answer as well
(Douglass, *Narrative*, pp. 38–39).

Here is the combination of balance, denunciation, and spare,
direct statement that give the assertive force so typical of Douglass
throughout all three works. He had just learned the technique of
antithetical clauses, and sometimes used them for their own sake:
the sentence, "his words were in perfect keeping with his looks,
and his looks were in perfect keeping with his words," for example,
is simply a display, an exercise; the content does not demand
an antithetical arrangement. In the final clause, the balance of
"sparingly . . . words" with "bountifully . . . whip," brought together
and modified by the next phrase, define and delineate the character of Gore in such a way as to compress his whole life into two
poles: giving orders and giving punishment.

When he came to write the *Life and Times*, Douglass no longer
displayed language for show; he had mastered antithesis, and,
when the occasion required, married it perfectly to the tone and
content of whatever he wished to say. His eulogy of John Brown is a
case in point:

All over the North men were singing the John Brown
song. His body was in the dust, but his soul was marching
on. His defeat was already assuming the form and pressure
of victory, and his death was giving new life and power
to the principles of justice and liberty. He had spoken
great words in the face of death and the champions of
slavery. He had quailed before neither. What he had lost
by the sword he had more than gained by the truth. Had
he wavered, had he retreated or apologized, the case had
been different. He did not even ask that the cup of
death might pass from him. To his own soul he was right,

> and neither "principalities nor powers, life nor death,
> things present nor things to come," could shake his
> dauntless spirit or move him from his ground. He may
> not have stooped on his way to the gallows to kiss a
> little colored child, as it is reported he did, but the act
> would have been in keeping with the tender heart, as well
> as with the heroic spirit of the man. Those who looked
> for confession heard only the voice of rebuke and warning
> (Douglass, *Life and Times*, p. 324).

The antithetical style in this passage, though more subdued, is the only one suited to carry the paradox of victory in defeat, the relationship between martyrdom and execution, truth and the sword, the contradiction of a "tender heart" residing in the same breast with a "dauntless spirit," and the ascendance of rebuke and warning over confession and uncertainty.

The alternation of long, periodic sentences with short loose ones is something which Douglass did in order to isolate and emphasize the most important point or effective statement of a paragraph:

> Trained from the cradle up to think and feel that their
> masters were superiors, and invested with a sort of
> sacredness, there were few who could rise above the con-
> trol which that sentiment exercised. I had freed myself
> from it, and the thing was known. One bad sheep will
> spoil a whole flock. I was a bad sheep. I hated slavery, slave-
> holders, and all pertaining to them, and I did not
> fail to inspire others with the same feeling wherever and
> whenever opportunity was presented (ibid., p. 145).

What stamps this passage with the personality of Douglass is his cheerful, ironic admission to being what his enemies called him, the proud acceptance of an identity as what they most feared: the "bad sheep." The term that summarizes his effect both on his fellow slaves and on the imagination of his master is the one isolated by the short sentence. The duality of its meaning, and behind that, the irreconcilable antagonism of the slave's and master's viewpoints, are thus emphasized and amplified.

Wordplay and puns are not common in Douglass, but when they occur, they have the same political motive, incisive tone, and ironic perception that one finds everywhere in his work. The following pun, for example, conveys his determination to be free:

> At the close of the year 1834, Mr. Freeland again hired
> me of my master, for the year 1835. But, by this time, I
> began to want to live *upon free land* as well as *with
> Freeland*; and I was no longer content, therefore, to live
> with him or any other slaveholder (Douglass, *Narrative*,
> p. 91).

And the account of his fight against Jim Crow on the Eastern Railroad, in New England, combines pun with understatement in such a way as to enlist the sympathy and respect of the reader:

> As usual, I had purchased a first-class ticket and paid the
> required sum for it, and on the requirement of the
> conductor to leave, refused to do so, when he called on
> these men to "snake me out." They attempted to obey
> with an air which plainly told me they relished the job.
> They however found me much attached to my seat,
> and in removing me I tore away two or three of the
> surrounding ones, on which I held with a firm grasp, and
> did the car no service in some other respects (Douglass,
> *Life and Times*, p. 225).

Other black abolitionists who met Jim Crow on Northern railways fought back with the same mixture of tough humor and defiance. Sojourner Truth used to run after the street railway in Washington, shouting "I want to ride! I want to ride!" until she had attracted a crowd big enough to stop the car. Assaulted once by a conductor, she brought a lawsuit against the company that eventually resulted in complete integration of the trolleys. "Before the trial was ended, the inside of the cars looked like pepper and salt."[2]

Making humor out of resistance to racial oppression is a response which Douglass shares in common with all the militant autobiographies, including works by H. Rap Brown, Bobby Seale, and Eldridge Cleaver. It seems obvious, inevitable, and exactly correct, but the reasons for its correctness, as for laughter itself, are difficult to analyze. It is a marked trait of "black styles" in general, especially when the audience is white; and the basis of it is the absurdity of the white man's racial attitudes: the incongruity of his deadly serious purpose (three men assemble to beat up a passenger on a train) and the trivial and despicable goal to which it is directed (ejecting the passenger from the first-class car because of his color); the contradiction between his concept of the "Negro" (docile, easily cowed, and in need of whippings to teach him his place) and the reality of Douglass tearing the seats off the floor and smashing up the car. To respond to tyranny with laughter is also a control on the feeling of helpless anger, a way of belittling the tyrant at times when it is not possible to overthrow him. The laughter is scorn at his diminished humanity, faith that he can be defeated, but also acknowledgement of the terrible price, in punishment, insecurity, and lives, which must be paid by the rebels.

How much mockery and accusation the black writer can include with the humor and still retain the sympathy of a white audience depends on the intensity of their racism and the degree of their social perceptiveness. The other aspect of black satire is the frontal attack, with no concern whatever to pamper the racism of the white reader, but instead to provoke it, expose it, and demand that it be reformed. This aspect was uppermost in Douglass, and reflected his viewpoint that freedom must be won by the enslaved themselves, through force; whites are persuaded by power more than by pity.

> A swarm of imps in human shape—the slave-traders and agents of slave-traders—who gathered in every country town of the state watching for chances to buy human flesh (as buzzards watch for carrion), flocked in upon us to ascertain if our masters had placed us in jail to be sold. Such a set of debased and villainous creatures I never saw before and hope never to see again. I felt as if surrounded by a pack of fiends fresh from perdition. . . .
>
> Yes, they were the legitimate fruit of slavery, and were second in villainy only to the slaveholders themselves who made such a class possible. They were mere hucksters of the slave produce of Maryland and Virginia—coarse, cruel, and swaggering bullies, whose very breathing was of blasphemy and blood. . . .
>
> To talk to those imps about justice or mercy would

have been as absurd as to reason with bears and tigers.
Lead and steel were the only arguments that they were
capable of appreciating, as the events of the subsequent
years have proved (Douglass, *Life and Times,* pp. 172–74).

Irony, satire, denunciation, and bitter determination to survive—
the vehicles of his attacks on racial oppression—are the most typical
features of Douglass's tone. A comparison of the *Narrative* with
the *Life and Times* shows that the cutting edge of his style sharp-
ened with age and use, and his skill in the handling of polemics
increased with the passage of time.

The opening paragraph of the *Narrative* states simply that he was
born in Tuckahoe, Talbot County, Maryland and explains that
his uncertainty of the exact date was due to the policy of slaveholders to wipe out the identity of the slave. His characteristic irony
and force show in the implied comparison between horses and
slaves: "By far the larger part of the slaves know as little of their
ages as horses know of theirs, and it is the wish of most masters within
my knowledge to keep their slaves thus ignorant." In the opening
pages of *My Bondage and My Freedom*, there is a considerable
amount of wordplay on the name "Tuckahoe," and more comment
on the local inhabitants. But in *Life and Times*, the first paragraph
has been honed into a rapier:

> In Talbot County, Eastern Shore, State of Maryland,
> near Easton, the county town, there is a small district of
> country, thinly populated, and remarkable for nothing
> that I know of more than for the worn-out, sandy,
> desert-like appearance of its soil, the general dilapidation
> of its farms and fences, the indigent and spiritless char-
> acter of its inhabitants, and the prevalence of ague and
> fever. It was in this dull, flat, and unthrifty district
> or neighborhood, bordered by the Choptank River,
> among the laziest and muddiest of streams, surrounded
> by a white population of the lowest order, indolent and
> drunken to a proverb, and among slaves who, in point of
> ignorance and indolence, were fully in accord with their
> surroundings, that I, without any fault of my own, was
> born, and spent the first years of my childhood.

> The reader must not expect me to say much of my
> family. Genealogical trees did not flourish among
> slaves (Douglass, *Life and Times*, p. 1).

Readers of John Barth's *The Sot-Weed Factor*, with its memorable portraits of the thieves, whores, drunken lawyers, corrupt judges, crooked doctors, and illiterate planters of colonial Maryland, will have a special appreciation for the accuracy of Douglass's verbal marksmanship. It is a typical sample of the skill with which he combines epithet and cumulative parallel clauses. The understatement beginning the next paragraph acts as an anticlimax to the first, providing a kind of tonal silence, or rest, that leaves his adjectives still ringing in the mind. The *persona* created by them is an aggressive, educated, highly literate veteran of social misery, who has succeeded in defeating every obstacle put in his path by his origins, rising above those who tried to keep him down and break his spirit and has won the right to pour on them his unmitigated contempt. This, with some additions, is the *persona* maintained throughout the rest of the book. It is maintained by the events he describes, by the positions he takes toward them, by the people he admires, but most of all, by style—a style developed through fifty years of immersion in political struggle—and in the kind of writing it demands: oratory, polemics, persuasion, letters, articles, and propaganda.

We have seen that the basis of the humor in the scene where Douglass is ejected from the first-class railroad car is the absurdity of the white man's racial attitudes. Indeed, most of the irony, parody, and denunciation in Douglass, as in all black autobiographies which use these methods, stem from social contradiction: between how whites are perceived by themselves and how they are perceived by blacks, between their political and religious ideology and their actual social system, or between their concept of black people and the reality of the black outlook and identity. In Douglass, satire was informed and animated by revolutionary passion.

> Mr. Auld . . . at once forbade Mrs. Auld to instruct me
> further. . . . To use his own words . . . "If you give a nigger
> an inch, he will take an ell. A nigger should know nothing
> but to obey his master—to do as he is told to do. . . ." All
> this, however, was too late. The first step had been

taken. Mistress, in teaching me the alphabet, had given me the *inch*, and no precaution could prevent me from taking the *ell* (Douglass, *Narrative*, pp. 49, 53).

As in the passage where Douglass accepted the identity of a "bad sheep," he defied slavery by using ironically the master's terms. Irony results when the meaning of the terms is changed, or when the favorable meaning which they have for the slave is superimposed on the unfavorable, threatening meaning which they have for the master. Parody results when the terms are used in a context that exaggerates and unveils the oppression and brutality behind them and so indicts the callousness and ignorance of slaveholders who think in those terms:

> Our food was coarse corn meal boiled. This was called *mush*. It was put into a large wooden tray or trough, and set down upon the ground. The children were then called, like so many pigs, and like so many pigs they would come and devour the mush; some with oyster-shells, others with pieces of shingle, some with naked hands, and none with spoons. He that ate fastest got most; he that was strongest secured the best place; and few left the trough satisfied (Douglass, *Narrative*, p. 44).

The revised version of this passage in the *Life and Times* is one of the few instances where Douglass blunted his barbs and watered down the sting of the rhetoric in the rewriting process; it is worth comparing the two versions for what it shows about his feel for the effect of words at his best. The second passage reads:

> Our corn meal mush, which was our only regular if not all-sufficing diet, was, when sufficiently cooled from the cooking, placed in a large tray or trough. This was set down either on the floor of the kitchen, or out of doors on the ground, and the children were called like so many pigs, and like so many pigs would come, some with oyster-shells, some with pieces of shingles, but none with spoons, and literally devour the mush. He who could eat fastest got most, and he who was strongest got the best place, but few left the trough really satisfied (Douglass, *Life and Times*, p. 72).

The short, snappy clauses of the early version, end-stopped with semicolons, bristling with controlled anger, have been changed into longer, more discursive sentences of reminiscence. The power of the word "mush" in the *Narrative* resides in its emphasis by italics, and its location at the end of the sentence; it mimicks the / dinner call that probably summoned the children. In this way it does more than answer the proslavery argument that slaves were well fed; it exposes, through mockery, the condescending, patronizing assumptions of debating the treatment of the slaves at all. Emphasis and location alone raise it to the level of parody, for in *Life and Times* it became mere description, despite the fact that the metaphor of the pigs had been retained. The power of the stark assertions, "set down upon the ground," "they would come and devour the mush," which help to convey the animal simplicity of the secene, has been dissipated by time and qualification. The purpose, in fact, seems to have shifted from polemic to historical narrative.

It is by comparison with the second version, also, that we recognize how in the first the use of stronger punctuation, the omission of modifiers, and the brief parallelisms—"He that ate fastest got most; he that was strongest secured the best place"—sketch out the swift, brutal wolfing of food. The use of the relative pronoun "that," rather than the more grammatically accurate "who," suggests indirectly that the slaves were considered animals and things rather than people, and the understatement of the final clause (which becomes only statement with the addition of "really") says more than is possible by adverbs about the starvation portions of their food allowance.

Elsewhere, Douglass achieves the tone of outrage and mimickry by repetition:

> ... there was in Boston ... a menagerie. I had long desired to see such a collection ... and as I approached the entrance to gain admission, I was told by the doorkeeper, in a harsh and contemptuous tone, *"We don't allow niggers in here."* I also remember attending a revival meeting in the Rev. Henry Jackson's meetinghouse, at New Bedford, and going up the broad aisle for a seat, I was met by a good deacon, who told me, in a pious tone,

"We don't allow niggers in here." Soon after my arrival in
new Bedford from the South, I had a strong desire to
attend the lyceum, but was told, *"They don't allow niggers
there."* While passing from New York to Boston on the
steamer *Massachusetts,* on the night of the 9th of Decem-
ber, 1843, when chilled almost through with the cold,
I went into the cabin to get a little warm. I was soon
touched upon the shoulder, and told, *"We don't allow
niggers in here."* A week or two before leaving the
United States, I had a meeting appointed at Weymouth.
. . . On attempting to take a seat in the omnibus to that
place, I was told by the driver (and I never shall forget
his fiendish hate), *"I don't allow niggers in here."* Thank
Heaven for the respite I now enjoy! I had been in Dublin
but a few days when a gentleman of great respectability
kindly offered to conduct me through all the public
buildings of that beautiful city, and soon afterward I
was invited by the Lord Mayor to dine with him. What
a pity there was not some democratic Christian at the
door of his splendid mansion to bark out at my approach, *"They don't allow niggers in here!"*
. . . The second day after my arrival in Liverpool, in
company with my friend Buffum, and several other
friends, I went to Eaton Hall. . . . As I walked through
the building the statuary did not fall down, the pictures
did not leap from their places, the doors did not refuse
to open, and the servants did not say, *"We don't allow
niggers in here"* (Douglass, *Life and Times,* pp. 245–46).

Douglass resembles Ward in contrasting his treatment in Britain
with that in America. Both anticipate the writers of the postslavery
period by directing their barbs toward racial discrimination and
attempting to steer the antislavery movement in the direction of
complete racial equality. They stand near the beginning of a
long line of black writers, from James Weldon Johnson to Leslie
Alexander Lacy, who exult over the sheer physical relief of being
away from the United States, able to confront themselves without
being imprisoned inside their own defenses.
   The style of Douglass shows the influence of his models; one

need only quote briefly from Garrison to demonstrate who was among his early mentors as a polemicist:

> As for those who defend the slave-holders, what are they, and who are they? Tell me not that they are respectable! They are not respectable in the eye of God; they are not respectable in the eye of Humanity. They are base, and Freedom loathes them. Tell me not that they occupy high stations in society! It only shows that society is corrupt. Tell me not that they are members of our churches! It only proves that our churches are anti-Christian. Tell me not that they occupy our pulpits! It only shows that they are blasphemers. We must unchristianize every man who does not regard man as man; or else we must be driven to the conclusion, that Christianity does not recognize the oneness of the human race, but allows the strong to oppress the weak.[3]

But, as we have indicated, Douglass was the slave neither of master nor mentor; he refused to remain in the role which many white abolitionists preferred him to occupy, that of eyewitness narrator to the facts of slavery; he presumed to become also theoretician, satirist, and orator, evolved his own principled differences with the Garrisonians, founded his own newspaper, and commanded style and rhetoric toward goals conceived by himself. He is superior, as a writer, to Solomon Bayley, Moses Grandy, Austin Steward, and dozens of other slave narrators, precisely because he did so much more than report what it was like to pick cotton and how he eluded the perils of escape.

To compare Douglass also with the rhetoric of Southern apologists for slavery is a great lesson in the political sources of ironic perception. In February 1837, when antislavery forces had petitioned Congress for the abolition of slavery in the District of Columbia, John C. Calhoun of South Carolina rose and spoke against even receiving the petitions. The next step, he feared, would be to consider and refer them to a committee, thus bestowing the legitimacy of due process on the abolitionist cause. His language marks a high point of moral schizophrenia in the history of the American self-concept:

I do not belong to the school which holds that aggression is to be met by concession. Mine is the opposite creed, which teaches that encroachments must be met at the beginning, and that those who act on the opposite principle are prepared to become slaves. In this case, in particular, I hold concession or compromise to be fatal. If we concede an inch, concession would follow concession—compromise would follow compromise, until our ranks would be so broken that effectual resistance would be impossible. We must meet the enemy on the frontier, with a fixed determination of maintaining our position at every hazard.[4]

The entire passage could have been written by Douglass. The formal diction, the literate, orational tone, the manly and dignified *persona*, all play their part in conveying the underlying assumptions of Calhoun's argument: that freedom, dignity, literacy, oratory, and manliness are properties of the ruling class, the Southern slavocracy, and that abolition, by challenging this ruling class, thereby threatens civilization itself. The only real differences between Calhoun's language and Douglass's are: (1) Calhoun is empty of concrete allusions to the facts of slavery, of common nouns like "cowhide," "bullwhip," "tobacco worms," "overseer," "ox-cart," and "chattel"; (2) Calhoun makes no use of irony or parody; and (3) his entire speech is based on a colossal lie, which extends its falsehood into his use of specific words such as "slave" and "resistance." It is in comparison with Calhoun that we can measure the achievement of Douglass. His dignity and manliness of tone eroded Calhoun's assumption that these qualities belong only to the ruling class; his ability to include the facts of slavery exposed what Calhoun's formal diction is designed to hide, i.e., the true brutality of the system; his irony and parody indicated a depth of insight beyond Calhoun's range, a double vision, a simultaneous grasp of the nature, and the absurdity, of class society's ideological underpinnings; and the fact that Douglass was right and Calhoun was wrong means that when the former used words like "resistance," "aggression," "slave," "freedom," "compromise," they connected him to reality, time, and the historical process, whereas when the latter used them, they divorced him from the truth, from humanity, and from himself, consigning him to the limbo of obstacles ("things," if you will) which more enlightened men and women have had to circumvent, or sweep aside, in order to advance the growth of human culture.

It is, conversely, by comparison with Douglass that we measure the hollowness of Calhoun's fine words and test the faith that the effects of lies erode their own viability, thus confirming the ultimate triumph of the truth. To speak of the facts of slavery would weaken his position; hence he must lose touch with facts. To speak of concession to the antislavery position as becoming a slave, he must "double-think" on two levels: slaveholders are apostles of freedom, and abolitionists are enslavers, that is, "freedom is slavery." Hence, he lost touch with reason. To take himself this seriously, to be unaware of the irony in his speech (and to be able to sleep at night), he must suppress John Calhoun the man, who ate, slept, and felt pain like the slaves, and give full scope to Hon. John Calhoun the senator, who kept them down. Hence, he lost touch with his own identity as a human being, apart from his role of politician. Most significant, the slaveholder's inhumanity is what forces Douglass to become human—to acquire the ironic perception, the dignity, the reason, the close grasp of facts, the insight into the structure of society, and the meaningful ideals. Calhoun helped to create the very forces that redeem society from his actions.

Douglass, in addition to his mastery of language on the level of rhetoric, also had the ability of the novelist to create character and dramatize feelings and scenes of confrontation. These talents appear to their best advantage in the *Life and Times*, which is so full of memorable portraits and incidents that to select some as examples seems an injustice to the others. His portrait of John Brown, in particular, stays in the mind, because it is based on direct personal knowledge of the man, because it completely contradicts the image of Brown given by popular American historians as an insane fanatic,[5] and because Douglass poured into this description all his talent for giving life to the concept of the hero, his hatred of slavery, his admiration for resistance to oppression, and his growing conviction that the only arguments respected by enslavers are bullets and bayonets. He calculated his effects to build suspense

and evoke for Brown the maximum interest and awe. He began
by describing Brown's house, "a small wooden building on a back
street, in a neighborhood chiefly occupied by laboring men and
mechanics," passed on to the furniture, or rather lack of it, noted
the reverence toward him of his wife and children, and, finally,
gave a physical description:

> In person he was lean, strong, and sinewy, of the best
> New England mold, built for times of trouble and fitted
> to grapple with the flintiest hardships. Clad in plain
> American woolen, shod in boots of cowhide leather, and
> wearing a cravat of the same substantial material, under
> six feet high, less than 150 pounds in weight, aged about
> fifty, he presented a figure straight and symmetrical as
> a mountain pine. His bearing was singularly impressive.
> His head was not large, but compact and high. His hair
> was coarse, strong, slightly gray, and closely trimmed,
> and grew low on his forehead. His face was smoothly
> shaved, and revealed a strong, square mouth, supported
> by a broad and prominent chin. His eyes were bluish-
> gray, and in conversation they were full of light and
> fire. When on the street, he moved with a long, springing,
> racehorse step, absorbed by his own reflections, neither
> seeking nor shunning observation.
>   Such was the man whose name I had heard in whispers
> —such was the spirit of his house and family—such was
> the house in which he lived—and such was Captain John
> Brown, whose name has now passed into history, as that
> of one of the most marked characters and greatest heroes
> known to American fame (Douglass, *Life and Times*,
> pp. 272–73).

Nothing in the entire portrait is arranged without purpose; Douglass employed most of the classical methods for delineating character, including the character's surroundings, his appearance, his
friends and family, his enemies, and his thoughts, and ordered
them in a progressive sequence, from the neighborhood and house,
to the interior, to the other people in it, to Brown himself, and
then to his plans.

John Brown's original plan impressed Douglass deeply and

gained his support: to establish small bands of armed men in the Appalachian Mountains, who would periodically raid plantations, convey some slaves to the North, recruit others as soldiers, and destroy the value of slave property in county after county, state after state, by rendering it insecure. As explained by Douglass, the plan sounds like an early American primer on guerrilla wars of national liberation. Douglass also defended Brown's Kansas exploits; "how he met persecution with persecution, war with war, strategy with strategy, assassination and house-burning with signal and terrible retaliation. . . ." The ground of his defense is that the violence of the slaveholders made it impossible to fight them by any other method. He admits a shudder at the "horrors" wrought by John Brown's "iron hand," but "it is the shudder which one feels at the execution of a murderer. . . . To call out a murderer at midnight, and without note or warning, judge or jury, run him through with a sword, was a terrible remedy for a terrible malady" (ibid., p. 303). Although disappointed and dismayed when John Brown cast aside his plan of prolonged guerrilla warfare in favor of the attack on Harper's Ferry, Douglass even then refused to disassociate himself from Brown's general views. His conclusion on Brown is delivered in his best polemical style:

> While it shall be considered right to protect one's self against thieves, burglars, robbers, and assassins, and to slay a wild beast in the act of devouring his human prey, it can never be wrong for the imbruted and whip-scarred slaves, or their friends, to hunt, harass, and even strike down the traffickers in human flesh. If anybody is disposed to think less of me on account of this sentiment, or because I may have had a knowledge of what was about to occur, and did not assume the base and detestable character of an informer, he is a man whose good or bad opinion of me may be equally repugnant and despicable (Douglass, *Life and Times*, p. 312).

The portrait of Brown is a reflection of the viewpoint toward the use of arms which Douglass developed in response to his own experience with slaveholders. Essentially that viewpoint was that the slave does not discover himself, does not become a man, and does not overcome the inhibitions on his will to freedom placed there by his master's teachings, until he resists the master and is prepared to defend that act with force. In the confrontation scene between Covey and Douglass, "the last flogging," the importance of force is primarily psychological; Douglass no longer "feels" like a slave, although in fact he has not yet escaped. Once having found out that the slave system is not omnipotent, nor himself powerless, he knows that actual freedom is only as far away as the first chance to run.

The drama of the "last flogging" is preceded by a portrait of "Covey, the Negro Breaker," and the narrative of that period in his life when Douglass was forced to drink the "bitterest dregs" from the cup of slavery: sixteen-hour work days, beatings on the one hand for not knowing how to drive oxen, and on the other for doing it imperfectly when forced, beatings for getting sick, beatings for taking a rest, and beatings simply to wear down and break his spirit. "I saw in my own situation several points of similarity with that of the oxen. They were property; so was I. Covey was to break me—I was to break them. Break and be broken was the order."

Bruised, battered, bleeding, and driven to run away, Douglass returned to his master to complain of his treatment, "all clotted with dust and blood," scarred and torn by briars around the legs; but was sent back to Covey. Covey's attempt to punish him for this escape was what precipitated the resistance. In the course of the fight, Douglass whipped Covey's cousin Hughes, stimulated two other slaves to disobey orders, and knocked Covey full-length into a pasture of cow dung. Throughout the account, we recognize the origin of the aggressive, bitter power so evident in his language. It was forged in the process of risking his life to save his spirit.

> He only can understand the effect of this combat on my spirit, who has himself incurred something, or hazarded something, in repelling the unjust and cruel aggressions of a tyrant. . . . I was no longer a servile coward, trembling under the frown of a brother worm of the dust, but my long-cowed spirit was roused to an attitude of inde-pendence. I had reached the point at which I was *not afraid to die*. This spirit made me a freeman in *fact*,

> though I still remained a slave in *form*. When a slave
> cannot be flogged, he is more than half free. He has a
> domain as broad as his own manly heart to defend, and he
> is really "a power on earth." From this time until my
> escape from slavery, I was never fairly whipped (Douglass,
> *Life and Times*, p. 143).

Listening to the cadence of the language, we notice certain
words that linger in the ear, because of their position at stressed
points, and color the whole statement with an aura of nobility:
"spirit," "tyrant," "coward," "dust," "roused," "independence,"
"not afraid to die," "flogged," "free," "heart," "defend," "power on
earth." These charged phrases are repositories of the Western
ideals of *liberty* and *equality*, as they have come down through
the chief documents of the English, French, and American Revolutions. They dignify the story in terms to which every bosom returns an echo; the diction is elevated and general; the sentiments
are universal; the mind reposes on them as on the stability of
truth.[6]

Equally important in Douglass, and equally well expressed, is
the effect on the spirit of knowledge; that which spoils a man
for slavery, because it enlarges his view of life's possibilities, enables
him to understand the basis of the master's power, and makes him
the intellectual equal or superior of the master. The profound,
angry discontent which follows that knowledge is another theme
common in black autobiography, and appears again in Du Bois,
Wright, Redding, and Malcolm X. It was probably never better
articulated, however, than by Douglass:

> And as I read, behold! the very discontent so graphically
> predicted by Master Hugh had already come upon
> me. I was no longer the light-hearted, gleesome boy,
> full of mirth and play, that I was when I landed in Balti-
> more. Light had penetrated the moral dungeon where
> I had lain, and I saw the bloody whip for my back
> and the iron chain for my feet. . . . As I writhed under
> the sting and torment of this knowledge I almost
> envied my fellow slaves for their stupid indifference. It
> opened my eyes to the horrible pit, and revealed the

teeth of the frightful dragon that was ready to pounce
upon me, but alas, it opened no way for escape. I wished
myself a beast, a bird, anything rather than a slave. I was
wretched and gloomy beyond my ability to describe.
This everlasting thinking distressed and tormented me,
and yet there was no getting rid of this subject of my
thoughts.
. . . I do not exaggerate when I say that it looked at me in
every star, smiled in every calm, breathed in every
wind and moved in every storm (Douglass, *Life and
Times*, p. 86).

We have chosen and discussed a number of single passages to
demonstrate that Frederick Douglass, among his other eminences,
was a superior literary artist; but the strength of the whole book
cannot be captured by quoting passages. His greatness as an autobiographer derives ultimately from two sources: (1) he held up
to humanity an image of heroism that is wholly consistent with the
idea of "manhood" as conceived in American culture but that is
devoid of the chauvinist frontier "individualism" associated with
the worst aspects of our history: murder of the Indians, rampant
capitalism, the exploitation of the poor and weak, the amassing of
huge fortunes, and the imperialistic contempt for the cultures
of other countries. He proved that it is possible to survive and defeat
the ugliest forms of tyranny with a sane mind and a spirit intact;
he is a standard by which to measure the meaning of the word
"freedom" and represents, at their best, the traditional Western
values of liberty, progress, energy, social concern, and involvement
in the material affairs of this world. (2) He blended the "life"
with the "times" so well that they are indistinguishable. Like
Richard Wright and W. E. B. Du Bois, Douglass conveyed an image
of man *in society*, the individual as shaped by social and class
forces at a particular time and place in history, and in turn shaping
and changing the balance of those forces by his participation in
the mass movements of his age. We have seen how this social involvement affects his language, by producing a polemical style
that takes advantage of all the resources of oratory, that is designed
to provoke tyrants and rouse friends of liberty to action, that renders

the material facts of social relations in clear detail, and that is weighted toward irony, parody, and blistering indignation; a style, in short, which is a fighting weapon. The disadvantage of the style is that it must rely heavily, for persuasion, on public formulas and so tends to slip into stock phrases and bombast. But it is a meaning-oriented language; it assumes a moral universe with right and wrong actions, for which we are responsible; it rebukes the audience for doing wrong and demands that they do right.

One of the most important critical lessons of the slave narratives is that the literary achievement proceeds *through* and *from* the political involvement of the writer. Douglass is great as a literary figure mainly *because* of the demands made on him in his political life; the one is not incidental to the other. It is impossible to appreciate his work as art without relating it constantly to his politics; there can be no such thing as a "purely aesthetic" standard of evaluating slave narrative literature.

It is an interesting fact that the slave narrative period, which represents an extraordinary outpouring of black literary activity and which produced at least one great book and several good ones, overlaps the same fifteen-year span as *Walden, Leaves of Grass, The Scarlet Letter, Representative Men*, and *Moby Dick*. But because Douglass, Thompson, Pennington, Ward, Bibb, Wells Brown, and the Crafts have never been accepted as part of the established canon of classical American literature, we have never been able to see the classical white authors in a complete context. *My Bondage and My Freedom* is equal to *Walden* in literary excellence, yet until recently it has attracted little historical comment and scarcely any criticism. Marion Wilson Starling's *The Slave Narrative: Its Place in American Literary History* (1946), singles out Douglass as the best narrator, but her opinion of the narratives in general is that they are "low in aesthetic values" and "possess primary significance for the social historian."[7] There is no mention whatever of Frederick Douglass or any other slave narrator in F. O. Matthiessen's monumental study, *American Renaissance*. This fact is a measure of the poverty of our understanding. It cannot be merely coincidental that the "American Renaissance" occurred during the time that the question of slavery was reaching a crisis. Among the black writers of the *Renaissance*, the race issue was the passionate foundation of their whole achievement. It is beyond the scope of this work to explore the relationship between the race concept of the white authors and that of the black, between the language and viewpoint of the whites, and between the literature of both races and the politics of the 1850s. But the results would tell us a great deal, about ourselves and the role of the race issue in our history, and about the causes of literary flowerings.

Part two
The Period of Search
ca. 1901-1961

From the Dark Tower

We shall not always plant while others reap
The golden increment of bursting fruit,
Not always countenance, abject and mute,
That lesser men should hold their brothers cheap;
Not everlastingly while others sleep
Shall we beguile their limbs with mellow flute,
Not always bend to some more subtle brute;
We were not made eternally to weep.

The night whose sable breast relieves the stark,
White stars is no less lovely being dark,
And there are buds that cannot bloom at all
In light, but crumple, piteous, and fall;
So in the dark we hide the heart that bleeds,
And wait, and tend our agonizing seeds.

—Countee Cullen

Chapter 5 *In search of a unified self*

THE sixty years from 1901 to 1961 cover a period of deep alienation and identity crisis in black writing. The year 1901 marks the appearance of Booker T. Washington's *Up from Slavery*, perhaps the last true slave narrative; 1961 is the date of James Baldwin's classic, *Nobody Knows My Name*, a collection of essays that stand on the threshold of civil rights, black power, and rebellion in the urban ghettoes.

The distance between these dates is filled with violent change. On the whole, autobiography no longer moves in a definite direction, with the current of history. If anything, many writers seem to feel that they are opposing the current, that it may be sweeping them backward into a Tartarus of racism, Jim Crow, hunger, violence, and lynch law. No single literary structure dominates the books. Instead, we find a pervasive, anguished groping for identity, that is no longer provided by the categories of the fugitive slave in resistance to the tyrannical slaveholders and their system.

The question of what and how to resist had become much more complex. Black people were restricted by a maze of new caste rules, migrating to Northern cities, pulled into industry as unskilled workers, and terrorized whenever they tried to exercise the freedoms the law said were theirs. At the same time, the migration to the urban North increased the possibilities for cultural and political action: the Harlem Renaissance and the Universal Negro Improvement Association, for example, followed closely on the growth of a black ghetto in New York.

The writers have widely varied backgrounds: Booker T. Washington was a former slave; W. E. B. Du Bois grew up in New England and attended Harvard; James Weldon Johnson was raised in Florida and went to New York with Cole Porter to seek his fortune marketing songs; J. Saunders Redding became a college professor and historian; Richard Wright was the son of a sharecropper; Hosea Hudson left sharecropping to work in a foundry in

Birmingham; Ida Wells was the daughter of a slave that became a carpenter; Langston Hughes's father was a wealthy businessman in Mexico; Claude McKay spent his boyhood in the countryside of Jamaica.

Their politics range all the way from acceptance of segregation to communist revolution; but every writer in this group is driven to assert the fact of his blackness as the starting point of creating a free self. Most assault the racism of American institutions. In doing so, these authors fall back on the same values that sustained the slave narrators: education, work, resistance, restless movement, group loyalty. Religion is a much weaker influence, but Christian assumptions are deeply ingrained in the rhetoric of several major figures. The assertion of black identity means that the author takes pride in being black; but it also means that he must maintain and struggle to reconcile two contradictory identities: one as a black person, the other as an American. This problem results in a condition which we have already seen in the narratives of Samuel Ward, William Wells Brown, Frederick Douglass, and William and Ellen Craft: a kind of cultural schizophrenia, where the author must somehow discover roots in a country which does not accept him as a human being. If he identifies only with black people, to the exclusion of white America, then he is partly an alien in his own homeland, with the added burden of having to wear a mask, to act out the white stereotype of the "Negro" in order to avoid white violence. If he identifies with the values of white America, then he is in danger of cutting himself off from his black cultural heritage, or worse, actually becoming an agent by which white industrialists maintain control over the whole working class.

We have seen in the slave narratives that although their authors felt and expressed the pressures of this double identity, their experiences as fugitive slaves and the existence of the antislavery issue assured them a sense of being at one with a mass movement. The threat of slavery was so great that no Negro could feel secure in his freedom until the system was destroyed.

In the second period of black autobiography, a new dilemma has crept into the old one of double identity: as the individual author succeeds in the white world by virtue of his outstanding abilities, he is more and more removed from the black masses; the gulf increases between himself and his own people, and at the same time he can never wholly enter the white American mainstream because of his color. He is doomed to alienation from both worlds. This identity crisis occurs most acutely in W. E. B. Du Bois, J. Saunders Redding, and Richard Wright, in the sense that it seems the center of their books; but it is also found in a different form in Langston Hughes and Claude McKay. Its effect is that it forces them to reexamine and redefine the whole relationship of the Negro writer and intellectual to black people and political movements. They must articulate, not only what it means to be a black American, but what it means to be a black writer and political activist, and on what basis art and politics are to be reconciled.

It was W. E. B. Du Bois who gave the most conscious, explicit statement, in autobiographical form, of the struggle to unite and harmonize the pieces of the divided self. Du Bois, like Douglass before him, returned again and again to the account of his life. *The Souls of Black Folk* (1903), *Darkwater* (1920), *Dusk of Dawn: An Essay Toward an Autobiography of a Race Concept* (1940), and *Autobiography* (1968) all mingle personal narrative with political essay, declaring that the author's being is important primarily as a microcosm for the issue of race. "My discussions of the concept of race, and of the white and colored worlds," he wrote in *Dusk of Dawn*, "are not to be regarded as digressions from the history of my life." Rather, that history exemplifies and illustrates "what race has meant in the world in the nineteenth and twentieth centuries."[1] The divided self, then, mirrors the divisions in the world at large; he cannot harmonize the self without becoming deeply involved in defining, and changing, its relations with other selves. Because the class and race divisions among other people are experienced internally by the black writer, he can approach the task of understanding society in the modern imperial West with an added degree of insight.

"One ever feels his twoness," Du Bois wrote in 1903; "an American, a Negro; two souls, two thoughts, two unreconciled strivings; two warring ideals in one dark body."

> The history of the American Negro is the history of this strife,—this longing to attain self-conscious manhood, to merge his double self into a better and truer self. In this merging he wishes neither of the older selves to

be lost. . . . He simply wishes to make it possible for a
man to be both a Negro and an American, without having
the doors of Opportunity closed roughly in his face.[2]

The gift of double vision gives him the clairvoyance, in *Darkwater*,
to see the souls of white folk "undressed and from the back and
side." He is "native, not foreign, bone of their thought and flesh of
their language."[3] Dual identity enables him to see the system
from within and without at the same time. Du Bois compared himself as a young man to a passenger on the "rushing express" of
industrialism, concerned mainly with his relations to other passengers rather than with its speed and destination (Du Bois, *Dusk of
Dawn*, pp. 27–28). Like William and Ellen Craft, who rode an
actual train to freedom, Du Bois wore a mask with the whites on
board, observing them from a vantage point they did not understand. The difference is that the Crafts knew where the train was
going and when to get off; Du Bois had to map the route in succes-
sive stages, not knowing where it led, certain only that the whites
knew less than he did about the human cost or the utimate goal.

What is more, the dilemma of having two souls and two unreconciled strivings no longer consisted only of the contradiction between
being black and American. Class and racial identity for the slave
narrators were almost the same thing. Even in the case of middle-
class Negroes like Samuel Ward and Charlotte Forten, their class
interests were to defend the slave; because as long as slavery
existed, all their class gains could easily be undermined by a law
such as the Fugitive Slave Act, or totally destroyed by a band of
kidnappers. In the second period, the writer must choose between
the Negro bourgeoisie and the black masses. To attend a university,
assimilate the culture and literary standards of white America,
address himself as a writer to a white audience, and "advance the
race" by advancing his own career, is at the same time to remove
himself from his black cultural roots. The result is a kind of rootless
limbo, for the color line makes it impossible ever to identify
wholly with the white world. The black autobiographer must attempt to develop himself as a writer without being swallowed by
the Negro bourgeoisie and without denying his American identity;
and he must somehow appropriate the literary traditions of the

white mainstream "beyond the Veil" without being separated from black experience and history.

The problem of the identity crisis is presented in tragic form by Du Bois in the tale of the coming of John (Du Bois, *Souls of Black Folk*, chap. 13). John Jones, "fine plough-hand, good in the rice fields," full of "bubbling good-nature and genuine satisfaction with the world," is sent away to the North to college. It so happens that a white John, son of a local judge, goes away at the same time. The white John comes back entirely at one with his family and culture. The black John is not so fortunate; he has seen the best which white civilization has to offer and been forbidden to partake of it by the color line. His education, meanwhile, has made him condescending and slightly contemptuous of his own people, their crude religion, and simple acceptance of poverty and segregation; he has lost his roots among them and become embittered by his knowledge and insight into the system of racial discrimination. When he returns to his home town to teach, the judge warns him not to upset Southern race relations by introducing any of his "new-fangled notions"; he is a marked man, his school is closed, and it is only a matter of time before some incident of racism drives him into open rebellion and he is lynched. That incident is provided when, returning home across a field, he discovers the white John in the act of raping his sister; the black John picks up a heavy stick and strikes him dead, thus committing the unpardonable crime of defending a loved one, asserting an elemental human right against a white man.

In the alienation of the black John from both worlds, his solitary bitterness, his struggle to find some political and cultural tie with his people and to avoid becoming an emasculated tool of the whites in power, we are given an image of the problems that beset Du Bois as a writer and intellectual. For Du Bois, the tragic conclusion of the tale of John is one possible result of the struggle; but the autobiographies are an effort to construct alternatives.

Du Bois was one of many black writers who felt caught between divided worlds in the second period. The dual identity crisis motivated J. Saunders Redding to abandon a comfortable life as a college student and immerse himself in the experience of the black farmer and worker in the South. He was returning, not, like

John, to discover and be defeated by his alienation from black people, but to overcome it. After several months of being the only Negro at a major Northern university, Redding "hated and feared the whites" and "hated and feared and was ashamed of Negroes."

> . . . at last I felt and knew that my estrangement from my fellows and theirs from me was but a failure to realize that we were all estranged from something fundamentally ours. We were all withdrawn from the heady, brawling, lusty stream of culture which had nourished us and which was the stream by whose turbid waters all of America fed. We were spiritually homeless, dying and alone, each on his separate hammock of memory and experience.[4]

The symbol of his identity crisis, in his family, is the fact that one of his grandmothers was light-skinned and religious, the other dark, a veteran of slavery, and passionate in her hatred of whites. His father used the white abolitionist speeches of John Brown, Wendell Phillips, Whittier, and Whitman "as battering stones hurled against the strong walls of a prison"; his mother rejected identification with black people and became upset when Negroes moved into their neighborhood (Redding, p. 24).

The Southern Negro college students of Redding's experience "were motivated by the desire to possess, as indeed they put it, yellow money, yellow cars, and yellow women." Unable to accept identity with the Negro bourgeoisie, Redding set out to find the values that would hold good for him as a black American and a man. The remainder of the book is a record of his journey from state to state, searching for who he was in relation to his cultural roots. The identity crisis in Redding is the conscious drive behind the work.

The issue of one's relation to the Negro bourgeoisie becomes a family and generational feud for Langston Hughes, whose father was a capitalist in Mexico and hated "niggers" and Mexicans. Hughes's desire to be among and identify with the working-class Negroes of America resulted in a final break with his father. His feelings about the Negro bourgeoisie of Washington, D.C., were that "they were on the whole as unbearable and snobbish a group of people as I have ever come in contact with anywhere."[5] The iden-

tity crisis is not stated as such in either *The Big Sea* or *I Wonder
As I Wander*, but we find it in a poem which he used often in readings to regain the attention of a flagging audience:

> My old man's a white old man. . . .
> My old mother's black.
> But if ever I cursed my white old man
> I take my curses back.
>
> If ever I cursed my black old mother
> And wished she were in hell,
> I'm sorry for that evil wish
> And now I wish her well.
>
> My old man died in a fine big house,
> My ma died in a shack.
> I wonder where I'm gonna die,
> Being neither white nor black.[6]

The poem brings out both the racial and class factors in the speaker's dual self. One side of him is white *and* bourgeois ("My old
man died in a fine big house"); the other is black *and* poor ("My ma
died in a shack"). The question, "I wonder *where* I'm gonna die,"
is at heart a question of his class identity, his place in the social
scale. But it is posed, in the final line, by the issue of color.

Langston Hughes's attitude toward the Negro bourgeoisie was
shared by Claude McKay. "Blacks in stiff-starched white facades
and black uniforms," he wrote, "like a flock of crows, imagining they
are elegant—oh no!"[7] Both writers experience alienation from
their black roots in the university atmosphere; McKay "quit college" because "the spirit of the vagabond, the daemon of some
poets, had got hold of me." Hughes begins *The Big Sea* with the
dramatic gesture of throwing all his books into the ocean from
the deck of the merchant ship on which he had signed as a common
seaman. These acts are rejections of a middle-class identity and
of education alone as a solution to anything.

Each book begins with an image of setting out: McKay is on a
railway car, Hughes on a ship. The problem of identity is not felt
acutely as a crisis in either work, because there is a sense very
early that they have made their choices, they have already determined where their loyalties and values lie. The main subjects

of *The Big Sea* and *A Long Way From Home* are the problems and
identities of their authors as poets, and the events of their careers
on the way to literary success. But even here the identity crisis
is a background force: they must set out, they must leave the values
of the Negro bourgeoisie, before they can discover a voice, a form,
or a subject matter. The problem of how to assimilate their experience into art necessarily implies the problem of what voice will
speak in the poems, and, therefore, what identity.

Du Bois pointed out as early as *The Souls of Black Folk* that
split identity wrought havoc with the artist, in particular, because
he had to decide what audience to address. The beauty of black
culture "was the soul-beauty of a race which his larger audience
despised" (Du Bois, *The Souls of Black Folk*, p. 5), and he could
not speak for that larger audience because it was white. James
Weldon Johnson rejected the idea of writing in dialect for precisely
the reason that a dialect poet remained "dominated by his audience . . . the white reading public"; and what he wrote "bore little
relation, sometimes no relation at all, to actual Negro life."[8]
Dialect fastened the poet inside the mask, the "Negro" identity
as conceived by whites, without permitting him to speak as a member of humankind.

What, then, were the steps that the autobiographies took to
create a "better and truer self," to reconcile being black with being
American, to break down the gulf that separated them from the
"heady, brawling, lusty stream" of black culture?

The most important step was the acceptance of their blackness as
a subject of pride. Even Booker T. Washington, the most conservative figure of the period, wrote that he would "rather be what I
am, a member of the Negro race, than be able to claim membership
with the most favored of any other race."[9] W. E. B. Du Bois first
discovered his own black identity through Negro music. "Ever
since I was a child these songs have stirred me strangely." They
are "full of the voices of my brothers and sisters . . ." (Du Bois,
Souls of Black Folk, pp. 250–51). In his last *Autobiography*, he
describes how, as a young man, he refused "integration" with white
culture, was "firm" in his criticism of whites and dreamed of a
self-sufficient Negro culture. He believed that "they who did not
know me were the losers, not I." The historical experience of the
Negro in America has made his cultural heritage "unique and

marvellous," and should be preserved by Negroes educated to support a school of black art and literature.[10]

At the beginning of *Along This Way*, James Weldon Johnson establishes his descent from Haitian ancestors who fought in the great slave insurrections with Toussaint L'Ouverture. These family and cultural roots are part of an identity which is conceived in both political and racial terms. Later he describes his "race superiority" complex as a child: "all the most interesting things that came under my observation were being done by colored men" (Johnson, p. 31). And he articulates the theme that "black is beautiful" in describing the "rich coloring," "gayety," "laughter and song" of black women (ibid., p. 121). The race problem, says Johnson, must be solved primarily in the South, by the black masses themselves, who are the most reliable hope for the "persistent movement forward of the race." The black masses laugh at the white man with a deep laughter which "should be the most ominous sound that reaches his ears" (ibid., pp. 120, 314–15). It is related to the ironic laughter of Frederick Douglass at the littleness of the men who attempt to eject him from his seat on the train, and the caustic laughter of the black revolutionary satirist at a doomed system that can only seal its doom further by exacting from him the toll of suffering he knows in advance he will have to pay.

A character in Redding's *No Day of Triumph* (1942) maintains, "I'd rather be a niggah myse'f. No, suh! I ain't a'ter no change. Niggahs got all de good bottom gravy, ter my way o' thinkin'." The qualities that Redding finds among the black masses of the South—"integrity of spirit, love of freedom, courage, patience, hope"—are, he asserts, the enduring qualities found in the mass of humankind all over the world. Black identity and pride, for him, were not merely racial, but means to discovering the common denominator of humanity in everyone.

In the autobiography of Ruby Berkley Goodwin, *It's Good to Be Black* (1953), pride in black identity is the central motif. The book was written, as the author explains, to disprove her white psychology instructor's statement that "all black children grow up frustrated." It debunks a liberal stereotype by asserting blackness as a positive cultural tradition. Parts of the narrative sound like themes from Faulkner's novels; at one point, when a new church burns down and the people determine to rebuild it, there is born in the author, as she watches her grandfather, "a great respect for the black man's strength":

> His is the strength of the beaver and the ant. The strength of the tireless little people of the world to build and rebuild. Patience and the ability to make a dream grow in the barren soil of nothingness—this is the black man's strength, sometimes seemingly powerless but always magnificent and—indestructible.[11]

"Black was a mark of distinction, not of condemnation." At the end of the book, she recalls her father's words, spoken to help her cope with an incident of racial discrimination:

> Black ain't nothin' to be ashamed of. . . . I'm proud when somebody calls me a black man. . . . The Bible says God made man out of the dust of the earth. I've seen red dirt, brown dirt, black dirt, and yellow clay, but all my life I ain't never seen no real white dirt. . . . I want you to be proud you're black, Reuben. Black is powerful! (Goodwin, p. 252).

The same theme of black identity appears in Claude McKay's *A Long Way From Home* and in the autobiographies by Langston Hughes, *The Big Sea* and *I Wonder As I Wander*. McKay and Hughes construct their identities primarily as poets and human beings, making it a point to argue that friendship and art should cut across the color line. Both writers, for example, feel more in common with white poets and with the masses of Soviet Russia than with the American black middle class, but blackness is an essential part of their identities as poets. McKay writes that he will raise his voice to make a canticle of the "mighty throbbing force" of America, its "bitterness" burning in his "black body" (McKay, p. 4). A discerning person reading his poems "would become immediately aware that I came from a tropical country and that I was not, either by the grace of God or the desire of man, born white" (ibid., p. 28). He recommends that black American school children, instead of being assigned Homer, should read the African poet Antar. And for political action, he advises that Negroes organize and officer their own group. "Group soul," according to McKay, is what Negroes have that is peculiarly theirs and could

not have been given them by any white civilization (ibid., p. 349).
What he means by the term "soul," interpreting the context, is
synonymous with negritude, shared culture, race pride, and black
communal values.

It is specifically with working-class Negroes that McKay and
Hughes feel their black identities; "blackness" is as much a class as
a racial category in their work. The racial and class aspects of
identity here are inseparable. "I was a Negro," says Hughes, "and
I liked Negroes very much." But the Negroes to whom he refers
are the Negro workers just up from the South, with their laughter
like "thunderclaps," their troubles, their "discussions of the war
and the men who had gone to Europe from the Jim Crow South,
their complaints over the high rent and the long overtime hours
that brought what seemed like big checks, until the weekly bills
were paid" (Hughes, *The Big Sea*, p. 54). The passage in *The Big
Sea* where Hughes attempts to identify with Africans on his voyage
to Africa is a record of rejection and hurt. They laugh at him,
shake their heads, and say, "you, white man! You, white man!"
(Ibid., pp. 102–3). It is obvious from this incident, and from many
others like it, that awareness of color is socially conditioned, and
that color is conceived as a social category by most of these authors.

Black identity in all the books is quite different from acknowl-
edging that someone has red hair and is six feet tall. It is a center of
experience, an organizing principle for the autobiography. Indeed,
only when blackness becomes this does it function as "identity,"
for identity in an autobiography consists of the speaking *persona*
which the experiences selected by the writer are supposed to have
shaped. The assertion of black pride is a defense against racism
and racial discrimination. Washington defends the capacity of
Negroes to learn skilled trades, work hard, and achieve economic
power; Du Bois and Redding assert their common humanity, pride,
integrity, and endurance; McKay and Hughes assert their warmth,
aesthetic sense, and responsiveness to poetry; Johnson and Goodwin assert their beauty. Even when not directly stated, black
identity always has an underlying social and political content. It
is always part of the fight against racial oppression.

How black identity leads to a greater feeling of kinship with
humankind is magnificently illustrated by the career of Paul
Robeson. In *Here I Stand*, he narrates the story of his growth from

a minister's son in Princeton, N.J., to actor, singer, communist, Pan-Africanist, and champion of freedom for all oppressed people. Though *Here I Stand* is not a full-scale autobiography, it is written from the same needs and solves the dilemma of the split self in a way that does not come to full flower in black writing until the great upsurge of the 1960s. Robeson simply refused to practice the values or think the frightened thoughts of a bourgeois Negro, even when this cost him his career as an actor and singer, his right to travel, and his reputation. The press distortions he encountered forced him to state his views in writing; but his views took their significance from his life. The need to write about his life, therefore, as in all black autobiography, is political. The direction of the narrative is toward political awakening.

"Yes, I heard my people singing!" Robeson said of his early years in Princeton;[12] later he would sing to audiences of workers, soldiers, and farmers everywhere, including the miners of Wales and the Loyalist brigades of the Spanish Civil War. He would also learn their songs and sing them to audiences in the United States and Canada, even while being harassed by the State Department and attacked by anticommunist mobs. Black songs meant an opportunity to immerse himself in the historical experience of his people and make it understood to other cultures. It also meant a bridge to the world's great folk music. But it was the "ominous drumbeat of history" that forced him to stand among the masses whose songs he had adopted.

In London, the heart of the British Empire, he would meet Kwame Nkrumah, Jomo Kenyatta, and the African seamen of the ports of London, Liverpool, and Cardiff. From them he would learn the great advances of the African past, the significance of African culture to black American self-esteem, and the emptiness of the claim that Africa was not ready for self-government. It was an African that called his attention to the progress the Soviet Union had made in wiping out discrimination against minorities. Like Langston Hughes, he visited the USSR in the 1930s and saw with his own eyes that "colored people walked secure and free as equals," where before the Revolution they had been segregated (Robeson, pp. 35–36). Through his interest in attaining full freedom for black people, Robeson came to study socialism and was won over to its principles as well as its achievements.

Contact with the various peoples of Britain taught him that "the essential character of a nation is determined not by the upper classes, but by the common people," who are "truly brothers in the great family of mankind" (ibid., p. 48). Filled with this conviction, he was free to accept the American aspect of his background despite the fact that he was persecuted as "un-American" by the federal government. His felt connections with the workers of other lands overcame the Negro/American dilemma: there need be no antagonism between being American and being Negro, if "American" means identity with the common people. The experience of blacks as participants in the most progressive movements of American history—the Revolution, abolitionism, the organization of labor, the fight against fascism—affords the basis on which to reconcile the divided self. The answer to "cultural schizophrenia" must be political. To fight for the freedom of black people is to fight for the future of democracy in America. To fight for socialism, realizing that full freedom can only be attained through the possession of all wealth and power by the peoples of the earth, is to fight for the future of mankind. True black identity, then, is a means of breaking through the isolation of the color line and joining hands with the rest of humanity. In no sense does this mean abandoning black interests; "the Negro people's movement must be led by Negroes" and have a "single-minded dedication" to the welfare of blacks. Only in this way can they cease being dominated by the idea that "white is right."

In practice, Robeson did experience a great deal of alienation in his own country, both from the white world of power and from black organizations afraid to be associated with him. When *Here I Stand* was published, white commercial newspapers and magazines in the United States ignored it. *The Crisis*, organ of the NAACP, gave it an unfavorable review; but several black-owned newspapers nevertheless had the courage to speak in its favor. The Chicago *Crusader*, the Baltimore *Afro-American*, and the Los Angeles *Herald-Dispatch* all broke the silence of the media by praising parts of the book and publicizing its ideas.

This fact indicates that an important change had taken place in the audience of black autobiography during the second period. The slave narrators, as we have seen, addressed themselves primarily to European and American whites—in particular, educated whites who would have the influence to help their cause. The white capitalist class, by the turn of the century, was in a position to manipulate both the audience and the reception of black writing as a means of reinforcing their own power. The Northern business interests that supported Booker T. Washington, for example, wanted to "discipline" the white working class by using Negro strikebreakers imbued with the Washington ethic of docility and worship of manual labor. Washington's writing, therefore, was reviewed and popularized by the major commercial news outlets, while the work of Du Bois was largely ignored, and funding for his studies cut off.[13] The same business interests tried to silence Robeson in 1958. Their failure is a measure of how far the black writer had turned toward different avenues of publicity since 1901.

The groundwork for this change was done in the 1920s. Ida Wells addressed her autobiography (1928) to the "young people who have so little of our race's history recorded." Her object is to redeem black history from oblivion, correct the false accounts of white historians, and make future black generations aware of their proud heritage.[14] These motives were certainly not absent from Frederick Douglass and Samuel Ward; but the need to be independent of the white reader and reviewer had come to the surface and inspired a whole new current of black literature. Du Bois "believed in the higher education of a Talented Tenth" who could take the intellectual leadership of black civilization out of white hands and guide the group "into self-realization and to its highest cultural possibilities" (Du Bois, *Dusk of Dawn*, p. 70). Langston Hughes published his early poems in *The Crisis*, received encouragement from Negro critics and editors, and built up an audience from among the Negro colleges of the South. Other writers of the Harlem Renaissance professed to care little for white critical opinion. It is true that the black audience which they tried to cultivate was confined too exclusively to the middle class for many years; but the effort was made. It had to be made; black identity could only be sustained in relation to a black public.

The social base of autobiography was still more or less the same as the base which produced the slave narratives: that is, the existence of racial and class oppression, the fact that black people could not vote, could not come and go as they pleased, had little or no legal redress, were forced to work under slave conditions and were brutalized at the whim of white mobs. But where the slave narratives dealt with the problem chiefly on the level of politics and religion, selecting and organizing experience according to what would best contribute to the antislavery struggle, these autobiographies of the second period dealt with oppression chiefly on the level of culture. The central motive of the former works was to fight a social system; the central motive of the latter was to resolve an identity crisis, to discover "who I am." Experience, therefore, was selected with that in mind, not necessarily for the needs of an objective movement. But this resolution is also a political act on a different plane. Once having discovered who he is, the writer may be led back into direct political struggle, because he has secured a kind of subjective "base camp," so to speak, from which to fight; he has worked out the terms on which to reenter the world of objective class relations and mass movements and decide what his role there is going to be.

Chapter 6 *In search of a social role*

ONLY a meaningful social role, in the long run, could reconcile the split identities of black authors. Since the source of identity crisis was the oppression of the author and his people by white power, that role had to be a form of revolt. Selfhood had to be conceived in political terms. Black solidarity and politicized education, restless movement and the legitimacy of fighting back—these are the values passed on by the slave narratives that the generation of Du Bois and Wright found most adaptable to their needs. Christian faith and fundamentalist religion, on the other hand, have almost run dry. But even here, we find no sharp break in continuity; the slave narrators had always recognized that religion was employed as a tool to support slavery, and their faith coexisted with a deep skepticism of the power of Christianity to change the world unless accompanied by political action. The values harvested from the second period in greater and greater abundance are socialism, communism, Pan-Africanism, and identification with the interests of the wage working class, black and white. Vaguely prefigured during slavery, they come forward after the Harlem Renaissance to fill the vacuum left by religion.

Christian faith is viewed with distance in the autobiography of J. Saunders Redding and with cynicism and hostility in Richard Wright. Langston Hughes seems detached from the religion itself but deeply interested in it as part of the life-force of working-class Negroes. Angelo Herndon, in *Let Me Live*, rejects Christianity as an opium of the workers. W. E. B. Du Bois treats it the same way that he treats the "Sorrow Songs," as the voice of the downtrodden hungering for the promised land, a kind of great taproot feeding all the branches of the black family tree. For James Weldon Johnson, religion is a resource of art. McKay has very little to say about it, although he was eventually to become a Roman Catholic. Booker T. Washington's religion is the Protestant ethic of Benjamin Franklin, and, in some respects, it is closest of all to the slave narrative heritage because of his belief that the special suffering of the Negro people is a mark of Providential favor.

The patronizing attitude of Redding, Johnson, Wright, and Hughes toward the rural evangelism of Southern Negroes is part of their alienation from black culture. Johnson "returns" to the grass roots by transmuting religious belief into art, but from the age of nine there is no question of his accepting it literally. Led to the mourner's bench to be consecrated to God, he knelt and tried to feel a conviction of sin; but he fell asleep instead. When the others shook him by the shoulder to wake him up, he kept very still and convinced them he was in a trance. Later on he "awoke" and recounted a vision to save himself from punishment (Johnson, p. 26). We sense here the detached perspective, the aesthetic and humorous distance, that was necessary for Johnson to make conscious use of religion as folk material in *God's Trombones*. His attitude in the poems is equally clear: the sophisticated artist may admire folk religion as "quaint," or as an emanation of the tireless strength of the people to endure; but this is quite different from the literal faith of Samuel Ward, J. W. C. Pennington, Noah Davis, and John Thompson.

Redding treats religion as an object of satire and journalistic description and a powerful psychological force straining against the walls of poverty and grief:

> On the periphery of awareness was the sound as of someone praying with quiet insistence in the next room. Flat and solid in the very center of consciousness was the heat in the kitchen. No one seemed to think of opening the window, though the air was thick and foul with the odor of simmering food, of flowers, and of our own yeasty body sweat. The pitcher went around a third time, but no one seemed to be drinking much. A thin scum of sweat put a sheen on all our faces. Slowly one took refuge in the sound of the praying voice from the other room. It rose and fell with expert, insinuating cadence, broken now and then by the fierce, low keen of a woman's voice (Redding, p. 270).

Here again there is no question of literal faith. The author is present as an observer, and a good one, for he captures the odor of humanity and the deep poetic hunger for self-transcendence rising from within the prison of material conditions. But he is outside the experience, looking in. The faith is not what sustains him as a value.

For Langston Hughes, faith makes little difference in the conduct of the individual. "Auntie Reed," he says, "was a Christian and made me go to church and Sunday school every Sunday. But Uncle Reed was a sinner and never went to church as long as he lived, nor cared anything about it" (Hughes, *The Big Sea*, p. 18). Yet both were equally "good and kind," and from them he "learned to like both Christians and sinners equally well." His own first experience with "salvation" was similar to that of Johnson and Wright. Taken to church as a child so that he might "see Jesus," Hughes watched boy after boy go up to the altar to be saved and kept waiting and waiting for something to happen. But nothing did. Finally, because he was tired, hot, and under pressure from the congregation, he got up and pretended to be called. Everyone was happy except him. Late that night he cried because he couldn't bear to tell his aunt that he had deceived everyone in the church and "didn't believe there was a Jesus anymore, since he didn't come to help me" (ibid., p. 21).

The most embittered rejection of Christian faith occurs in Angelo Herndon and Richard Wright. For Herndon, who was forced to work as a coal miner at the age of thirteen, religion was nothing but a distraction from the "sordid realities" of his life and a means by which the mining companies instilled "false humility and meekness" in the workers.[1] Richard Wright's experience with religion is a tale of sadism, cruelty, hypocrisy, and hatred. The meaning of religion is in "the hunger of the human heart for that which is not and can never be, the thirst of the human spirit to conquer and transcend the implacable limitations of human life" (Wright, *Black Boy*, pp. 131–32). But far from offering him any effective way of coping with the oppression in his environment, it simply reinforced the obstacles on the way to self-discovery; it was one more limitation that had to be overcome.

> While listening to the vivid language of the sermons I
> was pulled toward emotional belief, but as soon as I went
> out of the church and saw the bright sunshine and felt
> the throbbing life of the people in the streets I knew

that none of it was true and that nothing would happen (ibid., p. 113).

In the case of his Aunt Addie, religion was part of a sadistic and fanatical personality which took pleasure in organizing games for school children that knocked the wind out of them. In one incident, he defended himself against her assaults with a kitchen knife, and they "rolled, kicking, scratching, hitting, fighting as though we were strangers, deadly enemies, fighting for our lives." Wright's final comment on the battle is, "God blessed our home with the love that binds . . ." (ibid., pp. 120–21).

One also finds in Frederick Douglass an exposure of the social role of Christianity as a tool of oppression and character sketches of personalities whose sadism and cruelty were in direct proportion to the intensity of their faith. But Douglass made a distinction between "true" and "false" Christianity and professed loyalty to the former. What is different in Wright, Herndon, Redding, Hughes, and Johnson is the total absence of any such distinction or any political need to make one. If Douglass supported the "Christianity of Christ," it was because he did not wish to offend the religious sensibilities of the white reading public, and because the "true Christianity" was a powerful ideological weapon against slavery. The need to justify Christianity we find in Douglass no longer exists in the more complex black life here. The authors examine religion now, not in the light of the needs of an external political movement, but in the light of their own social and psychological needs. What they discover, on the whole, is that Christian faith has no real relevance to their lives except as cultural symbol and material for art.

In these roles it connects them to a stream that leads back to Africa. God appears with the immediate presence of a tribal deity when, in Johnson's "The Creation," he spits out the seven seas, makes valleys by treading the ground, and bends over the clay image of man "like a mammy bending over her baby." Reference to charms, fetishes, and conjuring also attest to a living African religious tradition behind a few autobiographies that were less diluted by Christianity. Hughes observed a conjurer in Georgia performing rites with chalk, powder, and burning sulfur to ward off the malevolent influence of a client's distant cousin in Brooklyn. Hughes's comment on the scene is "I guess if you really believe in a burning sulphur-stone dripping a cross, it might perhaps be good for what ails you" (Hughes, *The Big Sea*, p. 298). In Ruby Goodwin's autobiography, there is a dramatic and successful conjuring incident reported with all seriousness by her characters, without the tongue-in-cheek detachment typical of Hughes. "Big Chick," who had been languishing close to death for days, was the victim of an evil charm. A conjurer discovered it inside his mattress, neutralized it with a counterspell, wrapped it in a bundle, and sent someone to throw it into the creek. On the way something "swooped down from the trees" and tried to snatch the bundle, but it was safely sunk below the water level. The noise then ceased; Big Chick had recovered (Goodwin, p. 139).

We are reminded of the various charms and spells used by the slave narrators to ward off an overseer's wrath, secure a woman's love, or identify a thief. But an interesting shift of attitude has taken place in Ruby Goodwin's account. Douglass, Bibb, Grandy, and others who dealt with the slave's use of magic generally viewed conjuring as a superstitious vice they had fallen into during their unregenerate youth. Sandy, the slave in Douglass's *Narrative* who prepares a charm to defend him from punishment, even informs to the whites about a runaway plot. The escaped slaves generally were anxious to leave this part of their heritage behind, because it served them no advantage in the white world. Ruby Goodwin handles it without the need to divorce herself from the past. For her, it is part of the poetry of having a black childhood, and, at the least, a way of mobilizing psychological energy that lies beyond the understanding of Western rationalism.

The Souls of Black Folk gives the most comprehensive and moving explanation of the meaning of religion in the culture of black people in the chapter entitled "Of the Faith of the Fathers." But this is not a statement of the faith of Du Bois. It includes the description of a Negro revival as practiced in the backwoods of the South, a history of Negro religion from the voodoo of Africa to the modern Negro church, and an analysis of its importance in Negro social life. Du Bois concludes:

> But back of this still broods silently the deep religious
> feeling of the real Negro heart, the stirring, unguided
> might of powerful human souls who have lost the guiding

star of the past and seek in the great night a new religious
ideal. Some day the Awakening will come, when the
pent-up vigor of ten million souls shall sweep irresistibly
toward the Goal, out of the Valley of the Shadow of
Death, where all that makes life worth living—Liberty,
Justice, and Right—is marked "For White People Only"
(Du Bois, *Souls of Black Folk*, p. 206).

In this passage, and in the story of Alexander Crummell, the first
Negro Episcopalian minister in America, it is clear that Du Bois
shares the poetry, the political struggle, the yearning for a promised
land of equality *in this life* inherent in black religious faith; but
he does not enter into the faith itself, as did so many of the slave
narrators. Indeed, he thought that Negro religion had entered a
"critical stage," in which it was wavering between bitter revolt
and unctuous, flattering hypocrisy, and that only a "new religious
ideal" would reconcile its contradictions (ibid., pp. 202–6). Du
Bois is deeply religious in a secular sense; he represents the quality
of "group soul" as an almost Neo-Platonic hunger for a fulfillment
that combines politics and economics with mysticism. We shall
see later that his is the style most influenced by Biblical rhetoric in
the second period, and that his "new religious ideal" bears a close
resemblance to the function of myth as conceived by Yeats, Joyce,
Pound, and Eliot.

Booker T. Washington and Ida Wells are the writers whose
religious attitudes stem most directly from the tradition of the
slave narrative. Religion as Douglass and Ward practice it is wholly
missing in Washington, for his faith is not in the militant abolitionist tradition; but he professes religious values for political ends,
to conciliate and gain the support of a white reading public; the
Protestant ethic is the basis on which he identifies with American
culture; he condemns racism because of its effects on the morals
of the white man (Washington, 165–66); and he interprets the
suffering of the Negro as a sign of special attention from God. In
these respects *Up from Slavery* resembles the slave narrative. Its
purpose is to further a program external to itself, and its values are
constructed according to whether or not they serve that program.

The Christlike work which the Church of all denomina-
tions in America has done during the last thirty-five

years for the elevation of the black man would have made
me a Christian. In a large degree it has been the pennies,
the nickels, and the dimes which have come from the
Sunday-schools, the Christian Endeavour societies, and
the missionary societies, as well as from the Church
proper, that have helped to elevate the Negro at so rapid
a rate.

My plan was to have them, while performing this service,
taught the latest and best methods of labour, so that the
school would not only get the benefit of their efforts,
but the students themselves would be taught to see
not only utility in labour, but beauty and dignity, would
be taught, in fact, how to lift labour up from mere
drudgery and toil, and would learn to love work for
its own sake (ibid., pp. 193, 148).

Religion in these passages is valued because of its works, because it
serves material interests in the world of practical affairs. Work is
holy, and holiness is good works. Like Noah Davis, Washington
also praises his early supervisors for educating him in the virtues
of cleanliness, work, and thrift (ibid., p. 44). The special place
of the Negro in the designs of Providence is suggested by the fact that
he has already been led out of the wilderness of slavery and is "in
a stronger and more hopeful condition, materially, intellectually,
morally, and religiously, than is true of an equal number of
black people in any other portion of the globe" (ibid., p. 16).

The fire of abolitionist religion in Ida Wells, however, makes
Washington's pious tributes to the Christian Church seem like dead
ash. She did more than keep herself "spotless and morally clean,"
in obedience to the strictures of her slave mother; she appealed
to the Christian conscience of Britain and America to condemn
lynching without equivocation and pressure the federal government into having it stopped. She demanded of the churches in the
North that they threaten their Southern affiliates with expulsion
unless those affiliates ceased to support discrimination against
Negroes. Her forthright demand for simple justice was too much
for Washington, who disassociated himself from her "radical"
views (Wells, pp. 44, 101, 167, 233, 265).

In educational philosophy, Du Bois is also closer to the slave narrative than is Washington. When they spoke of education, the slave narrators stressed, first, learning to read and write; then, assimilating the best of European and American culture from such figures as Webster, Phillips, Whittier, Lowell, John Quincy Adams, William Pitt, John Bunyan, and the Bible, and turning their ideas to the needs of black people. Their concept of those needs was to buttress the ideology of abolition, afford proof of the mental equality of Negroes, and provide them with black intellectual leadership. Their concept of education was overwhelmingly humanist and literary. Douglass may have requested money of Harriet Beecher Stowe for the founding of a Negro school of industrial arts (Du Bois, *Life and Times*, p. 284), but he never lost sight of the necessity for an education of ideas. In these respects Du Bois is in the direct line of the abolitionist tradition, and Washington, with his emphasis on training for skilled labor in trades and factory jobs, is a departure from it and a compromise with slavery. Speaking of the Negro universities of the South, Du Bois wrote:

> The function of the university is not simply to teach bread-winning, or to furnish teachers for the public schools or to be a centre of polite society; it is, above all, to be the organ of that fine adjustment between real life and the growing knowledge of life, an adjustment which forms the secret of civilization (Du Bois, *The Souls of Black Folk*, p. 84).

The Negro scholar, according to Du Bois, should be made "a missionary of culture to an untaught people." Recognizing the need for artisans, he felt that "to seek to make the blacksmith a scholar is almost as silly as the more modern scheme of making the scholar a blacksmith; almost, but not quite." In his final *Autobiography* (1968) Du Bois warned as strongly as ever that unless Negroes were prepared by liberal education to lead movements for black culture and political equality, whites would capture the leadership of these movements (Du Bois, *Autobiography*, p. 236). The wisdom of the humanities, not business and labor skills, was for Du Bois the most important means of fighting racial oppression on the level of education. Referring to his study of the Philadelphia Negro (1899), he wrote, "I counted my task here as simple and clear-cut; I proposed to find out what was the matter with this area and why" (ibid., pp. 197–98). The value of scholarship to a solution of the race problem is essential. His practice in the application of scientific method to the study of a social group enabled him to grasp easily "the idea of a changing developing society rather than a fixed social structure" (ibid., 205–6) and hence prepared him to accept later the combination of science and commitment to change in the ideology of Marxism.

Angelo Herndon, in *Let Me Live*, arrives at a similar view of education from a proletarian direction. Denied access to the formal education of Du Bois, Herndon nevertheless saw the most valuable education as that which armed the worker with ideas rather than merely skills. "Education," his father taught him, "was a powerful weapon with which to fight poverty and the handicaps of racial discrimination. . . . Even to this very day it remains a spur and an inspiration to me—to seek knowledge and to widen my sympathies for suffering mankind" (Herndon, p. 14). The education most useful to him as a worker came through communism:

> The education I longed for in the world I had expected to find it, [sic] I surprisingly began to receive in my new Communist circles. To the everlasting glory of the Communist movement may it be said that wherever it is active, it brings enlightenment and culture (ibid., p. 87).

After acquiring the ideology of communism, he puts it to work as a "missionary of culture" in fighting the racism of his fellow white workers, thus providing the intellectual leadership necessary to unite against the mine companies. Angelo Herndon's concept of education is thus fully in accord with the abolitionist tradition of the slave narrative: it is an education of ideas rather than skills, its value to be judged by its service in the struggle of the oppressed against their oppressors. He never perceived his intellectual kinship with Du Bois, however, and referred to the latter as a "tool and lickspittle of the white ruling class."[2]

Hosea Hudson, another Communist, acquired his education by fighting for his rights. A foundry worker in Alabama during the 1930s, Hudson learned firsthand all the tactics of business managers to divide and control their employees. He saw them pit white workers against black, fire or murder union organizers, exclude all black people from positions in the local government, and use the police to intimidate rebels and crush strikes. He was followed and harassed for years by FBI agents, who told his friends and employers that he was a subversive, a spy, and a criminal. But it was the Communist party that taught him how to stand up for himself: he learned to organize, speak in public, "write postcards and letters of protest . . . put out leaflets," study politics from the standpoint of what political events meant to the working class, and develop a "bulldog determination not to be pushed down."[3] At communist meetings, he acquired the ideology of Marxism-Leninism, but it was day-to-day experience in shops, committees, picket lines, and open battles with the Ku Klux Klan and the National Guard that made the ideology meaningful as a guide to victory. Education in the abstract was useless; the point was to learn what would liberate the slave.

Education is intensely important to Washington, Du Bois, Hudson, and Herndon as a means to improve the position of the Negro people. The importance they place on education, as in the slave narratives, is both American and black: American because of its faith in mass culture, in the basic equality of rich and poor and the ability of the poor to aim high and make good; black because education must be more to them than a path to individual success; it must benefit the whole race, it must show the way to the Promised Land. The difference between them is in what kind of education to provide, and to whom.

In Hughes, McKay, and Redding, there is a strong current of antiintellectualism which we have already encountered in the episodes where McKay quits college to wander, Hughes throws his books into the sea, and Redding leaves the university to find his identity among the Negroes of the South. These authors say little about education directly, although Hughes delivers a short polemic in favor of Negro professors and Negro subject matter. McKay feels that black children should study Antar rather than Homer and to that extent is an early nationalist. But in general their outlook is much less political than Du Bois, Herndon, and Washington. The most evident thing in their attitudes toward the academic career is their disillusionment with it. These are writers deeply affected by the dual alienation, from the white world because of their color, and from the black world because of their learning. In choosing to wander, they have opted to attend the "college of experience"; and so education of one sort or another remains important in their work. The object is not to "advance the race" in a political sense. For Redding it is to rediscover the roots of black culture and the verities that hold good for humanity everywhere; for Hughes, McKay, and Johnson, it is to collect material for poems, to immerse themselves in the life of the people and give back that life transmuted by art. Du Bois had argued for a Negro intelligentsia that would be educated to support a school of art and literature in order to preserve the "unique and marvellous" cultural heritage of the Negro; Hughes, McKay, Redding, and Johnson were reinforcing Du Bois's efforts to create that art and literature.

But Hughes and McKay were not addressing themselves to the Negro intelligentsia. They had quite consciously scorned the intelligentsia and chosen to live among and write about and to the people. Hughes gave poetry readings all over the South to black audiences, and one of the highlights of McKay's autobiography is his reading of the sonnet "If We Must Die" to an audience of Negro railway porters. "I was in love," said McKay, "with the large rough unclassical rhythms of American life."

> I am partial to the idea of an artist being of and among the people, even if incognito. The puritan atmosphere of America was irritating, but it was not suffocating. I had written some of my most vigorous poems right through and straight out of the tumult and turbulence of American life (McKay, p. 244).

The "tumult and turbulence," the restless wandering, and the pride in work are all values that relate them both to the slave narrative tradition and to the American mainstream. Again, the values of black writers seem like the values of America writ large. In Fenimore Cooper, Mark Twain, Steinbeck, Hemingway, and Truman Capote, characters wander ceaselessly in search of self-hood and freedom, never for long part of a stable community and never accepting a definite social role. In the slave narratives the wandering was *flight,* in a definite direction, toward a clear social role in the abolitionist movement. In McKay, Hughes, and Redding, it is searching, "the spirit of the vagabond," but always with the desire to be close to the people. They reject the isolation of Natty Bumppo and the Hemingway hero. For Redding the direction is reversed; there is no clear social role in the North any longer; the abolitionist heritage transmitted by his parents is useless to him, and he must return to the source of Negro life. McKay and Hughes travel across four continents. The black wandering is distinguished from the white by group identity, by ties with the masses of humanity that are viewed by white characters, with some exceptions,[4] merely as threats. Huck Finn wants to leave Mrs. Watson and the Widow Douglas as far behind as possible, but Jim wants to escape up the Ohio River and return to steal his family out of slavery.

Pride in work, for the slave narrators, was part of their Protestant ethic and a means to uplift the race and disprove the white stereotype that Negroes are lazy. Work continues to have this importance, as a value, in the second period. In Washington it was also important to convince white people that Negro training represented a good economic investment. Redding remembers as a child that he and his father harvested a cornfield in record time as an act of defiance against their white employer, who had insinuated that it would take them longer than a white man (Redding, p. 22). Du Bois recounts having been driven to excel whites in his studies in order to overcome the color bar. "The secret of life and the loosing the color bar . . . lay in excellence in accomplishment" (Du Bois, *Autobiography*, p. 75).

In Hughes, McKay, Du Bois, Hudson, and Herndon, "pride in work" also takes on the additional significance of pride in the black working class. Everything most worth writing about, for Hughes, comes from his contact with work and Negro workers.

> Seventh Street is the long, old, dirty street, where the ordinary Negroes hang out, folks with practically no family tree at all, folks who draw no color line between mulattoes and deep dark-browns, folks who work hard for a living with their hands. On Seventh Street in 1924 they played the blues, ate watermelon, barbecue, and fish sandwiches, shot pool, told tall tales, looked at the dome of the Capitol and laughed out loud (Hughes, *The Big Sea*, pp. 208–9).

The Big Sea does not so much depict work as a means to solve a problem or a pathway to individual success, but as part of a class identity, a link with humanity, and a source of joy. The author is a worker because this is the current of his life and art. This is where one finds energy, passion, sorrow and hope. Work has the same importance to McKay; he does not work hard to prove that Negroes are ambitious and capable, to succeed in the white world, or to advance the struggle, but because he is a worker and the source of his poetry is the lives of Negro workers. In constructing class identities as workers, McKay and Hughes do not empty "work" of its racial content; it is simply the class aspect of the Negro's position in American society that interests them, or rather the merging of racial and class identity in the working-class Negro.

Workers, in particular Negro workers, interest McKay and Hughes because they are the vital wellspring of life and art. They interest Du Bois and Herndon because they are the wellspring of revolutionary change in capitalist society. For the slave narratives, work would free the Negro; for the black Communists, the *working class* will free him, by abolishing capitalism and doing away with the economic basis of racial oppression.

> In China the people—the laboring people, the people who in most lands are the doormats on which the reigning thieves and murdering rulers walk, leading their painted and jeweled prostitutes—the people walk and boast. These people of the slums and gutters and kitchens are the Chinese nation today. This the Chinese believe and on this belief they toil and sweat and cheer (Du Bois, *Autobiography*, p. 51).
>
> The change of my viewpoint was almost fabulous, emerging from the urge to escape the cruelties of life in religious abstractions into a healthy, vigorous, and realistic recognition that life on earth, which was so full of struggle and tears for the poor, could be changed by the intelligent and organized will of the workers . . . (Herndon, pp. 78–79).

The value of work in these communist autobiographies is still inside the tradition of the slave narrative, in that it is seen as a means to the end of Negro freedom; but it does not appear as an abstract category. The "dignity of labor" in Washington is almost metaphysical, for no specific object of labor is distinguished from any other except that it should have sale value. Labor in the abstract is what is beautiful, so that presumably the labor of a Negro child in a coal mine or a cotton field for twenty-five cents a day has just as much dignity as the labor of the Chinese people to build socialism out of a semifeudal colony. By exalting the revolutionary potential of the working class, rather than the "dignity of work," Herndon and Du Bois have placed the work ethic back in the realm of material social relations. Submissive, exploited work, alienated work that serves the interests of a ruling class, is not dignified, though it may be necessary at certain epochs. Work that organizes the revolution, and work under the control and for the interests of workers themselves, meaningful work that builds institutions the people can use, is the road to liberation.

One value that survived the slave narratives almost unchanged is militant resistance. Themes of armed resistance to white terrorism occur in every autobiography of this group, with the single exception of *Up from Slavery*. Even the relatively peaceful Du Bois armed himself and prepared for the worst when his family was threatened by a lynch mob, declaring that "if a white mob had stepped on the campus where I lived I would without hesitation have sprayed their guts over the grass" (Du Bois, *Autobiography*, p. 286).

We have seen earlier how James Weldon Johnson took pride in his descent from the Haitian rebels who fought with Toussaint L'Ouverture. Elsewhere he describes an incident in which his black neighbors armed themselves and occupied a row of buildings in order to save a black prisoner from being lynched by whites:

> The whole affair, especially the arrest in the middle of the night, makes an impression of terror on my mother's mind that she cannot rid herself of. I am deeply moved by her recital of these happenings, and I feel an exultant pride in the men who manned the windows and housetops to safeguard the prisoner, and in the women who brought them food and coffee (Johnson, p. 132).

A character in J. Saunders Redding's book stands up in the same way, gun in hand, to white intimidation during lynch fever (Redding, p. 190). Redding himself, at a ferry crossing, refused to give up his place in line to a threatening white man, prepared to sink his fist into the man's stomach, and was saved from a fight only by the timely intervention of two other white passengers. Claude McKay, during the period when he wrote the sonnet "If We Must Die," carried a revolver whenever his train stopped in a strange city, and once fought off a racist Italian with a knife. Langston Hughes took pride in his descent from Sheridan Leary, one of the black members of John Brown's raid (Hughes, *The Big Sea,* p. 13), and defended the violence of the Bolshevik government in dealing with enemies of the Russian Revolution (Hughes, *I Wonder As I Wander,* pp. 143, 147). Ruby Goodwin recalls with sympathy and approval that, during a mining strike, her father and other miners went out to meet the company-imported scabs with guns (Goodwin, pp. 174–75). Angelo Herndon, after knocking down his overseer in the mines, decided from then on "to return two blows for every blow I got, to take two eyes for one taken from me, to defend my rights as an upstanding man, to defend the elementary dignity of the human being in me against all aggressors" (Herndon, p. 69). Richard Wright fought his Aunt Addie and Uncle Tom with fists, razors, and knives from the time he was a boy and fantasized resisting white mobs with a rifle. The theme of violent resistance often implies racial solidarity against white workers and bosses, but in Goodwin, Hughes, and the communist autobiographies, it also implies class solidarity against the rich. In Wright it is directed against a whole environment, as a kind of existential defense of his right to grow.

The politics of these authors show a marked trend in the direction of socialism and class identity, rather than identity along purely racial lines; but this trend is by no means unanimous. Washington and Goodwin, for example, are anticommunist and republican. One can see a split beginning to develop between the ideologies of socialism and black solidarity and a struggle to reconcile the two.

James Weldon Johnson rejects working-class solidarity and politics as a solution to the race issue, because of the racism of white workers:

> We are told and we tell ourselves that as a race we belong
> to the proletariat and that our economic and political
> salvation lies in joining hands with our white fellow
> workers. Notwithstanding, it is true that the black worker
> finds getting into most of the white labor unions no
> easier than getting an invitation to a white bourgeois
> dinner party (Johnson, p. 45).

He does not believe that America will ever adopt communism, and
for the Negro to turn communist would mean taking on the
antagonisms that center against red as well as those that center
against black. The problem is to "change the hearts of men," and
political and economic revolutions do not change the heart. If the
Negro is forbidden entrance into the American mainstream, "there
will be only one way of salvation for the race that I can see, and
that will be through the making of its isolation into a religion
and the cultivation of a hard, keen, relentless hatred for everything
white" (ibid., p. 412). His alternatives are: either desegregation
and equality, or a movement for black separatism. He sees the
latter as a disaster both for the Negro and for America.

Johnson's caveat against taking on the hostility of anticommu-
nism received a reply in the autobiography of Benjamin J. Davis.
Davis became a Communist while serving as Angelo Herndon's
trial lawyer in Atlanta in 1933. For years active in the Communist
party and on the City Council of New York, Davis himself was
sent to a federal penitentiary in 1950. His attitude was that communism provided the knowledge needed by black people to fight
effectively. "Far from considering it a handicap to be a Negro and a
Communist simultaneously, I considered it a double weapon
against the ruling class." A Communist Negro is equipped with a
science "which alone can help realize his 300-year aspiration for
freedom and equality."[5]

Claude McKay and Langston Hughes both refused to become
members of the Communist party because they felt that, since the
party was based on discipline, they would have to accept political
directives on how and what to write. McKay also objected to
dictatorship of any sort. Hughes believed that poetry and fiction
"had to express as truthfully as possible the *individual* emotions
and reactions of the writer, rather than mass directives issued to

achieve practical and often temporary political objectives"
(Hughes, *I Wonder As I Wander*, p. 122). Nevertheless, McKay
approved of the fact that the Bolsheviks had "put a stop to the
vicious political exploitation of group and race prejudice" (McKay,
pp. 193–94). Hughes is also clearly in sympathy with the achievements of the Revolution. His perspective on the social changes
taking place in Turkmenistan during the 1930s reveal the race
issue to be fundamental to the meaning of the Bolshevik Revolution, whereas, to his traveling companion, Arthur Koestler, its
meaning lay far more in economics and government. "To Koestler,
Turkmenistan was simply a *primitive* land moving into twentieth-
century civilization. To me it was a *colored* land moving into
orbits hitherto reserved for whites." Hughes was especially impressed by the speed with which the Communists had done away
with Jim Crow in public accommodations:

> The old partitions that once separated natives from
> Europeans, colored from white, were still there when I
> arrived—I saw them. But now anyone sat anywhere in the
> Tashkent trams. In ten short years, Jim Crow was gone
> on trams, trains, or anywhere else in Central Asia.
> Russians and Uzbeks, Ukranians and Tartars, Europeans
> and natives, white or colored, all went to the same schools,
> sat on the same benches, ate in the same co-operatives,
> worked in the same shops or factories, and fussed and
> fumed at the same problems. Gains and defeats were
> shared alike. In Tashkent, whenever I got on a street
> car and saw the old partitions, I could not help but
> remember Atlanta, Birmingham and Houston in my own
> country where, when I got on a tram or a bus or a
> train, I had to sit in the COLORED section. The natives
> of Tashkent, about my own shade of brown, once had to
> sit in a COLORED section, too. But not any more. So I
> was happy for them. How had this change been
> brought about in so short a time? At the City Soviet
> I asked Kurbanov about it. He said, "Those who don't
> like it are almost all in jail—or dead" (Hughes, *I Wonder
> As I Wander*, p. 172).

Hughes reconciles the perspectives of class and race in his opinion of the Bolshevik Revolution just as he does in the content of his poetry; it is always the working-class, unemployed, and peasant colored people who draw his interest. Color alone is not a sufficient reason to identify with a group. In *The Big Sea*, class cuts entirely across color as a basis for contact with people when he abandons the usual tourist attractions of Italy and seeks out the slums and working-class districts (Hughes, *The Big Sea*, p. 189). The political importance of his attitude is that it represents a movement toward the broad goals of socialism: a system controlled by and for the masses, in which each ethnic or national group is free to practice its own culture and accepts all other groups as part of the great human family. Hughes succeeds in representing and identifying with the human qualities shared by all mankind, not by ignoring color or denying its importance, but precisely by interpreting the world through the class perspective it has given him. As a writer, his role is to hold up an image of the "better and truer self," the human being at one with his culture, class, and country.

The development of politics in black autobiography from desegregation to socialism is best exemplified by the half-century career of W. E. B. Du Bois. In *The Souls of Black Folk*, his political goals were "freedom of opportunity," "the power of the ballot," and access to everything in American life which was available to whites. He couched these goals in the rhetoric of the American Revolution, believing that Negroes, as a group, without relinquishing their black culture, should strive for self-development "in large conformity to the greater ideals of the American Republic, in order that some day on American soil two world-races may give each to each those characteristics both so sadly lack." He added that "there are today no truer exponents of the pure human spirit of the Declaration of Independence than the American Negroes . . ." (Du Bois, *The Souls of Black Folk*, p. 11). He begins, in essence, where the abolitionist movement left off: adapting the revolutionary tradition of 1776 to the black experience. Du Bois was later to conclude that he erred in not questioning the ideals of the white world that he wished to share. Yet his membership in the Communist party, and his decision to "help the triumph of communism in every honest way that I can," does not constitute a sharp break with what he wrote in his early work. For it was the theory and practice of the party, after the Comintern congress of 1928, to draw on the tradition of the American Revolution, support black nationalism as a revolutionary force, and defend the ideal of black cultural integrity within a socialist United States.[6]

Du Bois also saw the race question in America as one dimension of a world problem and so was moving in a direction that could be considered Pan-African: "The problem of the twentieth century is the problem of the color-line—the relation of the darker to the lighter races of men in Asia and Africa, in America and the islands of the sea" (Du Bois, *The Souls of Black Folk*, p. 13). James Weldon Johnson, Frederick Douglass, and Samuel Ward tended to consider the race question as a peculiarly American phenomenon that stuck to Americans "like their skins," and they looked to other countries as a refuge from the "man-Negro dualism" they felt at home. "Any kind of a Negro will do," said Johnson, referring to discrimination on railway cars in the United States, "provided he is not one who is an American citizen" (Johnson, p. 65). But Du Bois and Hughes perceived the dynamic relationship between colonialism in Asia and Africa and the color line in America. They anticipate in that respect the politics of Malcolm X.

We saw in the slave narratives that one of the great strengths of black autobiography is its perception of the close link between individual lives and mass movements and its ability to depict that relationship convincingly as a function of material human social organization. This special insight is the product of special oppression on the basis of color; for oppression forces a conscious black identity on the writer. He must examine his own life in relation to the history of other black people, because the color line ties his fortunes so closely to theirs; he must remain more than usually interested in and aware of politics, in its larger sense of the systematic relations between human groups; and he must watch closely any change in the dynamics of white society for the possible bearing it may have on the race question. Frederick Douglass, in the slavery period, was the writer who most successfully merged the "life" of the individual with the "times" of his political and social matrix. In the first half of the twentieth century, this strength continues to grow. It is deepened by the turning inward of the most alienated writers to reexamine and re-create their split selves and their ties with the rest of mankind. Finally, between 1903 and 1945, it is responsible for a whole line of the best autobiographies in our literature: *The Souls of Black Folk*, *Dusk of Dawn*, *The Big Sea*, *No Day of Triumph*, and *Black Boy*.

Du Bois links individual and historical life by a combination of autobiography, brilliant political essay, the use of myth, the motives of the "Sorrow Songs," and the music of his language in *Souls of Black Folk*. The details of his own life are threaded in and out of chapters on the history of the Freedman's Bureau, a justification of university education for black people, the history of public education and industry in the South, an economic analysis of the "black belt," a sociological analysis of the Negro church, a biography of Alexander Crummell, and a short story. The *Autobiography* spends the first sixty pages on a defense of communism and, in explaining the academic and political career of its author, supplies nearly as much material on the position of the black man in America as the more literary *Souls*. Hughes and Redding link the individual and history by their fully realized images of Negro life. Redding is especially skilled in creating the gestalt, the tension and balance, of a system of society by means of an accumulation of interviews, character sketches, and overheard conversations. Richard Wright, in *Native Son*, focused the whole complex of American race history through the glass of a single character, Bigger Thomas; in *Black Boy*, that glass is himself.

A fresh view of the relationship between art and politics has been made possible by what black writers have achieved in placing individuals within a historical context. White American critics tend to assume a dichotomy between "pure art" and "propaganda," and, in criticism, between standards which judge art on "aesthetic" grounds and those which evaluate it by "external" political criteria. We think especially of the "New Criticism" pioneered by John Crowe Ransom, Cleanth Brooks, Robert Penn Warren, and many others. In this dichotomy, aesthetic pleasure and political usefulness appear almost as mutually exclusive functions. Political criticism, to our best white artists and critics, has always been a heresy which suggests "totalitarian" control over the imagination; e. e. cummings, T. S. Eliot, and Anaïs Nin, for example, scornfully dismissed Marxist criticism in their essays, prefaces, and journals as inimical to the life of the free creative spirit. More recently, Norman Mailer, attacking the criticism of Kate Millette, illustrates how deeply ingrained is this reflex in the outlook of American literary figures; objecting to her analysis of the sexual politics of Henry Miller and D. H. Lawrence because it ignores the beauty of their language, he slips into a series of anticommunist clichés: she is "totalitarian to the core," ready to resort to "liquidation at the end of the road," "not so much Molotov as Vishinsky," a "literary lawyer" with a "social lust to make units of people."[7]

But the happy marriage of art and politics in the work of Hughes, McKay, and Du Bois shows that another view of political criticism is possible. The Communist critics who appear in *The Big Sea* and *A Long Way from Home*, like Robert Minor, or the cultural committees of the Stalinist regime, made the mistake of applying political criteria *directly* to art. A poem in their view was to be judged by whether it was "bourgeois" or "proletarian," that is, of what use it was to the revolution. Forgetting that culture is a doubly reflective concentration, and not merely a translation, of politics, they sought to explain one level by the rules of the other, as a mad chemist might attempt to account for all the events of psychology by reference only to the laws of chemistry. Hughes and McKay quite rightly rejected this crude application of Marxism to their art. They recognized that the material of the artist is in the first place his own concrete experience, not political theory, and that the latter, while it may clarify and reflect, should not ever dictate the former. But concrete experience is the stuff of politics. Because of their blackness and their sensitivity to its meaning, they were able to use their experience as a microcosm for that of whole classes and races, without at any point lifting it out of the world of material fact into metaphysics. Their concern was with the subjective impact of historical experience on individual identity. "I am not an organizer or an agitator," said McKay; the role of poet is distinct from the role of revolutionist, and the two should not be confused. The latter makes the revolution; the former distils the class and race forces behind it into art. "All I offer here," McKay said of his autobiography, "is the distilled poetry of my experience" (McKay, p. 354). The poet creates the image of the human face, as it is manifested through color, class, culture, geography, politics. The contribution of the black poet is that he does not conceive of a human face apart from these specific manifestations, these concentrations of history into a song or a flash of anger.

We turn now to the instrument which the authors used to realize their identities, values, and social roles: their language.

Chapter 7 *In search of a voice*

THE language and structure of black autobiography since the slave narratives became highly individualized. Du Bois and Hughes represent the two extremes of style, the one as elaborate and formal as an Elizabethan sermon, the other as colloquial as the talk of a work gang on a WPA project. Use of language in Hughes, Redding, Johnson, McKay, and Wright seems at first to have more in common with James Agee, John Steinbeck, Woody Guthrie, Ernest Hemingway, and other white writers of the 1930s than with Frederick Douglass or John Thompson. The movement in black writing from periodic to loose syntax, from formal and oratorical to informal diction, and from abstract to concrete language, in large part simply parallels what has happened to modern writing in general. Nevertheless we notice a marked difference in context and purpose, subtle currents of tone, cadence, and word order, that distinguish the black from the white. The difference ceases to be subtle in the 1960s, as black writers veer sharply in the direction of ghetto speech rhythms for their models.

To what extent do the stylistic traditions of the slave narratives survive in second-period autobiographies? To what extent do these earlier works prefigure the conscious black rhetoric of the 1960s and '70s? And in what ways does the language of the second-period writers express their black content? These are the questions that bear most directly on the "blackness" of the material and will indicate how it is distinguished from the white mainstream.

The structure of the slave narrative survives in at least four books: *Up from Slavery, Let Me Live, Black Worker in the Deep South,* and *Black Boy.* Its content and purpose live on especially in the Communist autobiographies, including William L. Patterson's *We Charge Genocide.* The slave narrative's basic pattern, it will be remembered, was an escape from South to North as well as a movement up the social scale from the status of slave to that of respected, educated citizen and vanguard of black politics and culture. The narrator began with a suppressed identity, kept down by seemingly irresistible forces, his time and body the property of an enemy class; he witnessed atrocities, experienced punishment and disillusion, and he was denied opportunity to advance himself. At a certain point in his growth he learned to read and acquired the will to resist in spite of all the obstacles placed in his path; he fought back—usually first against an overseer—and was forced to run away for fear of being entirely eliminated. Once on safe ground, he turned his energies to acquiring more knowledge and skill as a writer, orator, or political leader so that he could reenter the battle and fight the entire system of oppression instead of its immediate agents. His life goal became the promised land of freedom. The style of the slave narrative was largely an instrument of political struggle; its main purpose was to create public sentiment in favor of the abolitionist cause, and to that end it included descriptions of slave living conditions and Christian rhetoric.

The autobiographies of Washington, Herndon, Hudson, and Wright are each stamped with this basic pattern, although none corresponds to it in every particular. Washington was "not quite sure of the exact place or exact date" of his birth; on the plantation where he was a slave, "meals were gotten by the children very much as dumb animals get theirs." He made up his mind as a child to "get enough education" to enable him "to read common books and newspapers," and the sight of Hampton Institute, where he was a student, gave him "new life." The voice and concerns are the slave narrator's. He begins without a family tree, describes what it was like to live and work in the South, and dreams of education as a means to enter the promised land. As a slave narrative, *Up from Slavery* lacks only the themes of armed resistance and the physical movement from South to North (Washington, pp. 1, 9, 27).

Angelo Herndon's book contains the struggle against oppression and slavery, specific details of conditions in the mines and in Georgia prisons, and the dream of education as a way out and up from enslavement. In Georgia during the 1920s, he was "overwhelmed with the painful certainty that all of the world was a prison," until he found out that he could beat his overseer in a fight. He discovered then that Negroes "could improve our conditions only if we stuck together and made a collective effort." By becoming a Communist, he reenters the battle to fight the whole system of oppression rather than merely its effects and is educated by communist ideas to give leadership to a political movement. The purpose of the book is to support that movement, in particular, to appeal to the class interests of the whites (Herndon, pp. 55, 60, 69, 173). Herndon includes a number of atrocity stories about labor conditions in the South and responds to the Communists of Georgia the way Frederick Douglass responded to his first abolitionist meeting in New Bedford, Mass. Douglass attended "all the anti-slavery meetings held in New Bedford . . . my heart bounding at every true utterance against the slave system and every rebuke of its friends and supporters" (Douglass, *Life and Times*, p. 214). Communist meetings gave Herndon little less than the courage to live:

> Up to the time I had met the Communists I did not know how to fight the lynching of Negroes and Jim Crowism. I was bewildered, grief-stricken and helpless. All of a sudden I found myself in an organization which fought selflessly and tirelessly to undo all the wrongs perpetrated upon my race (Herndon, p. 89).

What links Herndon in an especially revealing way to the slave narrative tradition is the fact that he was later convicted and sentenced to prison under an old Georgia slave statute for "inciting insurrection."

The style and rhetoric of the slave narrative is less evident in the second-period works, but we find interesting examples in the autobiographies of Hosea Hudson and Benjamin Davis. A description of a prosecution assistant in Davis's work echoes the antithetical balances of former times: "Every day of the week he sent the little fry to the chain gang or to the gallows. On Sundays, he was also an ordained Methodist minister. . . . If one of his talents didn't get you, the other would" (B. J. Davis, p. 64). This could be the rhetoric of Douglass, describing his overseer Austin Gore or the sound of church bells punctuated by the slave driver's lash.

Hudson's fascinating little narrative is told in a straight, deadpan, factual style, absolutely devoid of rhetorical flourish of any sort. His career is the story of an industrial wage-slave who stayed where he was, the toughest area of the country to organize, and did his "anti-slavery" work in the heart of the slaveholder's territory. The issues were as clear as chains: either he would succeed in defeating racism and uniting black and white in a common front, or the workers of both races would remain slaves and he would be jobless, homeless, beaten and perhaps lynched. Eventually he had to run for his life, but before he went North, Hudson helped to unionize foundries and steel mills in the Birmingham area and get black representation in local politics. The language fits the issues as snugly as the rims that he used to weld onto the driving wheels of steam engines. "As I've said, all of us molders were Black, and because of this we were not recognized as molders. . . . If the working people knew their strength, they would not let themselves be pushed around and they wouldn't let themselves be divided. . . . The weekly *Southern Worker* and *Sunday Worker* had been brought to the shop. . . . These papers attracted the stoolpigeons like breadcrumbs attract pigeons in the park" (Hudson, pp. 123, 45). Political conclusions are preceded by descriptions of job tasks, attempts of the boss to forestall union and party organizing, and concrete activities of the workers to defeat the obstacles and make progress; so that every conclusion is tested by experience and laid on the page as a lesson to be used.

Du Bois is the writer whose language is most in the oratorical and Biblical tradition of the black abolitionists. His tone is exalted and formal, slipping frequently, like the slave narratives, into sermon and melodrama; and his syntax is full of repetition, metrical cadence, and parallelism. The melodrama, that is, rhetorical effect without sufficient cause in experience, occurs when the content has shifted from the sublime to the mundane, leaving the language still at peak level:

> I remember well when the shadow swept across me. I was a little thing, away up in the hills of New England, where the dark Housatonic winds between Hoosac and Taghkanic to the sea (Du Bois, *Souls of Black Folk*, p. 2).

But it is not long before he supports the rhetoric with another peak; he will then go on to narrate his first intimation that he was "shut out" from the white world "by a vast veil," and the style which was left hanging a moment ago sweeps the reader into his mood of injured nobility.

Nobility and grandeur, perhaps, best describe the atmosphere he is able to cast over history:

> So dawned the time of *Sturm und Drang*: storm and stress today rocks our little boat on the mad waters of the world-sea. . . . The war has naught to do with slaves, cried Congress, the President, and the Nation; and yet no sooner had the armies, East and West, penetrated Virginia and Tennessee than fugitive slaves appeared within their lines. They came at night, when the flickering camp-fires shone like vast unsteady stars along the black horizon: old men and thin, with gray and tufted hair; women, with frightened eyes, dragging whimpering hungry children; men and girls, stalwart and gaunt,—a horde of starving vagabonds, homeless, helpless, and pitiable, in their dark distress.

> In failing thus to state plainly and unequivocally the legitimate demands of their people, even at the cost of opposing an honored leader, the thinking classes of American Negroes would shirk a heavy responsibility,—a responsibility to themselves, a responsibility to the struggling masses, a responsibility to the darker races of men whose future depends so largely on this American experiment, but especially a responsibility to this nation, —this common Fatherland (ibid., pp. 10, 14, 55).

Here is the style developed and polished in the field of antislavery politics from pulpit and lectern and stump, with its vivid images in a context of measured, rhythmic periods, its cumulative emphasis of public moral formula words ("a heavy *responsibility*,—a responsibility to themselves, a responsibility to the struggling masses, etc."), and its use of emblems such as the endangered ship and the stars of freedom to represent the trials and hopes of the slave. The North Star of the fugitive during the time of the Underground Railway was used by Pennington as a symbol of his role in his family and by Douglass for the title of his first newspaper; here the symbolic stars guide the refugees into the Union camp.

The Biblical element in the style of Du Bois is best illustrated by the chapter, "Of Alexander Crummell." Du Bois has organized it as though it were a sermon, comparing the three temptations of Alexander Crummell, great churchman, scholar, and Pan-Africanist, the first Negro Episcopalian priest in the United States, with the three temptations of Christ.

> Three temptations he met on those dark dunes that lay gray and dismal before the wonder-eyes of the child: the temptation of Hate, that stood out against the red dawn; the temptation of Despair, that darkened noonday; and the temptation of Doubt, that ever steals along with twilight. Above all, you must hear of the vales he crossed,—the Valley of Humiliation and the Valley of the Shadow of Death. . . . Restless still and unsatisfied, he turned toward Africa, and for long years, amid the spawn of the slave-smugglers, sought a new heaven and a new earth (ibid., pp. 215–16, 224).

But this chapter contains effects which are seldom found in the slave narratives and which demonstrate the maturity of black autobiography into literary art. It is completely appropriate, from a literary point of view, that a piece on Crummell should be cast in the form of a sermon and Christian allegory and echo the Bible in style; the motive for the Christian framework is more aesthetic than religious or political, although it draws on the political tradition of abolitionist rhetoric. Moreover, Du Bois has assimilated into the language the theme of the "Sorrow Songs." The purpose of the music in the book is to represent the hungering soul rising in melody and rhythm from Negro history and culture. To that end, the style shades into poetry, the music of language. In "Of Alexander Crummell" there is a whole succession of iambic pentameter lines within sentences:

> This is the history of a human heart, . . .
> Instinctively I bowed before this man,
> as one bows before the prophets of the world. . . .
> —that mocking world which seemed to me at once
> so light and dark, so splendid and sordid. . . .
> Faint cries burdened the Southern breeze. . . .
> A form that fell in vast and shapeless folds. . . .

> Like some grave shadow he flitted by those halls. . . .
> For there had passed a glory from the earth. . . .
> And cast his robe upon the floor and writhed. . . .
> Leaving the watcher wingless and alone. . . .
> So surged the thought within that lone black breast. . . .
> But in that soul lay deeper death than that. . . .
> But Alexander Crummell it gave back. . . .
> He turned at last home across the waters,
> humble and strong, gentle and determined. . . .
> He sat one morning gazing toward the sea. . . .
> And then the soul I loved fled like a flame
> across the Seas, and in its seat sat Death. . . .
> While round about the morning stars sat singing.

We hear the voice of Wordsworth in the lines, "this is the history of a human heart," and "there had passed a glory from the earth." By this echo, the meaning of Negro music intersects the general meaning of the Romantic movement—to reclaim the lives of humble people as serious literary material. Four frames of reference meet in that single chapter: abolitionist rhetoric, the Christian sermon, Negro music, and Romantic poetry.[1]

A comparison of the way Du Bois describes a cotton field with the work descriptions of slave narratives will also show how the emphasis of black writing has shifted from giving information to giving pleasure:

> Have you even seen a cotton-field white with the
> harvest,—its golden fleece hovering above the black earth
> like a silvery cloud edged with dark green, its bold white
> signals waving like the foam of billows from Carolina
> to Texas across that Black and human Sea? I have some-
> times half suspected that here the winged ram Chry-
> somallus left that Fleece after which Jason and his Argo-
> nauts went vaguely wandering into the shadowy East
> three thousand years ago; and certainly one might frame
> a pretty and not far-fetched analogy of witchery and
> dragon's teeth, and blood and armed men, between the
> ancient and the modern quest of the Golden Fleece in
> the Black Sea (Du Bois, *Souls of Black Folk*, pp. 135–36).

The object is not primarily to inform readers of actual working conditions in the South, although Du Bois is skillful at this kind of precise description, too, when the occasion requires. The object is instead to capture the mixture of beauty, energy, poverty, exploitation, and sordid industrial greed which make up the economy of the Black Belt since the Civil War; and to lend the significance and elevating power of myth to the lives of black share-croppers. In his choice of a classical myth, Du Bois is asserting whatever claim the black masses may choose to make to the classical heritage of "white" civilization on American soil, by actively demonstrating its relevance to their history.

Another chapter which applies classical myth to the meaning of the industrial South is the one entitled "Of the Wings of Ata-lanta." The myth of Atalanta, used by Swinburne in a work which Du Bois would certainly have read,[2] describes how Hippomenes caught the "tall and wild" Atalanta by placing three golden apples along her path; and when she stopped to pick them up, she lost the race. In Du Bois, the city of Atlanta is in danger of losing in the quest for Beauty and Truth by stooping to pick up the materialistic apples of profit; and not only Atlanta, but the Southern Negro.

This chapter, and the quotations that head the other chapters, contain an important key to Du Bois's use of language. We saw that the drive behind the work is the identity crisis, the struggle to merge the Negro's two selves into a "better and truer self." The identity crisis of the individual is linked to the fate of the whole country. America also suffers an identity crisis, for the black self is split from the white, resulting in a failure of civilization for both. The dream of Du Bois, the Promised Land, is a country where "some day on American soil two world-races may give each to each those characteristics both so sadly lack." The Promised Land is conceived as an Ideal of learning and culture; the chapter headings, by juxtaposing in each case a quotation from white poetry with a theme of Negro music, bring together the cultural achievements of both races to reflect the specific subject of the chapter. They are the Ideal within the material reality of history and fact. The language contains that Ideal, lofty, exalted, poetic, and musical, as manifested in words, the light of a cultural North Star guiding a fugitive country past prejudice, hate, profit and greed, to a unified self and civilization, "in large conformity to the greater ideals of the American Republic."

> From out the caves of evening that swing between the strong-limbed earth and the tracery of the stars, I summon Aristotle and Aurelius and what soul I will, and they come all graciously with no scorn nor condescension. So, wed with Truth, I dwell above the Veil. Is this the life you grudge us, O knightly America? Is this the life you long to change into the dull red hideousness of Georgia? Are you so afraid lest peering from this high Pisgah, between Philistine and Amalekite, we sight the Promised Land? (Du Bois, *Souls of Black Folk*, p. 109).

The larger meaning of the "Veil" metaphor in Du Bois becomes apparent here as well: it is not only the "Veil" of the color line separating black from white, but the Veil of material reality, of business, profits, wages, and industrialism separating the self from the Promised Land and the Negro worker and sharecropper from the values of Western Civilization.

The incident in which the black John is ejected from a Northern theater during a performance of Lohengrin's Swan is a masterful exposition of the Veil theme:

> The infinite beauty of the wail lingered and swept through every muscle of his frame, and put it all a-tune. He closed his eyes and grasped the elbows of the chair, touching unwittingly the lady's arm. And the lady drew away. A deep longing swelled in all his heart to rise with that clear music out of the dirt and dust of that low life that held him prisoned and befouled. If he could only live up in the free air where birds sang and setting suns had no touch of blood! Who had called him to be the slave and butt of all? And if he had called, what right had he to call when a world like this lay open before men? (ibid., pp. 236–37)

Immediately thereafter he is tapped on the shoulder by the usher, given back the money for his ticket, and asked to leave. The close connection between use of language and Du Bois's theory of the "talented tenth" in education is obvious: it is the talented tenth, exposed to classical Western culture, who will lead the black man beyond the Veil to within hearing of the Swan. Their role is paralleled in the lyricism of the style. The style is the music of the Swan to the "dirt and dust" of Negro slavery and discrimination.

The vague Idealism of Du Bois's vision of the Promised Land, his use of myths to structure and exalt individual chapters, his comments on Negro religion, and the place of Negro music in the organization of *Souls* indicate that he was feeling his way over the same ground later covered by other writers immediately before and after World War I: the search for a unifying myth, comprehensive enough to espouse the history of a people with the conflicts of the artist. The organizing myths of our major twentieth-century white artists—the legend of the Grail and Fisher King in Eliot, the arrangement of the Bach fugue in Pound's *Cantos*, the *Odyssey* in James Joyce, the system of the gyres and the great wheel in Yeats—are far more carefully and thoroughly worked out than the impulses in that direction that occur in *Souls*; but the fundamental reason for this fact lies in the difficulty of appropriating a European myth system to espouse the history of American black people with the conflicts of the black artist. This seems to have been what Du Bois wanted to do. But if the European poet had to deal with the alienation of the artist from bourgeois society, the black American poet had to deal with the alienation of black from white, of the black masses from America, of America from Europe, of the bourgeois Negro from the white ruling class and from the black masses, and of the black poet from all three. Despite these nearly insurmountable obstacles, Du Bois came very close, in the musical themes, to providing a "myth" that would have the same relationship to *Souls* as the Grail legend has to the *Wasteland*.

Du Bois's use of language, then, though far from a colloquial black idiom, is related to the rhetoric of abolition, to the black identity crisis of the second period, and to his own politics and educational theory. In allowing "black" to represent manual labor and "white" to represent Lohengrin's Swan in the split self of America, he also anticipates the dualism of "Omnipotent Administrator" and "Supermasculine Menial" in Eldridge Cleaver's *Soul on Ice*.

Du Bois carries on a black tradition of style in two other respects: he can shift rapidly between history, personal narrative, and polemics, and he is an excellent satirist. There is no bogus "objectivity" in his treatment of historical events. If personal narrative is important only as an illustration of the meanings in history, then the converse is also true: history is an extension of personal life. It is made by groups of persons in conflict, trying to create meaning and insure that their meaning will prevail. It makes all the difference in the world whether we see Reconstruction as the brave attempt of conquered whites to overthrow a conspiracy of carpet-baggers and ignorant Negroes to crush the South, or whether we see it as a bid for freedom on the part of the emancipated slaves that still remains unfinished business. When Du Bois writes history, he is narrating who he is and how he came into being. The issues are partisan; it is not until we take sides, or realize we have ended up on a side by default, that we become a subject instead of an object.

> After Emancipation, it was the plain duty of some one to assume this group leadership and training of the Negro laborer. . . . to see that these workingmen were not left alone and unguided, without capital, without land, without skill, without economic organization, without even the bald protection of law, order, and decency . . . (ibid., p. 168).

Like Douglass and Baldwin, Du Bois has the power of honest subjectivity. He interprets the past in order to change the present. If freedom remains unfinished business, then the problem is to find out why it remained unfinished, and to finish it. The past is alive and continuous, animated in Du Bois by the impassioned vigor of oration. Autobiography and social analysis are inseparable; the individual has no meaning except through the group.

As a satirist, Du Bois was most brilliant on the subject of the white man's burden. *Dusk of Dawn* slyly pretends to agree with the assumptions of white thinking in order to follow them to the point of logical absurdity. The Christian gentleman believes in Peace; to insure Peace, he must support a system of Justice; but Justice cannot be maintained without Defense; and since the best defense is a good offense, he has to be prepared for War, provided others do the fighting. Similarly, Christian Good Will requires the practice of Manners. Manners are best cultivated by a leisure class of whites and therefore imply the necessity of Caste; but Caste is founded on discrimination and generates Hate. Each Christian ethic, as practiced by American whites, leads in this way to its opposite. "They believe in liberty under a firm police system backed by patriotism and an organization of work which will yield profit to capital." Liberty demands Police, who are indoctrinated and sup- ported by Patriotism, which reinforces Exploitation. Liberty is Exploitation. "Possibly they are playing acrostics." Like the slave narrators, Du Bois condemns the white supremacists out of their own mouths. The position of the white man's burden is more than a lie; it seems a delusion, a form of insanity (see Du Bois, *Dusk of Dawn*, chap. six).

In his formal and oratorical style, Du Bois is an exception to the second-period autobiographies. Hughes, Redding, Johnson, and McKay all represent a trend toward loose syntax and concrete diction. But the quality of writing in these authors, their ability to modulate sound, hold interest, sustain metaphor, and adapt style to purpose does not lag far behind the best of Du Bois. A glance at Redding's description of the neighborhood where he lived as a child shows also a range well beyond the general run of slave narratives:

> Our street was quiet and shaded with elms that in summer formed an archway over the cobbled street. There were porches and hedge-bordered patches of front yards, and deep back yards with grape arbors and flowers. But below us on the east the streets became gradually more naked and sly, until, flinging off the last rag of pride, they prowled with brutal defensiveness past the huddled houses, the big-windowed corner saloons, the dark, dirty grocery stores, and the obscene, blank-walled factories to the river (Redding, pp. 12-13).

The appeal of the writing lies not only in the subdued personifica- tion of the streets as brute energy, but in the contrast between neighborhoods, the precarious balance of Redding's street, with its elms and tended yards and other pretensions of middle-class status, on the precipice of the eastern slum. Under the surface of this image is the deeper meaning of the relationship of middle-class Negroes to the mass of the proletariat.

The more concrete writers also employed irony, caricature, and polemics when dealing with racial themes, and so carry on a black writing tradition begun in the slavery period and continued in the 1960s. The tradition of concrete language and description seems distinctly "black" in diction and syntax only in the work of Langston Hughes, but in the other three it draws on the black experience by the way it expresses their identities and values.

The following passage by McKay, for example, makes use of methods that belong equally to Dos Passos and Steinbeck, but its preoccupations reveal a distinctly black, and also, perhaps, rural immigrant point of view:

> I liked to walk under the elevated tracks with the trains clashing and clanging overhead. There was excitement when the sudden roaring of the train abruptly blotted out conversation. Even the clothes suspended in the canyon tenements appeared endowed with a strange life of their own. In the stampeding hours of morning, noon, and evening, when the crowds assumed epic proportions, I was so exalted by their monster movement that I forgot that they were white. . . .
>
> The black giants of the New York Central, belching flame and smoke and dust along the facades of the fine palaces, created a picture like a caravan of modern pirates coming home in a rolling cloud of glory. The grim pioneer urge of the great pragmatic metropolis was a ferment in my feeling (McKay, p. 133).

Only a black writer would measure his exaltation by whether or not he forgot the crowds were white, a detail delayed to the end of the paragraph, where its impression is strongest. And in discovering a grandeur in the city that transcends color, he is reconciling a "black" with an American identity and putting the latter foremost in importance. It is best not to insist on the symbolism of the black locomotives, but they dirty the facades of the fine palaces like the ghost of "poor, painful black face" to whom McKay refers later as haunting the "pale devils." One also sees an image of democratic, pragmatic America dirtying the facades of aristocracy. The rural immigrant point of view is reflected in his fascination with the sheer spectacle of the city's energy and power; city dwellers who live under those elevated tracks all their lives and are caught day after day fighting the epic crowds, are apt to be much less exalted by them. Out of such feelings of ferment and exaltation, McKay wrote the poems in which a "discerning person" notes that he was "not, either by the grace of God or the desire of man, born white."

The purpose of satire in McKay expresses the predominance of racial over class identity in his politics. In the following quotation there is a racial slant, a theme of black versus white, rather than black worker versus white power structure. Satire is directed at the white man and white civilization undifferentiated by class.

> Poor, painful black face, intruding into the holy places of the whites. How like a specter you haunt the pale devils! Always at their elbow, always darkly peering through the window, giving them no rest, no peace. How they burn up their energies trying to keep you out! How apologetic and uneasy they are—yes, even the best of them, poor devils—when you force an entrance, Blackface, facetiously, incorrigibly, smiling or disturbingly composed. Shock them out of their complacency, Blackface; make them uncomfortable; make them unhappy! Give them no peace, no rest. How can they bear your presence, Blackface, great, unappeasable ghost of Western civilization! (ibid., p. 145).

Aside from the repetition and the parallel clauses, this paragraph is interesting because of the way in which the minstrel-show portrait of the obsequious black clown, supposedly terrified of graveyards, by a slight shift of tone becomes a terrifying ghost himself, a more real and persistent ghost than the white-sheeted night riders of the Ku Klux Klan would have imagined possible, haunting the white man with the very stereotype he has created to allay his Negrophobia. The larger social context of the passage reflects McKay's political outlook and gives added power to the language: the ghost of Western Civilization is white oppression of the Negro; keeping away the "black face," for the white man, keeps away the direct confrontation with his own guilt, yet reinforces the oppression and gives cause for even more guilt;

hence, the ghost is "unappeasable," for it cannot lie down decently exorcised in the grave of time until racism and race oppression come to an end.

James Weldon Johnson draws a picture of his father ironically from the viewpoint of a child:

> My first definite thought about the hotel was that it belonged to my father. True, there was always around in the office a Mr. Campbell, a rather stooped man with a short reddish beard, who habitually gave me a friendly pat on the shoulder, and who evidently had something to do with the place. But just to the right, at the entrance to the big dining room stands my father, peerless and imposing in full-dress clothes; he opens the door and takes me in; countless waiters, it seems, are standing around in groups; my father strikes a gong and the waiters spring to their stations and stand like soldiers at attention; I am struck with wonder at the endless rows of tables now revealed, the glitter of silver, china, and glass, and the array of napkins folded so that they look like many miniature white pyramids. Another gong, and the waiters relax . . . . My father snaps his fingers, waiters jump to carry out his orders, and guests smile him their thanks. He lords it over everything that falls within my ken. He is, quite obviously, the most important man in the St. James Hotel (Johnson, p. 16).

The essence of the irony is the difference between the child's perception of the dinner, which centers on the splendor of the tables, the gong, the father's clothes, and his command over the physical movements of the scene, and the reader's perception (shared by the author), with its full awareness of the racial and class nuances that escape the child. The adult understands that the elegance and glitter is to impress the customers, the father is head waiter and outfitted like the "house nigger" of the plantation, and the whole relationship of the customers, the white owner with the "short reddish beard," and the black servants is institutionalized racism. One also considers the social fact that the child will some day have to grow up to face: the restriction of Negroes to jobs where they are waiters, stewards, maids, janitors, and porters for whites. The complete context of American race relations lies under the surface of the passage; we perceive it only indirectly, in the background of a picture; it works the way literature works, by falling and growing slowly on the periphery of awareness rather than commanding attention from the lectern at the front of the hall.

Johnson has an "impish" sense of humor, to borrow his own adjective for his childhood religious hypocrisy, that links him with a stylistic tradition looking backward to Douglass and forward to Dick Gregory, Julius Lester, and H. Rap Brown.

> When I was born, my mother was very ill, too ill to nurse me. Then she found a friend and neighbor in an unexpected quarter. Mrs. McCleary, her white neighbor who lived a block away, had a short while before given birth to a girl baby. When this baby was christened she was named Angel. The mother of Angel, hearing of my mother's plight, took me and nursed me at her breast until my mother had recovered sufficiently to give me her own milk. So it appears that in the land of black mammies I had a white one (Johnson, p. 9).

The Southern white man, elsewhere in the book, is the butt of much of this humor, especially when he is most grimly serious about his racial "superiority."

No Day of Triumph contains several good examples of satire. A Jewish entrepreneur, proud of his liberal race attitudes because he hires colored factory hands, introduces Redding as "Mr. Redding" to another white man. And following this egalitarian gesture, he insists "you don't owe me nuthin.' " There is also a long anecdote which describes a sadomasochistic relationship between "Slug," a black vagrant, and a middle-class woman who taunts him into beating her up before she allows him to make love with her. Malcolm X describes a similar relationship with a rich white woman in his *Autobiography*; the couple act out the violence, dualism, and inferiority/superiority syndromes of race antagonism, but with the object of reversing the roles. Redding's incident, like the anecdotes of incest in Ellison's *Invisible Man*, waver between caricature and serious psychological case material (see Redding, p. 90). The essentials of Redding's satirical method can be seen in this caricature of a Negro doctor who is completely dependent on whites and serves their interests like an emasculated puppet in the black community:

> I had said good-by to the doctor the night before, but in the morning he had come down in his pajamas and a velvet-silk robe that reached to his ankles. He sat at table with me while I ate fruit and drank coffee. His teeth were out and his jaws and lips were collapsed in spongy weakness. He looked much older. Speech came grotesquely from his rubbery lips (ibid., p. 95).

Langston Hughes is probably the funniest writer in the second period, although his humor is not always satire on the race issue and does not, as a rule, contain the scornful epithet of Douglass and Malcolm X. These two figures exhibit the scars of social contradiction on the surface; Hughes tends to keep his scars in the background and his laughter out front. Typical of *The Big Sea* is his account of Bruce, a Negro cook in a Paris hotel.

> He was an enormous brownskin fellow, with one eye, stout, and nearing fifty. He wore a white apron, a white cap, and a very fierce frown. He could look at you so fiercely out of his one eye that you would quake in your shoes. His other eye was closed tight. But the one he had looked like three (Hughes, *The Big Sea*, p. 158).

The French proprietor fires Bruce because his salary is high and "the income of the place low," adding, as he delivers his last paycheck, "*Oui*, you may go right now, if you like. I'm tired of your impudence and that frown of yours you carry all the time."

> Bruce said: "Alors?"
> The boss said: "Allez!" and went back to his cash desk behind the bar, leaving Bruce's money on the kitchen table.

His "huge dark face" standing out like a "Dixie moon" under the chef's hat, Bruce selects "the longest of the butcher knives from the kitchen rack." He walks out to the cash desk, raises the knife, and demands, "Now, *qu'est-ce-que vous voulez, m'sieu?*" The boss "dived beneath the bar." The manager, who runs forward to insist that he is fired, is backed "right out into the street." One after another, he chases out the customers, the danseuses, and the bartender. "By this time Bruce had the place to himself, except for the orchestra, that stopped playing to laugh." He returns to the kitchen, replaces the knife, and goes back to work.

"Jim, did you see me?" he asked.
"I saw you, Bruce," I said. "You really did your stuff."
"Talking about *I'm fired!*" he snorted indignantly.
"You saw *who* left here, didn't you?"
"The boss!" I said.
"And all his assistants, little and big! Lit out and gone!" He rolled his one good eye and it rested on me. "But we still here, ain't we?"
"We're right here," I said.
"And here we'll be," he affirmed. "Life's a bitch, but I'll beat it—and stay here, too."
His final statement was absolutely correct (ibid., pp. 158, 182–3).

Here is caricature, but not of a white racist, a bourgeois Negro, or a racist institution. The environment is workingclass; the contradiction between worker and boss is not even, as elsewhere in Hughes, a question of racial exploitation. Until the last few lines, the fact that Bruce is black means no more than to underscore his formidable demeanor. It is only in retrospect that we realize the story leans heavily on two traditions of racist comedy and stereotype: the Negro with a knife, and the Negro servant who bullies his master, slyly pushing at the boundaries of his "place." But the purpose is to demonstrate endurance. "Life's a bitch, but I'll beat it—and stay here, too." Laughter in black autobiography is usually sardonic in intent, and directed *at* some aspect of racial oppression. To paraphrase a proverb by William Blake, it is often "excess of sorrow." The laughter in this case is *with* the characters, exulting in their triumph over the "bitchiness" of life. It is a shared affection rather than a shared hostility, whose message is the irrepressible resilience and will to survive of the Negro worker. The racist cliché is transvalued by its new context.

Indignant humor is not the rule in Hughes's personal narratives, but the poems contain that rage which is the impulse of satire, and one occasionally finds good examples of it in the prose. The following two passages of satire come from the common ground that is most typical of black autobiography, the contradictions of racial and class antagonism:

> Haiti, land of blue sea and green hills, white fishing boats on the sea, and the hidden huts of peasants in the tall mountains. . . . A surge of black peasants who live on the land, and the foam of the cultured elite in Port au Prince who live on the peasants.

> I went outside [in Savannah, Ga.] on the sidewalk and around into the white waiting room where I bought the *Sunday Times* without incident. But, coming out of the station, just at the door, a white policeman stopped me.
> He yelled, "You can't come in and out this door."
> "There's no newsstand in the colored waiting room," I explained.
> "I don't care nothing about that!" he barked. "You can't come in this door. This is for white folks."
> "Oh," I said. "I am going out now."
> "You can't go out this way neither," said the cop as I started through the door.
> This puzzled me, as there was no other way out of the station except through the train sheds. "I just came in this way," I said.
> "Well, you can't go out this way," barked the cop. "Niggers can't use this door."
> "How do I get out then?" I asked.
> "Only way I can see," said the cop seriously, "is for you to walk the tracks" (Hughes, *I Wonder As I Wander*, pp. 15, 53 respectively).

In the first example the language builds up a dramatic tourist-brochure impression of Haiti, only to undercut and parody the whole effect in the last phrase. It is a method that suits perfectly the way Hughes saw the country, as a tourist trying to step outside the tourist role, looking for the human struggle and sweat behind the facade. It points up the difference between the perceptions of the white tourist, who would probably see only the tourist-brochure impression, and those of the Negro, who sees the exploitation and the international color line. His mind is playing, at the end, with the possibilities of a metaphor which caps a *surge* of black peasants with a *foam* of cultured elite. Like the rhythms of Negro blues, which he had described with the same metaphor in *The Big Sea*, the black peasants have the persistence and "deep-rooted power" of the waves, while the elite have the effervescence, and impermanence, the airy nothingness, of the white froth on top. Herein lies the chief distinction between Hughes and Douglass or Baldwin, both of whom are much better polemicists: Hughes seems more interested in what he can do with the language than in actually reforming the injustices of the subject matter. In the second example, the satire is a matter of simple presentation: the pathetic stupidity of the white cop, and the system he is defending, speaks for itself. Hughes's response is to "burst out laughing as I walked along with my paper from Manhattan." The incident is more absurd than outrageous, although its offensiveness is not ignored. He comments later, "When I thought about these things seriously, they were not funny. They were boorish and stupid" (ibid., p. 54).

A more evident way in which Hughes carries on and refines black traditions of style is to speak with a plain, repetitive, colloquial, concrete voice. He stands out, in the modern trend toward loose syntax and concrete diction, as a *black* voice, because looseness, simplicity, repetition, etc., suit his racial and class viewpoint as a black writer. Simplicity in Langston Hughes has nothing to do with "primitivism"; he attacks the idea that Negroes are any more "primitive" than other people. Simplicity has far more to do with paring away all pretentiousness and ornament, so that the basic patterns of his language will come close to the basic patterns of life, as lived by the Negro workers and tenant farmers who fill his books. Like Hemingway, he relies on subject-verb clauses linked together by "and," "so," and "but" and avoids complex subordination, antithesis, conceit, periodicity, and personification. When he needs emphasis, he will repeat a parallel series of quick, simple sentences, often letting one sentence stand alone as a paragraph. Hughes was consciously influenced in his poetry by the rhythms of the blues:

> Like the waves of the sea coming one after another,
> always one after another, like the earth moving around

the sun, night, day—night, day—night, day—forever, so
is the undertow of black music with its rhythm that never
betrays you, its strength like the beat of the human heart,
its humor, and its rooted power.

> *I'm goin' down to de railroad baby,*
> *Lay ma head on de track.*
> *I'm goin' down to de railroad, babe,*
> *Lay ma head on de track—*
> *But if I see de train a-comin',*
> *I'm gonna jerk it back* (Hughes, *The Big Sea*,
> p. 209).

The prose style of *The Big Sea* is affected by the same blend of
repetition, simplicity, and humor that he admired so much in
the music. In this way it is given a black slant that distinguishes
Hughes from Hemingway or Steinbeck. During his visit to
Genoa, Hughes ordered a piece of meat at a restaurant and "could
smell it afar off. It was liver. And ripe. In small restaurants in
Italy they have no ice boxes. . . . Anyway, this was an old piece
of liver. A *very old* piece." Not knowing how to ask for his money
back or order anything else, he ate the liver so as not to waste
the three lire, "every leaping morsel."

> I could taste it in my mouth and it was a thousand years
> old. I could feel it boiling in my stomach. I could smell
> it green as maggots on my breath (ibid., p. 195).

The pattern of the three short sentences which conclude this
passage resembles the three-line structure of the blues song: they
are set up in parallel forms, with the strongest and most vivid
line saved for last.

Often the rhythm of a Hughes passage resembles the refrain
and lines of a song lyric. We can hear in its cadence the same voice
of "The Negro Speaks of Rivers," "The Weary Blues," and
"Blues at Dawn":

> Hunger came, too. Bread and cheese once a day couldn't
> keep hunger away. Selling your clothes, when you didn't
> have many, couldn't keep hunger away. Going to
> bed early and sleeping late couldn't keep hunger away.
> Looking for a job and always being turned down

couldn't keep hunger away. Not sleeping alone couldn't
keep hunger away (ibid., p. 151).

In George Orwell's *Down and Out in London and Paris*, hunger is
the subject of a reporter's investigative curiosity, a new experience
considered with the directness of the second-person pronoun "you."
But in Hughes it becomes a refrain, marking time like the sound
of feet on the pavement looking for a job, a basic rhythm of life.

Simplicity and concreteness in Langston Hughes also mean
closeness to material facts, politics grounded solidly in experience,
and the ability to project the nature of a social system or the importance of a social movement by detailed realization of single incidents. We have noted this quality during his visit to Turkmenistan, in *I Wonder As I Wander*, where Hughes was able to perceive
the world meaning, closed to Koestler, of the Bolshevik dictatorship. For Hughes the meaning came through observable fact, such
as the presence of Uzbec workers in the best hotels, the disappear-
ance of Jim Crow on the trams, and the empty harem kennels that
had once been filled with wives belonging to the potentates
Koestler had seen in prison. Hughes turns the same vision on
colonialism during his visit to Africa. The ship he worked on had
been carrying a "little family of Africans" down the coast. When
they came to the gang-plank to go ashore, the English inspector
refused to let them off because "their papers called for a French
colony." The captain came "fuming down from the bridge" and
tried to strike them with his cane, "but they ran." Looking like "the
father of the Katzenjammer Kids, very fat and German in his white
suit," he chased them around for a while, but "they ran too fast,
man, wife, and offspring, like deer."

> It looked very funny—this chase—and I wanted to laugh,
> but somehow I couldn't laugh, because it is too much
> like today's Africa, real, beyond humor—the raised club,
> the commanding white man, and the frightened
> native (ibid., p. 113).

For white writers of the twenties and thirties, the rediscovery of
sense experience and sense language was a reaction to the moral and
political abstractions that had rationalized World War I, and,
even earlier, bourgeois Victorian society. The meaning of the

detailed sense impressions of food, warmth, the touch of physical
objects, and the movements of people in Hemingway's *A Farewell
to Arms* is that they represent life, and expressions like "freedom,"
"glory," and "in vain" represent the language of death. Hemingway, however, rejects all politics and ideology as either "opium"
or "catharsis." Sense experience is all there is and means nothing
beyond itself. Hemingway is a "primitivist" in the worst sense
of the term, because he cannot see well beyond the immediate light
of his symbolic campfire. Death, hardship, and struggle for him
lead only to *nada*—isolation and nihilism. Where death is given
dignity and purpose, it is purely in terms of an individualist code.
For Hughes, concrete language is a tie to a political tradition and
a class identity; it is a microcosm for that larger insight into
society and social conflict without which no real understanding of
World War I, the Bolshevik Revolution, or race discrimination is
possible.[3]

Concreteness in J. Saunders Redding has the same importance.
The beauty of *No Day of Triumph* is in the way its author enters
into the voices of his characters and lets their experience draw the
picture of class structure and race relations in the South. Redding
had gone South to break out of his isolation, to lose the narrow,
split "self" of the bourgeois Negro and find a larger self in the
stream by whose turbid waters all of America fed. Appropriately,
he keeps himself offstage for most of the book and allows his various
interviewees to give what they have to offer in their own words.
His narrow "self" is thus sloughed off in the artistic method. The
work is a collection of short stories and precise observations
organized around the theme of his search for the "highest common
denominator of mankind." But his material is selected carefully
for what it reveals about the whole system of society in the areas
where he traveled. His descriptions of the mines and working conditions for the miners recall the descriptions of slave labor and
cotton picking in the slave narratives (see especially Redding, p.
103). And the following dialog by a semiliterate miner, commenting
on a Negro lawyer, penetrates to the utter uselessness of the petty
capitalist ethic as a solution to the problems of black workers:

> "Funny thing, but if you ain't got nothin' seems like
> there ain't nothin' you can do, an' if you got something,

you's afraid to do anything. It ain't nobody's fault, I
don't guess, but it sure looks like we'se in a poke. I heard
Coe say that if Lawyer Cartwright would live twenty-five
years more, he might be worth a half a millyun dollars.
Now what can a nigger with that much money do for
anybody but hisself? But, pshaw, he ain't goin' a live that
long, an' what he's got now's goin' back to the white
folks" (ibid., p. 104).

Throughout *No Day of Triumph* we are given a clear understanding of the way human beings in a particular area produce and
distribute wealth, buy and sell commodities, work together, exploit
labor and cope with exploitation, what they think of themselves
and each other, how they associate, and how their values and ideas
are related to the way they earn their living (ibid., pp. 76, 211,
256, especially). Redding's autobiography is full of wages, factories,
bosses, workers, shacks, cotton fields, sharecroppers, and important
economic detail of every sort. These facts have aesthetic, as well
as sociological, importance, for they contrast with and complement
the verbal tradition of abolitionist oratory in his family background, and thus help to structure the work. They are also the
basics of his larger, human "validities," their content and mode
of existence.

We may conclude that the language of second-period autobiographies is affected by their black viewpoints in various ways, that
they continue the lines of development in the slave narratives and
prefigure the language of the 1960s. The structure of the slave
narrative survives in several works, especially the ones by Communists. Its Biblical and orational rhetoric survive primarily in
Du Bois, and its polemics, irony, satire, caricature, and sense description survive to some degree in almost every author. Irony and
satire continue to spring from the experience of racial and class
oppression and attack these things obliquely, by exposing their
foolishness, absurdity, or inhumanity. Black autobiography has
gained greatly in the range and depth of its art; the methods
have become more subtle and sophisticated, the goals less *directly*
political and more cultural and literary. Looseness and concrete
language, while superficially part of a general trend in all American
literature, is distinguished from white writing by its class per-

spective, politics, and social matrix; black music affects the styles of both Du Bois and Langston Hughes; the former is influenced by the spirituals, the latter primarily by the blues. Although there is as much difference between these two styles as between any other two American writers, both reflect the black-oriented values and identities of their authors.

The high quality of black writing in the second period, though more indirectly than in the slave narratives, continues to be a function of the "black viewpoint." In a general sense, the "black viewpoint" means a sharper awareness of social relationships, acquired through having to direct constant attention to the social relationship of color. Style is no longer primarily a weapon but still bears the mold of political consciousness.

The full value of the black autobiography, as art, cannot be appreciated by reference only to the art object itself but must be taken in the social context where the author places it. The "blackness" of the work demands such consideration, because "black" is nothing less than its social context.

Chapter 8 *Richard Wright*

ICHARD Wright's *Black Boy* is the autobiography most worth reading of all the works of its kind in American literature, whether black or white. It has the tough, pure beauty of a desert cactus, squeezing life energy from the dry sand, rich in water beneath the protective spines, putting forth roots, flowers, seeds, and curiously shaped stalks in a land of death and buzzards. Only *Walden*, of the autobiographies by white authors, contains as deep a vision of life's possibilities or forges an identity so solid in its grasp of the actual, yet fluid enough to go on growing and changing with the changes in the social climate. Only *Walden* stays in the mind as long, extending awareness of the meanings in our experience over time, and inspiring us with the difference made therein by how and what we think. One should feel apprehensive about making such a statement, because the real objectives of literature are so often and easily forgotten in the game of "mirror, mirror, on the wall, tell me the fairest of them all." And it must be remembered that any critic's judgment of a book is always in terms of why it is good *for him*. But the purpose of making such judgments is to stress what is valuable in the work and why.

The qualities that make *Black Boy* great are mostly the same ones we have already discussed in black writing and that appear in some form as early as the slave narratives. Like Douglass, Wright is affected by a host of influences which he assimilates and masters. *Black Boy* includes the identity crisis, the alienation, the restless movement, and the views on education, knowledge, and resistance that were demonstrated to be traditional in black autobiography as a whole. Wright's prose also shares the trend toward looseness and objective detail and the power of rendering the design of human social relations through the behavior of a single set of characters. He stands somewhat above his contemporaries because of the way he has used the material common to them all.

The structure of *Black Boy* belongs to the slave narrative. The author grows up in an environment of poverty, violence, and constant hunger; most of the physical punishment he receives comes from his family, but they are only acting out the oppressive relationship of white over black in the society at large. He teaches himself to read, acquires a passion to know the meaning of his life which the social system around him discourages and suppresses; he is driven on several occasions to settle family quarrels with knives and razors and is forced to go North because he cannot adapt to the role of racial inferiority expected of him by whites. He is unable to wear the mask, and white violence, the punishment for black integrity, threatens to kill him or emasculate him. Although the book ends where he leaves for Chicago, we know that later he reentered the struggle as a writer and, for a time, as a Communist party member, to fight against the social system of capitalism and provide intellectual leadership within a political movement. All the elements of slave narrative structure are present: self-taught literacy, education as a means to understand a brutal environment, resistance that preserves one's integrity and goals as an individual human being, inability to fit the mold of slave, anger and bitter discontent, the journey to the North, active group politics, and movement up the social scale. The reason they are present is not so much that Wright has consciously imitated the slave narrative (although the material could have been shaped with that form in mind), but that his childhood and adolescence closely resembled the patterns of slavery, and so the literary forms developed as a response to slavery have continued to serve a purpose.

The identity crisis and alienation that we have recognized in the other authors exist also in Wright. It is more than awakening to the absurd, however, and in using the term "alienation" to describe his isolated feelings, it is necessary to point up the differences between Wright and the existentialist friends he was later to make in Paris. The foundation of the wall separating Wright and his world is the role of "nigger" forced on the vast majority of black children in American society. Wright is forbidden and prevented from acting spontaneously on his own feelings or even on his intuition of what ought to be accepted and praised in any system. He must be what he is not. He is forced to hide his feelings in order to avoid being beaten for them. That he cannot suppress them entirely and learn to ape only permissible feelings means that, instead of being estranged from himself, he is estranged from others. "Alienation" as applied to Wright must often mean simply the chasm dividing what he is from what others expect him to be. Later it comes to signify the general homelessness of American blacks and the pain of the black man who cannot accept his people as they are and cannot be accepted by them.

His separation from his schoolmates results in part from his desire to be a writer, a goal beyond their world of possibilities and beyond their belief in what a black person has any reason to expect:

> The mood out of which a story was written was the most
> alien thing conceivable to them. They looked at me with
> new eyes, and a distance, a suspiciousness came between
> us. If I had thought anything in writing the story, I had
> thought that perhaps it would make me more acceptable
> to them, and now it was cutting me off from them
> more completely than ever (Wright, *Black Boy*, pp. 184–5).

But Wright's sense of isolation began at a very early age, in his curiosity and tenderness of feeling and his constant refusal to obey orders, to accept the substandard life imposed on him. Even as a child there was a part of him that remained detached from and embarrassed by the formulas of his own culture:

> In shaking hands I was doing something that I was to do
> countless times in the years to come: acting in conformity
> with what others expected of me even though, by the
> very nature and form of my life, I did not and could not
> share their spirit (ibid., p. 45).

His tenderness of feeling and sensitivity show in the incident where his Uncle Hoskins, in a playful mood, drives their horse and cart into the Mississippi River and convinces the boy Richard that he is heading straight for the middle "so the horse can drink." Richard takes him seriously and jumps out of the cart in a panic. Catching him by the foot, his Uncle drags him back and turns the cart around but has to force him to stay in the seat. The boy finally lunges free and lands in the dust.

> "Are you really that scared?" he asked softly.
> I did not answer; I could not speak. My fear was gone
> now and he loomed before me like a stranger, like a man I
> had never seen before, a man with whom I could never
> share a moment of intimate living (ibid., p. 61).

The action of Uncle Hoskins is part of a process of acculturation
that prepared black children for a world of random violence and
danger; but with Richard, the process does not "take." He sees only
that his being, his personality, has been ravaged, and he refuses
to accept a relationship where this can happen. His answer is to
withdraw, to regard Hoskins as a stranger.

Alienation and the struggle to grow are the heart of the narrator's
development in *Black Boy* and more completely and persuasively
portrayed here than in any other work. Wright traces the history
of his alienation in terms of gradual estrangement from his family,
points out the transference of that feeling to the white world,
generalizes brilliantly from direct experience to its meaning in
the formation of his character and special insights, and explains its
source in the racist organization of society.

In school, Wright never had anything for lunch and watched
the other pupils split open loaves of bread and "line them with
juicy sardines," declaring, with a shrug of his shoulders, "Aw, I'm
not hungry at noon, ever." If he had gone home to eat his plate of
greens, he would have been kept in, and he preferred to "tramp with
a gang into the woods, to rivers, to creeks, into the business district,
to the doors of poolrooms, into the movies when we could slip in
without paying, to neighborhood ball games, to brick kilns, to
lumberyards, to cottonseed mills, to watch men work." He deliberately "starved" in order to learn about his environment. Speaking
of the members of his gang, he broadens the meaning of "hunger"
suddenly to include his sense of separation from them:

> Again and again I vowed that someday I would end this
> hunger of mine, this apartness, this eternal difference;
> and I did not suspect that I would never get intimately
> into their lives, that I was doomed to live with them but
> not of them, that I had my own strange and separate road,
> a road which in later years would make them wonder
> how I had come to tread it (ibid., p. 140).

On one of his first jobs, as an agent selling worthless insurance to
black sharecroppers, he "saw a bare, bleak pool of black life and I
hated it; the people were alike, their homes were alike, and their
farms were alike." The "essential bleakness of black life in America" he ascribes to the fact that "Negroes had never been allowed
to catch the full spirit of Western Civilization . . . they lived
somehow in it but not of it" (ibid., p. 45). His family's reaction of
pleasure and pride at the money he was making simply increased
the distance between them and gave him added insight into the
hypocrisy of their religion. "To Granny, I had accomplished a
miracle," he wrote, "and some of my sinful qualities evaporated, for
she felt that success spelled the reward of righteousness and that
failure was the wages of sin." Elsewhere he saw in religion only a
"naked will to power":

> Wherever I found religion in my life I found strife, the
> attempt of one individual or group to rule another in the
> name of God. The naked will to power seemed always
> to walk in the wake of a hymn (ibid., pp. 150–1).

His jobs for white bosses were full of pitfalls and minor disasters
because he had never learned to play the obsequious "nigger."
Asked seriously by a white woman, "Do you steal?" his response is to
laugh and say, "Lady, if I was a thief, I'd never tell anybody."
When the woman reddens and snaps back, "What do you mean?"
he realizes that he "had made a mistake during my first five minutes
in the white world" (ibid., p. 160).

> I was tense each moment, trying to anticipate their wishes
> and avoid a curse, and I did not suspect that the tension
> I had begun to feel that morning would lift itself into the
> passion of my life. Perhaps I had waited too long to start
> working for white people; perhaps I should have
> begun earlier, when I was younger—as most of the other
> black boys had done—and perhaps by now the tension
> would have become an habitual condition, contained
> and controlled by reflex. But that was not to be my lot;
> I was always to be conscious of it, brood over it, carry it in
> my heart, live with it, sleep with it, fight with it (ibid.,
> p. 165).

The problem worsens when he asks two Southern whites to teach him how to grind lenses while working for an optical company, and they beat him up, threaten him with death, wave an iron bar in his face, call him a "black granny-dodger" and run him off the job. The tales of lynchings that come to his ears compel him to give his entire imagination "over to white brutality," an act which "blocked the springs of thought and feeling in me, creating a sense of distance between me and the world in which I lived (ibid., p. 190). Called back by the Yankee owner of the optical company to tell which of the white men had "bothered" him, he is unable to speak because of fear:

> I felt drenched in shame, naked to my soul. The whole of my being felt violated, and I knew that my own fear had helped me to violate it. I was breathing hard and struggling to master my feelings (ibid., p. 212).

He walks away as though having been "slapped out of the human race." In his statement of the net effect of this alienation on his perceptions, we are able to understand clearly how the special experience of the black writer leads to his special grasp of social organization and the link between individual and class:

> I knew what was wrong with me, but I could not correct it. The words and actions of white people were baffling signs to me. I was living in a culture and not a civilization and I could learn how that culture worked only by living with it. Misreading the reactions of whites around me made me say and do the wrong things. In my dealing with whites I was conscious of the entirety of my relations with them, and they were conscious only of what was happening at a given moment. I had to keep remembering what others took for granted; I had to think out what others felt (ibid., p. 215).

The identity crisis in Wright resembles the dual alienation of Du Bois and Redding: his singularity, his genius, the height of his aspirations, cut him off from the black masses at the same time that racism cuts him off from acceptance in the white world, and the bitter affronts to his pride by whites kill any desire to work for their approval. Unlike Redding, Richard Wright could not solve this crisis by returning to identify with the people. He was "flabbergasted" by their "simple unaffected trust." In fact he could overstate his distance from the black masses so heavily that he may have provided white racism with ammunition:

> (After I had outlived the shocks of childhood, after the habit of reflection had been born in me, I used to mull over the strange absence of real kindness in Negroes, how unstable was our tenderness, how lacking in genuine passion we were, how void of great hope, how timid our joy, how bare our traditions, how hollow our memories, how lacking we were in those intangible sentiments that bind man to man, and how shallow was even our despair . . . [ibid., p. 45].)

This passage may provide a clue to explain the alleged overstatement in the character of Bigger Thomas, who is likewise crude, unstable in tenderness, devoid of real kindness, simple and shallow even in his despair. Bigger Thomas may represent what could have happened to Wright if he was prevented from growing in a constructive direction. Wright's purpose in *Native Son* is the valid one of demonstrating how the distortions in black culture are caused by the organized racism of white society, and how, given the racism and the distortions, blacks must cope with them by rather ugly methods if they are to survive at all. But the overstatement, the fact that he could say what he did, reveals how deep the dual alienation in Wright actually went. What is important is whether the insights into human life that result from it are worth the price he paid in anguish and distorted vision. And for the reader, they are.

Being cut off from all reason to live, beyond sense enjoyment, creates the gulf out of which springs resistance. The violence in the world around him necessitates a violent response from the narrator. His resistance begins at the age of four, when he refuses to submit to a spanking after setting fire to the house. As an older child, he was sent to the grocery store three consecutive times and robbed and beaten every time by a gang of boys. He tried to hide inside his apartment. But his mother gave him a stick, slammed and locked the door in his face, and promised to whip him if he didn't come home with the groceries. He "had the choice of being beaten at home or away from home." If he were beaten at home, he reasoned, there was nothing he could do about it, but if he were beaten in the streets, he could fight back.

> They closed in. In blind fear I let the stick fly, feeling it crack against a boy's skull. I swung again, lamming another skull, then another. Realizing that they would retaliate if I let up for but a second, I fought to lay them low, to knock them cold, to kill them so that they could not strike back at me. I flayed with tears in my eyes, teeth clenched, stark fear making me throw every ounce of my strength behind each blow. I hit again and again, dropping the money and the grocery list. The boys scattered, yelling, nursing their heads, staring at me in utter disbelief (ibid., p. 25).

When the parents rush out to defend the boys, Wright tells them he would "give them the same" if they bothered him. He carries the reader with him at every step, in complete sympathy, because the conclusion of the tale is what every child who has ever been beaten up by a gang fantasizes and longs to have done in his own case. The rapport between reader and narrator thus established remains when Wright moves on to narrate the battles that were more political or more peculiar to his individual background.

The narrative accumulates the stories of white violence that came to Wright in his childhood: the murder of his Uncle Hoskins, the sight of black chain gangs in the road, the folk tale of the Negro woman whose husband was lynched, who went humbly to the whites to beg for the body, withdrew a shotgun, and killed four of them firing "from her knees." These stories oppress his imagination with the knowledge that "there existed men against whom I was powerless, men who could violate my life at will." He resolved that if he were ever faced with a white mob, he would "conceal a weapon," pretend that he had accepted their cruelty as the law of his life, and at the last moment, "kill as many of them as possible before they killed me." The fantasy enables him to keep his "emotional integrity whole," so that his personality could "limp through days lived under the threat of violence." When he finally reaches the age where gang fights with white boys are a regular part of his life, he has been prepared for the role by everything he has learned in his culture:

> We were now large enough for the white boys to fear us and both of us, the white boys and the black boys, began to play our traditional racial roles as though we had been born to them, as though it was in our blood, as though we were being guided by instinct. All the frightful descriptions we had heard about each other, all the violent expressions of hate and hostility that had seeped into us from our surroundings, came now to the surface to guide our actions (ibid., p. 93).

As an adolescent, he discovers some of the details of his grandfather's early manhood; and by this means, Wright now connects the resistance of his particular experience to a tradition, to the sweep of American history, concentrating history in the facts of his personal life:

> It was from Granny's conversations, year after year, that the meager details of Grandpa's life came to me. When the Civil War broke out, he ran off from his master and groped his way through the Confederate lines to the North. He darkly boasted of having killed "mo'n mah fair share of them damn rebels" while en route to enlist in the Union Army. Militantly resentful of slavery, he joined the Union Army to kill southern whites; he waded in icy streams; slept in mud; suffered, fought.... Mustered out, he returned to the South and, during elections, guarded ballot boxes with his army rifle so that Negroes could vote. But when the Negro had been driven from political power, his spirit had been crushed. He was convinced that the war had not really ended, that it would start again (ibid., p. 155).

The reader understands at this point that the "war" for the survival of the human spirit in black people is still being fought by the boy Richard, that a whole heritage of struggle is being expressed through his actions as though he were "guided by instinct." When the climax of the resistance theme occurs in the chapter where he confronts his uncle, razorblades in hand, and refuses to be whipped for the tone of his voice, it is Douglass fighting Covey the Negro-breaker, the woman of the folktale shooting her enemies from the knee, the will to freedom transcending the "implacable limitations" of oppression. "I'll be damned if I'm going to be beaten for your hurt feelings," Wright told his uncle. The uncle advanced, calling him "the worst criminal I ever saw," but the boy threatened and "sliced out with points of steel," until the man, chest heaving, stopped and concluded, "Somebody will yet break your spirit." "It won't be you!" was Richard's reply.

> We stood in the early morning light and a touch of sun broke on the horizon. Roosters were crowing. A bird chirped near-by somewhere. Perhaps the neighbors were listening. Finally Uncle Tom's face began to twitch. Tears rolled down his cheeks. His lips trembled.
> "Boy, I'm sorry for you," he said at last.
> "You'd better be sorry for yourself," I said.
> "You think you're a man," he said, dropping his arm and letting the switch drag in the dust of the yard. His lips moved as he groped for words. "But you'll learn, and you'll learn the hard way. I wish I could be an example to you. . . ."
> "You are not an example to me; you could never be," I spat at him. "You're a *warning*. Your life isn't so hot that you can tell me what to do. . . . Do you think I want to grow up and weave the bottoms of chairs for people to sit in?"
> He twitched violently, trying to control himself.
> "You'll be sorry you said that," he mumbled.

It is also the pathetic defeat of his family's effort to instill in him the meekness and obedience of the oppressed. The pride and integrity that Wright maintains in this scene causes a "huge wound, tender, festering," after he graduates from the beatings of his family to the organized hostility of the white world, which is not so easily confronted; for he must accept defeat and humiliation many times to save his life. Because his spirit has not been killed as a child, he is doomed to feel "numb, reduced to a lumpish, loose, dissolved state" as an adult, doomed to feel the "longing to attack" without

knowing how to appease that torment (ibid., p. 213). But the
pain of a raw and living spirit is quite different from the dumb
pain of the ox in the yoke. The latter has no meaning whatever, for
the ox. The former is the well of creative energy behind revolution, civilization, literature, science, and everything that makes
human life more than a blind mouth opening in the darkness.

The place of combat in *Black Boy* reminds us again of the creative
value given to revolutionary force by Fanon in *The Wretched of
the Earth*. Wright's family, like the colonized native, deal with
their impulses to violence against the white world by taking them
out on each other and by sublimating them in religious frenzy.
Wright overcomes his sense of helplessness by rising in rebellion
to attack his oppressors and reclaim his life for his own use. He also
lays bare the role of family organization in reinforcing the class
relations of master and slave, mother country and colony. He
extends his experience into the most sophisticated realm of political
theory, as he does with equal brilliance in *Native Son,* where the
facts of Bigger Thomas's life are placed in a theoretical and political framework by the trial speech of the lawyer Max. In both
respects, he prefigures the revolutionary period of the 1960s and
'70s.

Equal in importance to the theme of resistance is the hunger for
knowledge. Here, too, Richard Wright is bringing together
what has by now become a tradition in the viewpoint of black
autobiography. In the slave narratives, the hunger for knowledge
implies risks that are almost equal to the risk of open rebellion.
Knowledge is a threat to the system of slavery. Knowledge has this
significance in *Black Boy*. True to his method, Wright traces the
growth of his hunger for knowledge incident by incident, relating
it at every point to his objective experience, revealing how the
need for it is a response to the barriers of his stunted environment,
how it orders his confused emotions and hostilities. Only after
he has accumulated a wealth of material incidents, showing the
origin of the need in the social system, does he then give it a
theoretical formulation.

"Ella," he asks a schoolteacher boarding with the family, "what
are you reading?" Her answer is evasive, and he presses her further:
"But I want to know." It is the story of Bluebeard and his Seven
Wives.

The tale made the world around me be, throb, live. As
she spoke, reality changed, the look of things altered, and
the world became peopled with magical presences. My
sense of life deepened and the feel of things was different,
somehow. Enchanted and enthralled, I stopped her
constantly to ask for details. My imagination blazed. The
sensations the story aroused in me were never to leave
me. When she was about to finish, when my interest was
keenest, when I was lost to the world around me, Granny
stepped briskly onto the porch (ibid., p. 47).

The grandmother forbids the teacher to tell him any more stories
because it is "the Devil's work." But Wright "had tasted what to
me was life, and I would have more of it, somehow, someway."
Burning to learn to read, he steals novels and nags his mother into
telling him the meanings of words; they were "the gateway to a
forbidden and enchanting land." Later he questions her about
"white folks" and color differences, is put off, and insists, "I want
to *know*." He asks if his grandmother couldn't find out who her
father was.

"For what, silly?"
"So she could know."
"Know for what?"
"Just to know."
"But for *what*?"
I could not say. I could not get anywhere (ibid., pp. 56–57).

The same ceaseless questions arise when he notices a black chain
gang in the streets: "What are they? . . . What's a chain gang? . . .
What did they do? . . . Why don't the white men wear stripes?
. . . Why are there so many black men wearing stripes? . . . Why
don't all the black men fight all the white men out there?" (Ibid., pp.
67–68) In high school, the questions are broader, but they follow
the same pattern, and lead in the same direction:

What was it that made the hate of whites for blacks so
steady, seemingly so woven into the texture of things?
What kind of life was possible under that hate? How had
this hate come to be? Nothing about the problems of
Negroes was ever taught in the classrooms at school; and

> whenever I would raise these questions with the boys,
> they would either remain silent or turn the subject into
> a joke. They were vocal about the petty individual
> wrongs they suffered, but they possessed no desire for a
> knowledge of the picture as a whole. Then why was I
> worried about it? (Ibid., p. 181)

Although he does not find answers right away, he learns that reading
enlarges and clarifies the context of the questions, and writing
gives shape to the mood, the restless longing, that compels him to
keep asking. His first exposure to H. L. Mencken teaches him that
words could be used "as one would use a club," and Sinclair Lewis
enables him to identify his boss as "an American type." "I felt
now that I knew him, that I could feel the very limits of his narrow
life" (ibid., pp. 272–73). Knowledge defends him against the cultural oppression of helplessness and despair. But he risks violence
to pursue it, for he has to forge a white man's name on a permission
slip to get books out of the library.

   Through knowledge, resistance, and the restless movement that,
as in the slave narratives, takes the form of flight to the North,
Wright builds an identity out of the atomized solitude of alienation and preserves his integrity and freedom of spirit. It is an identity as a writer and a free human being, whose will and intelligence,
far from being eroded by oppression, have only been strengthened,
have taken root in the *ell* of culture which he wrested from a
system that was determined to withhold the *inch*.

> At the age of twelve . . . I had a conception of life that
> no experience would ever erase, a predilection for what
> was real that no argument could ever gainsay, a sense
> of the world that was mine and mine alone, a notion as to
> what life meant that no education could ever alter, a
> conviction that the meaning of living came only when
> one was struggling to wring a meaning out of meaningless
> suffering. . . .

The spirit he caught made him "strangely tender and cruel, violent
and peaceful," while his questions kept alive in him "that enthralling sense of wonder and awe in the face of the drama of human
feeling which is hidden by the external drama of life" (ibid., p. 112).

No more perfect instrument could be imagined for the meaning that he wrung out of meaningless suffering than Richard Wright's language and the organization of this book. It is a simple language of factual statement, spiny syntax, forceful narrative and dialog, full of exact detail about the living and working conditions around him. It contains occasional specimens of caricature, irony, and polemics, though very little real humor. Now and then it even rings with the faint echo of slave narrative oratory, and there are catalogs modeled after the poetry of Whitman and Sandburg. Like the identity and the values, the language brings together familiar traditions of black writing. But it is a language utterly without superfluity of any sort, bare as the bones of his environment, direct and honest. It is not therefore impoverished, for it contains everything essential to his purpose. No hint of Biblical allusions or Promised-Land rhetoric is anywhere to be found, save in parody of his relatives. Identity and meaning are to be created on the terms of hardship and realism compelled by survival in the present, not in the future or the hereafter. The plant cannot wait to grow in a garden if the seed falls in a railroad yard.

> My faith, such as it was, was welded to the common realities of life, anchored in the sensations of my body and in what my mind could grasp, and nothing could ever shake this faith, and surely not my fear of an invisible power (ibid., p. 127).

The organization of *Black Boy* is a swing between fact and interpretation, the latter never straying from the former and always summarizing, illuminating, and directing it toward "the picture as a whole," the whole picture of the narrator, his society, and the meaning of his life. The first page sets the tone. He is a child, standing before the fireplace, cooped up in a shack with his sick grandmother and ordered to stay quiet. He "crossed restlessly to the window and pushed back the long fluffy white curtains—which I had been forbidden to touch—and looked yearningly out into the empty street." There is a contrast between his daydreams of "running and playing and shouting" and the "vivid image of Granny's old, white, wrinkled, grim face, framed by a halo of tumbling black hair. . . ." A bird wheels past the window, and he "greeted it with a glad shout." The response from his mother is immediate suppression. Bored and angry, the child picks straws out of the broom, holds them in the fire, and touches them to the curtains to see what will happen. Before he realizes it, he has nearly burned down the house.

Here are the ingredients of the autobiography, assembled at the start: the child, the free human spirit, imprisoned by his environment, longing for release. The image of the bird suggests a combination of inner and physical freedom, a freedom that includes simply getting out but extends beyond that to the intangible flight of the mind. When the glad shout is suppressed, the child retaliates by destroying the environment. The effect is disastrous for him as well as for the adults, but the spirit is irrepressible: if it cannot get free in a constructive way, then it will get free by fire and destruction, but in either case it will spread wings and beat them on the air. "Freedom" in Richard Wright is profoundly individual and existential, without ceasing to imply class struggle and the freedom of an oppressed class.

Following that first incident, which captures so beautifully the major theme of the work, there are four points where the author pauses to take stock, give his experience a theoretical formulation, summarize and illuminate the detail, and direct its forward march toward the meaning. The first is his account of the final meeting with his father, years after he had become an adult and successful writer. It occurs after his childhood impressions of desertion and hunger, after the scene where his mother takes him to see the father and his new mistress in order to beg for money, and the father gives him a nickel. "You ought to be ashamed," the mother says; "Giving your son a nickel when he's hungry. If there's a God, He'll pay you back." Wright has drawn a picture of the father's huge belly, his gruffness and violence, and the mingled awe, fear, and hatred that he inspires in the children. The son was not to see him again for a "quarter of a century," when they met "standing alone upon the red clay of a Mississippi plantation," the father "clad in ragged overalls, holding a muddy hoe in his gnarled, veined hands." During this twenty-five years, Richard's mind and consciousness "had become so greatly and violently altered" that they spoke a different language, "living on vastly distant planes of reality." The elder Wright "was standing against the sky, smiling toothlessly, his hair whitened, his body bent, his eyes glazed with

dim recollection," his soul "imprisoned by the slow flow of the
seasons, by wind and rain and sun." His memories were fastened
"to a crude and raw past," and his actions and emotions "chained
. . . to the direct, animalistic impulses of his withering body."

> From the white landowners above him there had not
> been handed to him a chance to learn the meaning of
> loyalty, of sentiment, of tradition. Joy was as unknown to
> him as was despair. As a creature of the earth, he en-
> dured, hearty, whole, seemingly indestructible, with no
> regrets and no hope. He asked easy, drawling questions
> about me, his other son, his wife, and he laughed, amused,
> when I informed him of their destinies. I forgave him
> and pitied him as my eyes looked past him to the un-
> painted wooden shack. From far beyond the horizons
> that bound this bleak plantation there had come to me
> through my living the knowledge that my father was a
> black peasant who had gone to the city seeking life,
> but who had failed in the city; a black peasant whose life
> had been hopelessly snarled in the city, and who had at
> last fled the city—that same city which had lifted me in its
> burning arms and borne me toward alien and undreamed-
> of shores of knowing (ibid., pp. 42–43).

The great social forces of the "pragmatic metropolis" and the class
categories of sharecropper and worker meet in this individualized
portrait of father and son, with its smooth and quietly passionate
statement of the impact of history on subjective awareness, its
exact delineation of the productive relations against which human
beings beat the wings of their dreams. The two figures confront
one another as two periods in time, two social systems, torn apart
by the sea flow of migration and industrialism, the father's limitations located precisely in the routines of sharecropping, the
son's conflict and passion located in the "burning arms" of urban
ferment; yet they do not cease to be individuals who think and
feel and who can change their destinies by conscious action. The
line "toward alien and undreamed-of shores of knowing," the only
place where the language shades into the subjective and mystical,
recognizes that the "passion to know" is something more than
the animal desire to escape pain and approach pleasure, more than

wanting to understand why some people do not have comfortable
homes, friendly communities, and plenty of food in the kitchen; it is
hunger for the wild surmise upon a peak in Darien, hunger to see
the watershed, delta, ocean, and rain clouds at the same time that
one is being swept along by the river. Wright made economics
the food of this cosmic passion without substituting mind for
matter, without abandoning the cold sense of the materialist outlook.

The second theoretical formulation we have already seen in the
passage where, at the age of twelve, he acquires the conviction that
"the meaning of living came only when one was struggling to
wring a meaning out of meaningless suffering." The third occurs
after he had written his first stories, begun to aspire to be a writer,
and met only with discouragement, racism, and suppression at
every turn. In this summation we hear all that is left of abolitionist
oratory in Wright, the parallel clauses which progress toward a
climax, the dramatic metaphor, and the polemical razor edge directed at the Southern educational system:

> I was building up in me a dream which the entire edu-
> cational system of the South had been rigged to stifle. I
> was feeling the very thing that the state of Mississippi
> had spent millions of dollars to make sure that I would
> never feel; I was becoming aware of the thing that the
> Jim Crow laws had been drafted and passed to keep out of
> my consciousness; I was acting on impulses that southern
> senators in the nation's capital had striven to keep out of
> Negro life; I was beginning to dream the dreams that
> the state had said were wrong, that the schools had said
> were taboo....
> I was in my fifteenth year; in terms of schooling I was
> far behind the average youth of the nation, but I did not
> know that. In me was shaping a yearning for a kind of
> consciousness, a mode of being that the way of life about
> me had said could not be, must not be, and upon which
> the penalty of death had been placed. Somewhere in the
> dead of the southern night my life had switched onto
> the wrong track and, without my knowing it, the loco-
> motive of my heart was rushing down a dangerously

steep slope, heading for a collision, heedless of the warning red lights that blinked all about me, the sirens and
the bells and the screams that filled the air (ibid., pp.
186–87).

All mingled in the tone are the pride and joy of defeating an
enemy plan, living up to the enemy's worst expectations, the
wonder of his own growth, his powers unfolding leaf by leaf, the sad
acknowledgement of the cost in tension and suffering, the acceptance of the cost, the determination to follow the track through to
the end, and the ironic reversal of the concept of "putting a kid
on the right track." It is a "drama of human feeling," with bells,
sirens, screams, and warning red lights, the collision of a single
man moving for his freedom and a rigid system bent on using up
his life to maintain itself. The only drama more compelling is the
moment of social explosion when the underpinnings of the old
system are swept away by millions of people moving at the same
time.

Although the razor edge, the tone of the political essay, is present,
Wright's main interest is clearly in *how the system affects the
narrator*: what are the dangers to his growth, how they are overcome, and how the growth is distorted in the process. The object of
the political essay would be to attack the system; the object of
realistic literature is to understand its total impact on consciousness.

The fourth theoretical formulation is found at the end, where
Wright brings together all the ways in which his personality has
been shaped by the South, what courses of action he could pursue
if he stayed, and what he hopes to accomplish by leaving. *Black Boy*
thus begins with struggle and ends on a note of hope, uniting in
between the particular of his experience with the general of
society in America.

The pictures of Southern whites and Southern race relations
amount to irony and caricature, but there is no attempt, as with
Ellison, to transform them by literary method into surrealist
nightmare. They are simply presented. The boss's dog bites the
narrator in the thigh. The flesh is torn, the wound swells and hurts.
"If it bothers you, let me know," says the boss, wearing a cool
white suit, a Panama hat, and white shoes, "But I never saw a dog

yet that could really hurt a nigger" (ibid., p. 180). White workers approach Wright on his job: "Say, Richard, do you believe that I'm your friend? . . . We don't want you to get hurt . . . we like you around here. You act like a good boy. . . . Well, you better watch that nigger Harrison. . . . Harrison was waiting for you at the door of the building with a knife." The whites meanwhile have told Harrison the same thing about Richard; later the two are each given knives and paid five dollars apiece to fight. In another incident, Shorty, a black elevator operator, sings to a white man, " in a low mumble, smiling, rolling his eyes . . . 'I'm hungry, Mister White Man. I need a quarter for lunch.' " He is ignored, and stops the elevator five feet shy of the right floor: " 'This black sonofabitch sure needs a quarter,' Shorty sang, grimacing, clowning, ignoring the white man's threat. . . . 'Can't go no more, Mister White Man, unless I get my quarter.' " The white man asks what he would do for a quarter. "Shorty giggled, swung around, bent over, and poked out his broad, fleshy ass," offering to let himself be kicked.

> The white man laughed softly, jingled some coins in his pocket, took out one and thumped it to the floor. Shorty stooped to pick it up and the white man bared his teeth and swung his foot into Shorty's rump with all the strength of his body. Shorty let out a howling laugh that echoed up and down the elevator shaft.
> "Now, open this door, you goddamn black sonofabitch," the white man said, smiling with tight lips.
> "Yeeeess, siiiiir," Shorty sang; but first he picked up the quarter and put it into his mouth. "This monkey's got the peanuts," he chortled.

Wright asks, "How in God's name can you do that?" and Shorty answers, "Listen, nigger . . . my ass is tough, and quarters is scarce" (ibid., pp. 249–50).

In the elevator scene, Shorty has succeeded ironically in degrading the white man by charging him money to act out his racism. Shorty has deliberately, consciously used the race stereotype for his own benefit. The white man cannot ignore such a direct challenge to his supremacy; but, since Shorty has stayed within the limits of the clowning "nigger" role, he cannot be justified in a violent attack. His only choice is to buy his way out, to reassert his authority through his power to give away money. He salves his threatened ego by putting extra strength into the kick. He has been manipulated by the very power relations that he helps to maintain.

All these examples present the system of racism in naked, capsule form, understated, absurd, pathetic, and oppressive. But they are rendered as objective fact. The caricature is in the system, not in the perception of the author. The irony is in the behavior of the people, not in the style. To satirize needs no more than to keep the eyes open and report what they see.

Wright's caricature of his Aunt Addie is another good example. She goes through doors by kicking the door open ahead of her. At the Seventh Day Adventist school, she teaches children how to "pop the whip" at recess, a game in which they hold hands, run in a tightening circle, and toss the end boy off his feet, with the likelihood that he might break an arm or a neck. When the whip flung Richard "headlong through space" into a ditch, he "rolled over, stunned, head bruised and bleeding." It was "the first and only time" he ever saw Addie "laugh on God's holy ground" (ibid., p. 122).

Satire in Richard Wright, like other black satire, attacks racism, hypocritical religion, and race oppression, and it exposes the absurdity and contradictions of these practices through irony and caricature. But it is individualized by the objective, realistic method of presentation, the prose that never calls attention to itself and points unerringly at the content, the deadly seriousness of tone which assumes that the incidents are beyond laughter and are shocking past all comment. Douglass and Wells Brown satirized by verbal irony and invective; J. Saunders Redding by exaggerating certain details of his descriptions, such as the grotesque rubbery lips of the Negro doctor; Ward by pretending to argue his enemy's viewpoint, and Hughes by laughing him to scorn. Wright selects the most damning facts about his enemy and puts them on the page.

Concrete diction and loose syntax in *Black Boy* are almost devoid of self-consciousness or stylistic "technique" of any sort. It requires selection and method to be able to write without "technique," to make language such a perfect vehicle of content that the two are indistinguishable, but the method waits on the matter.

Method steps forward only in the summation passages, with their metaphors and echoes of oratory, and in the catalogs modeled after Sandburg and Whitman. The catalogs may feel somewhat intrusive, but they are the most economical way to arrange and concentrate a vast number of childhood memories.

> There was the tantalizing melancholy in the tingling scent of burning hickory wood.
>
> There was the teasing and impossible desire to imitate the petty pride of sparrows wallowing and flouncing in the red dust of country roads.
>
> There was the yearning for identification loosed in me by the sight of a solitary ant carrying a burden upon a mysterious journey (ibid., p. 14).

And as in Whitman, the serial arrangement of the catalog is seldom haphazard; we see a progression from melancholy to desire and identification. The oratorical tone of the summation passages is wholly justifiable because of their role in bringing together and interpreting the objective material, because they carry a weight of passion, and because the writer steps in through this tone and reminds us that we are reading specifically about a writer's development.

It is otherwise in the dialog and narrative. The special qualities of Wright's language stand out best in comparison with the concreteness of Langston Hughes. Hughes's style is distinctive by the deliberateness of his effects: he is comic, he likes intriguing metaphor, he repeats, he imitates the blues refrain, he emphasizes with short, choppy sentences, he is rhythmic. Wright generally stays away from such visible deliberation. There are moments of humor, but they shade quickly into curiosity, estrangement, or bitterness. The language of Hughes is a conscious mark of identity with the working-class Negro. Wright is brooding inwardly over a painful and stunting background, separated from the people around him by his dreams, his resistance, and his deadly seriousness. The language, typically, is full of unanswered questions, brief, direct statement, and, in moments of passion and wonder, clause piled on clause to catch the thrashing of the human spirit at war with a deadly threat.

I sensed some emotional problem in Aunt Addie other than her concern about my eating in school. Did my presence make her feel so insecure that she felt she had to punish me in front of the pupils to impress them?

Would someone say that I was a bad nigger and try to kill me here? What was keeping the woman so long? Would she tell other people that a nigger boy had said something wrong to her? Perhaps she was getting a mob? Maybe I ought to leave now and forget about Betsy? My mounting anxieties drowned out my hunger.

Ought one to surrender to authority even if one believed that that authority was wrong? If the answer was yes, then I knew that I would always be wrong, because I could never do it. Then how could one live in a world in which one's mind and perceptions meant nothing and authority and tradition meant everything? There were no answers.

The rhetorical question, a characteristic feature of *Black Boy*, expresses the theme of the thirst for knowledge and growth. The method of piling clause on clause is seen most often in the confrontations, the rushes of emotion, or the sudden changes in outlook that announce a line has been crossed in his maturity and he will never be the same again. The previous quotations abound in examples.

I stood fighting, fighting as I had never fought in my life, fighting with myself. Perhaps my uneasy childhood, perhaps my shifting from town to town, perhaps the violence I had already seen and felt took hold of me, and I was trying to stifle the impulse to go to the drawer of the kitchen table and get a knife and defend myself. But this woman who stood before me was my aunt, my mother's sister, Granny's daughter; in her veins my own blood flowed; in many of her actions I could see some elusive part of my own self; and in her speech I could catch echoes of my own speech. I did not want to be violent

with her, and yet I did not want to be beaten for a
wrong I had not committed (ibid., p. 119).

The last sentence of this paragraph presents the dilemma which
tears at the narrator throughout most of his childhood. Submit and
be crushed, or resist and be terrified. In Douglass, the sentence
would be arranged as antithesis and would call attention to itself
as a rhetorical device. Here it is a pair of simple clauses linked by a
conjunction, a direct statement of the problem. The entire paragraph in fact is organized around the same dilemma, but it is the
dilemma we notice and not the organization.

Wright's language suits his point of view by its terse clarity,
serious tone, loaded rhetorical questions, plain verbs and syntax,
short sentences, rapid accumulations of clauses, and shifts between
example and summary, bitter passion and implacable fact. The
serious tone and rhetorical questions follow from the seriousness
of what he is trying to do: wring a meaning out of meaningless
suffering. The terse clarity, bare verbs, and stripped syntax declare
that that meaning is to be sought on the terms of his environment,
which is plain, terse, and brutal. The short sentences and rapid
accumulations of clauses are like the alternation between struggle
and waiting, the flurries of the trapped bird dotted by moments
of rest and thought. The shifts between example and summary
discover the meaning in the whole system of relations in American
capitalism, linking individual and mass destiny with a literary
brilliance impossible to achieve by polemics alone. The implacable
fact is the only consolation to the bitter passion; it sets the limits
of freedom, but it is the only ground on which freedom can be won.

The greatness of *Black Boy* as literature is that it encompasses
history and politics *through* the individual experience of the boy
Richard, without ever leaving his personal story. The slave narrators, W. E. B. Du Bois, Redding, and Hughes all encompass
history and politics, but they mingle autobiography and essay;
they detach themselves momentarily from their personal stories to
discourse on religion, abolition, education, Jim Crow, and a host
of subjects not strictly autobiographical. It is of course a virtue of
black autobiography to do at least this, and it stems from their
vision of man in society; but Richard Wright communicates that

vision on terms that are not subject to sterile argument or distracting controversy. Instead of shifting his attention between man and society, he looks at society through the man. Politics in *Black Boy* is a matter of what he has seen and felt; we cannot "debate" his experience of seeing a Negro woman tortured in the back room of a store for nonpayment of debts, thrown out on the street, and then arrested for loitering. The political conclusions are left to the reader, but the experience is structured so that no thinking, feeling reader can escape them. Wright is completely successful at transcending the color line and pulling the white reader inside the boy Richard, isolating and portraying meanings that hold good for all of humanity under oppressive conditions. His responses above all seem *recognizable*; courageous, articulate, and creative enough to set a worthy example, yet fearful and weak enough to serve as a mirror for ourselves. At the same time, he achieves his purpose by the fullest realization of color identity.

Perhaps it is the boy's alienation from his own background, his existential loneliness and struggle *as an individual*, that travels so well across the color line, for existential loneliness is endemic in white American literature from Young Goodman Brown to Perry Smith. But *Black Boy* is an inspiration. Like the *Life and Times of Frederick Douglass*, it gives a valid definition to the word "freedom," valid for the poet and dreamer as well as for the janitor, sharecropper, convict, and punch-press operator. It sweeps the muck of abuse and hypocrisy from the American values of pragmatism, realism, equality, education, toughness; it shows how the class analysis of society is useful and important to one's personal life, and how it can be reconciled with American individualism. It pits a child against the full terror of family conflict, cruel and sadistic guardians, torn loyalties, racist oppression, and capitalist exploitation, and it shows how, with no other ally but his own brains and body, and with what few friends he can find, he can survive, grow, keep his integrity, fight back, and become a great writer. In *Walden* life is deliberately reduced to its bare essentials outside of society, consciously examined, and found to be worth it. In *Black Boy*, life is stripped down to less than those essentials inside society, consciously examined, and still found to be worth it.

Black Boy is also the bridge between the eclectic, groping, Bibleridden, alienated second period in black autobiography and the repoliticized militance of the third. Fundamentalist Christian faith and rhetoric here have died out. The slave narrative structure, irony, caricature, and polemics are preserved and adapted, continuing to fill a need. The materialist insight into social organization, the revolutionary viewpoint, ripen like the grapes of wrath, ready for harvest by the black revolution of the 1960s and '70s.

Part three
The Period of Rebirth
Since 1961

For My People

Let a new earth rise. Let another world be born. Let a bloody
peace be written in the sky. Let a second generation full of
courage issue forth; let a people loving freedom come to
growth. Let a beauty full of healing and a strength of final
clenching be the pulsing in our spirits and our blood. Let the
martial songs be written, let the dirges disappear. Let a race
of men now rise and take control.

—Margaret Walker Alexander

Chapter 9 *James Baldwin*
The growth of a new radicalism

W HEN James Baldwin published *Nobody Knows My Name* in 1961, the Civil Rights movement was well under way; Emmett Till had been dead for six years; Martin Luther King had already been assaulted and jailed for leading demonstrations in the South; the word "freedom rider" had entered popular usage, and the great Watts uprising was four years into the future. The year 1961 was a dividing line in American history, a time when all the race issues left unsettled by Reconstruction were coming back to the surface. Black organizations had once more begun to attack racism frontally with mass, militant action. The autobiographies written after *Nobody Knows My Name* belong to this new period of reawakened political commitment. It was no longer a time of middle class alienation and introspection; the black masses took the initiative, forcing the middle class to respond to their militance one way or the other.

Who are the writers of this third period? Claude Brown, toughest kid on the block, reform school inmate, narrowly escaping heroin addiction because his first snort made him so sick he never wanted to touch the drug again, dabbler in Muslim religion, law student and satirist; Leslie Alexander Lacy, son of a well-to-do Negro doctor, trapped between the white and the black worlds, departing for Ghana to find a black society which has solved the problem of white domination, only to discover that here, too, he is an outsider; Anne Moody, daughter of a poor Mississippi farmer, taking jobs in white people's kitchens so she could go to college, drawn into the Civil Rights movement where she is terrorized by the insane hostility of the whites, bewildered and discouraged by the apathy of the poor blacks, embittered when her people are sold out by the leaders of the March on Washington in 1963; Maya Angelou, awkward and insecure as a child, raped at the age of eight, learning the courage to get what she wants from a male-dominated world,

breaking the color barrier on San Francisco streetcars, deciding
to have a baby without resigning herself to marrying the father;
Eldridge Cleaver, Bobby Seale, and George Jackson, convicts,
unemployed ghetto dwellers, revolutionaries, members of the Black
Panther party, risking their lives to tell the black masses that
freedom grows out of the barrel of a gun; Malcolm X, pimp and
drug pusher, convict, Muslim minister, Pan-Africanist, pilgrim to
Mecca, lifting himself up to become one of the few men who
could have been the Lenin of America before he was cut down by
gunfire; H. Rap Brown, flamboyant SNCC militant, facing down
rednecks with his gun on lonely Mississippi roads, dogged continu-
ally by police and FBI agents, preaching that "violence is as American as cherry pie"; Julius Lester, civil rights activist, black power
advocate, writer, folksinger, struggling to synthesize the goals
of revolution with spiritual brotherhood, poetry, and joy; Donald
Reeves, immigrant from Jamaica, high school student in New
York City, manipulated by the administration, warned and threatened as he realizes he is being used, ostracized by other students
for having a white girlfriend, who is also using him, architect of a
high school bill of rights, refusing to accept any theory that does not
tally with his experience.

These figures come from all levels of society: urban slums and
rural shacks, well-to-do homes and rat-infested tenements. Most
see no way to go on developing themselves short of supporting
revolution and have taken active part in leftist organizations; but
there is no unanimous agreement as to goals and tactics. The center
of this period is the movement manifesto, the book which traces
the writer's gradual progress toward becoming a revolutionary.
At the same time, luminous and beautiful statements continue to
be written that, like Wright's *Black Boy*, attempt to create a meaning for living on strictly personal terms, without denying the
meanings found by the political activists.

Like their predecessors, many books are directed at a market
which is largely white and middle class. Sometimes the focus is even
narrower, directed specifically at white college students. Baldwin's
early essays were first published in liberal intellectual magazines
such as *Harper's, Esquire, Commentary, Encounter,* and *Partisan
Review.* Bobby Seale wrote *Seize the Time* to earn money for the
Black Panther party; the first installments of the work, appearing

in *Ramparts* Magazine, were clearly aimed at the white Left. The initial push behind Malcolm X's *Autobiography* came from the white reporter and ghostwriter Alex Haley, although the content of the book is meant equally for white and black. Cleaver was a discovery of *Ramparts,* and his work, *Soul on Ice,* has been adopted as required reading on college campuses throughout the country. Julius Lester also addressed the white Left in *Revolutionary Notes, Look Out Whitey! Black Power's Gonna Get Your Mama,* and *Search for the New Land.* George Jackson, on the other hand, wrote almost exclusively for his family, the letters having been collected and published later when his case became internationally known. H. Rap Brown, Donald Reeves, Leslie Lacy, and Maya Angelou all seem to regard the black audience as primary, although they are conscious of whites looking on from the wings.

James Baldwin deserves close attention because he makes the transition in his writing between the second and third periods. He follows his own path, independent and suspicious of all radical viewpoints, yet becoming radicalized himself through seeing what happens to black people who attempt to carry out their vision of change within American society as it is. He stays close to the purely personal side of autobiography, attempting to produce work which stands on its own artistic merits as consciously examined life, without the crutch of having the "correct" political views; yet he derives good political views through that very process of examination.

It becomes clear, looking back on Baldwin's essays after a decade of black militance, that his language and point of view are rooted in the second period. The preoccupations of his major work are those of Du Bois and Redding: alienation, identity crisis, the dilemma of being both American and Negro, the meaning of European culture to the black intellectual, the role of the Negro writer, the attitude of the Northern Negro toward the South.

The impact of the black revolution, however, has changed the tone of his most recent essays. In *Notes of a Native Son* (1955) and *Nobody Knows My Name* (1961), his values are Christian, and his language shares the moral assumptions of Christianity and political liberalism; but "An Open Letter To My Sister Angela Davis" (1970) is almost an act of revolution, though still marked by occasional sermon echoes and a certain quality of gentleness which comes through everywhere in Baldwin. And *No Name in the*

Street (1972) declares openly that there is no hope for peace as long as capitalism exists, and that some form of socialism will have to precede any lasting and meaningful change in the United States. The scope of his work illustrates the long, tortuous, self-examining, reluctant process by which black writing in general has concluded that America has no intentions of voluntarily redressing the wrongs of slavery and discrimination, that radical change is absolutely necessary for survival, and that henceforth blacks must be prepared to undertake massive, organized resistance against efforts to suppress them.

In the 1940s and '50s, there are few enough articulate voices from the black proletariat so that Baldwin can still speak for "the Negro" to a white audience. The language, in fact, makes it obvious that his audience is primarily white. He even uses the pronoun "we" in referring to white society.[1] Most of his work is a quest for selfhood in isolation from any political movement. Nevertheless, there is a distinct quickening of spirit when he writes on political subjects that suggests the beginning of a new period. His background in Harlem, his attacks on Faulkner's politics and on the covert, institutionalized racism of Northern cities, and his involvement in the early civil rights causes, link even the young Baldwin to the 1960s.

The problem of split identity is consciously and thoroughly examined in Baldwin, who, at the close of the second period, brings to a head its principal concerns, enlarges them, puts them under a microscope. His object is to find redemptive value in alienation, to turn evil into good, to discover and apply in his writing the special insights produced by special oppression. In *Notes of a Native Son*, Baldwin reveals flatly that he "hated and feared white people," and "despised" black people, "possibly because they failed to produce Rembrandt" (Baldwin, *Notes of a Native Son*, p. 4), a statement attacked by Cleaver in *Soul on Ice*. Baldwin's means of coping with his estrangement, at this time, is to identify wholly with "America," and, by extension, with European culture:

> I would have to appropriate these white centuries, I would
> have to make them mine—I would have to accept my
> special attitude, my special place in this scheme—other-
> wise I would have no place in *any* scheme.

> I love America more than any other country in the
> world, and, exactly for this reason, I insist on the right
> to criticize her perpetually. I think all theories are suspect,
> that the finest principles may have to be modified, or may
> even be pulverized by the demands of life, and that one
> must find, therefore, one's own moral center and move
> through the world hoping that this center will guide one
> aright (ibid., pp. 4, 6).

In the process, he attempts to reconcile being an American with
being a Negro, to discover the "truer and better self" which was the
dream of Du Bois. Negro identity is not denied but seems to be
regarded as a hardship forced on him by a racist homeland, an
obstacle to stealing the "sacred fire" of culture from Europe rather
than a positive cultural element in its own right. Cleaver has ac-
cused Baldwin of "the most grueling, agonizing, total hatred of
the blacks, particularly of himself, and the most shameful, fanatical,
fawning, sycophantic love of the whites," [2] a point which is stated,
or overstated, with the customary razor edge of black polemical
writing; but it underscores the fact that the burden of *Notes of a
Native Son* and *Nobody Knows My Name* is to resolve the problems of being a black American without rebelling against the mainstream culture. The object is not to resist it as a system, but to
change it through moral persuasion and thus affirm its tolerance
of dissent and individual freedom.

The positive value of Baldwin's struggle for wholeness is something he shares in common with Redding and Du Bois: he re-
examines and verbalizes what it means to be an "American" and
demonstrates that the identity crisis of the "Negro" is a crisis for the
entire country; it reflects our dangerous and hubristic blindness,
our bland assumption of cultural superiority and simple-minded
innocence of the tragic. Americans who are ignorant of black
identity are ignorant of their own. Black Americans, on the other
hand, because they are forced by the color line to find out who they
are, can also find out what an "American" is and thus give an
essential self-knowledge to whites. The question of color identity
poses the deepest questions of social existence on all levels.

> The goal of the student movement is nothing less than the
> liberation of the entire country from its most crippling

attitudes and habits. The reason that it is important—of
the utmost importance—for white people, here, to see the
Negroes as people like themselves is that white people
will not, otherwise, be able to see themselves as they are.[3]

The chapter entitled "Princes and Powers" in *Nobody Knows My
Name* is rich in examples of how the color question demands
definitions for such terms as "culture," "classic," "nation."
   Color also poses the question of the writer's role:

> I left America because I doubted my ability to survive the
> fury of the color problem here. (Sometimes I still do.) I
> wanted to prevent myself from becoming *merely* a
> Negro; or even, merely a Negro writer. I wanted to find
> out in what way the *specialness* of my experience could
> be made to connect me with other people instead of divid-
> ing me from them (ibid., p. 4).

Color identity, although it seems to be America's curse, can also
be our greatest strength, Baldwin tells us, if whites will look into
the mirror held up to them by blacks. His conclusion to *Notes of
a Native Son* comes close to the dream of Du Bois, the reconciliation
of the split selves of America, wherein the races give each to each
the qualities both so sadly lack, in large conformity to the greater
ideals of the Republic. The worst error of American white men
is that they "still nourish the illusion that there is some means of
recovering the European innocence, of returning to a state in
which black men do not exist." He does not think it too much
to suggest that the "American vision of the world," which is almost
ignorant of the tragic and which "tends until today to paint moral
issues in glaring black and white," is "dangerously inaccurate, and
perfectly useless," that it "owes a great deal" to the effort of whites
to maintain separation of the races, and "protects our moral
high-mindedness at the terrible expense of weakening our grasp
of reality." The price we will pay for persisting in this innocence
is to invite our own destruction, black and white, and turn our
nation into a monster.
   In resolving his crisis, then, Baldwin must handle the basic
questions of how society is put together and where it may be going.

The necessity to deal with color leads the black writer to answer questions about American society that most whites never get around to asking. But, as Cleaver and other black critics have maintained, the answers of Baldwin's early work seem inadequate. Although he has put the questions of alienation and identity, and the social insights resulting therefrom, at the center of the stage, and thrashed out their various implications in essay after essay, they did not, until recently, add up to a truer and better self, that is, a *political* self, whose backbone is the act of resistance against the system which creates the problem by shattering the self into contradictory fragments. Cleaver felt that Baldwin's insights did not link the individual with the movement of history in any realistic way but instead seemed to lead back precisely to the "innocence" of moral and political liberalism which we are supposed to abandon. "But ah! 'O masters,' it is Baldwin's work which is so void of a political, economic, or even a social reference. . . ." His essential weakness is that the "sacred fire" of European civilization, though it "could not burn the black off his face . . . certainly did burn it out of his heart" (Cleaver, *Soul on Ice*, pp. 105, 109). Baldwin's reason for not wishing to overstress the black component of his identity was that it could detract from the main task of becoming human:

> It is no longer important to be white—thank heaven—the white face is no longer invested with the power of this world; and it is devoutly to be hoped that it will soon no longer be important to be black. The experience of the American Negro, if it is ever faced and assessed, makes it possible to hope for such a reconciliation. The hope and the effect of this fusion in the breast of the American Negro is one of the few hopes we have of surviving the wilderness which lies before us now (Baldwin, *Nobody Knows My Name*, p. 215).

But the white face was not to be so easily dislodged from the power of this world, as millions of Vietnamese, Algerians, and Afro-Americans have learned to their cost. And "Blackness" is a political stance evolved to confront that power. To deny its importance too soon in the fight is to risk forfeiting the goals of the black revo-

lution; it is to make being "American" more important. If one is
bred here one cannot help being "American" in the sense of being
a product of this country's history and culture; but the black
revolutionaries have helped us to see that the dominant white
culture of America is a ruling-class culture, and must be rejected,
indeed, actively fought, by blacks *and* whites if the country as a
whole is ever to redeem the word "freedom" from the garbage
disposal of free enterprise.

Baldwin's former politics illustrate the danger of trying to construct an "American" identity without a sound grasp of how the
system operates. When Du Bois sent a telegram of protest to the
Negro-African Writer's Conference because the State Department
would not let him attend, Baldwin's loyalty to "America" impelled
him to describe it as an "extremely ill-considered communication"
(ibid., p. 18). In the same chapter he announces that it had never
been in the interest of the American Negro to overthrow the
machinery of the oppressor [!] because the possibility of making it
"work for our benefit" is "built in" (ibid., p. 21). He considers
it important for America to eliminate the sources of black discontent in "our own country," or else "we" will never be able to do
it "on the great stage of the world" (ibid., p. 82), a sentence which
apparently shares the Messianic belief of John Foster Dulles that
corporate America has a moral mission to go forth and civilize
the restless heathen. For the role of the Communist party in mobilizing public opinion around the Scottsboro defendants in the 1930s,
he can only say that the case gave communism "hideous opportunities" (ibid., p.145). He must concede, before he can defend
the action, that the black people who demonstrated in the United
Nations gallery after Lumumba's murder probably contained
"Stalinist and professional revolutionists acting out of the most
cynical motives" (ibid., p. 74). The sentence implies that "Stalinist,"
"revolutionist," and "cynical" are all synonymous. Most distress-
ing of all is his condescension toward almost every movement
which holds within itself the potential of an alternative to imperialist culture, from Aimé Cesaire to the Beatniks.

Baldwin's language reveals clearly that he shared the moral
assumptions of white liberalism. This paragraph, for example,
though quite beautiful on its own terms, contains the language of
religion, guilt, and atonement:

> But there is a complementary faith among the damned
> which involves their gathering of the stones with which
> those who walk in the light shall stone them; or there
> exists among the intolerably degraded the perverse and
> powerful desire to force into the arena of the actual
> those fantastic crimes of which they have been accused,
> achieving their vengeance and their own destruction
> through making the nightmare real (Baldwin, *Notes of a
> Native Son*, p. 29).

A glance back at the quotations from his American identity manifestoes in *Notes of a Native Son* will discover phrases that could
only proceed from an "end of ideology" perception of world
affairs: "all theories are suspect; . . . one must find one's own moral
center; . . . I insist on the right to criticize; . . . I love America more
than any other country in the world." This is the role of loyal
opposition. Finding "one's own moral center" poses a society like
Hemingway's, where morality as an individual construct stands
above class relations, a society which is an assemblage of individuals
and power interests going their own way instead of a system of
classes producing and exchanging wealth, asserting power, and
deriving "moral centers" from the social environment according
to an analyzable pattern. "All theories are suspect" is an academic
truism, at best, that tells us no more than to keep aware of new
evidence; in the liberal world view it simply functions to obscure
the relationship between "moral center" and social organization.
Baldwin's moral center is not merely his own; it is on lease from
the "black bourgeoisie," to borrow E. Franklin Frazier's title, a
social class whose position *between* the owners of capital and the
proletariat, and between the black poor and white society, fosters
the illusion that they think and work *outside* this structure.

An accumulation of passages from *Nobody Knows My Name*
suggests that here Baldwin views politics as a matter of "moral responsibility," "spiritual force," "national honor," "moral bankruptcy," and "rehabilitation."

> In trying to make their hovels habitable, they are per-
> petually throwing good money after bad. Such frustration,
> so long endured, is driving many strong, admirable men

and women whose only crime is color to the very gates of paranoia.

That hundreds of thousands of white people are living, in effect, no better than the "niggers" is not a fact to be regarded with complacency. The social and moral bankruptcy suggested by this fact is of the bitterest, most terrifying kind.

The wide windows look out on Harlem's invincible and indescribable squalor: the Park Avenue railroad tracks, around which, about forty years ago, the present dark community began; the unrehabilitated houses, bowed down, it would seem, under the great weight of frustration and bitterness they contain; the dark, the ominous schoolhouses. ...

If we are not capable of this examination, we may yet become one of the most distinguished and monumental failures in the history of nations.

It is the failure of the moral imagination of Europe which has created the forces now determined to overthrow it (Baldwin, *Nobody Knows My Name*, see pp. 60, 61, 63, 116, 214 respectively).

Terms like "moral bankruptcy," "moral imagination," are abstractions assuming a standard of right and wrong which transcends class and caste relations and mode of production and exploitation; they also assume "free will" in its abstract sense. To worry about whether or not America becomes a "monumental failure" as a nation is a little bit like worrying about our "national honor" and leads easily to a kind of politics where the institutions of government, however flawed, are assumed to represent the "will of the people," as though they were an imperfect reflection of the National Ideal rather than the other way around. (If the government is the reflection of an Ideal instead of the instrument of a ruling class, then the function of social criticism should be, not to attack it, but improve it—a course which utterly obscures both the role of the state and the locus of power in a capitalist system.) The metaphors "throwing good money after bad," "social and moral bankruptcy," conceive of social problems as moral failures, expressed in the imagery of commodity relations. The description of Harlem's "invincible and indescribable squalor" is the language of liberal reform. To solve a problem of "unrehabilitated" houses and people, one rehabilitates the houses or the people; one does not abolish a social system. Ghetto school houses are "dark" and "ominous" to the middle-class liberal who fears their meaning, i.e., that we need a social revolution; to the families of the schoolchildren they are outrageous and oppressive. The sooner the meaning is recognized, the sooner the conditions can be changed.

To compare Baldwin and Du Bois on how a society is organized underscores sharply the limitations of the former. Du Bois had analyzed what a "society" is in clear and comprehensive terms long before he discovered Marx: first, "the physical proximity of homes and dwelling-places, the way in which neighborhoods group themselves"; secondly, the "methods by which individuals cooperate for earning a living," that is, the mode of wealth production. Thirdly, he included the political relations, control of government, and tax patterns. Then there were "the interchange of ideas, through conversation and conference, through periodicals and libraries," and the formation of public opinion. There were also the "various forms of social contact," in travel, theaters, etc., and finally, the institutions of religion and moral teaching (Du Bois, *Souls of Black Folk*, chap. 9, p. 165). Du Bois arrived at this clarity of outlook because of his racial perspective, because he wanted to analyze the racial patterns in the society of the South. Baldwin, true to the tradition of black autobiography, takes up the inquiry into the "hidden laws" which govern society. "It is up to the American writer," he says, "to find out what these laws and assumptions are" (Baldwin, *Nobody Knows My Name*, p. 11). But nowhere is there a precise definition either of the "hidden laws" or of society. The language often precludes such a definition.

Baldwin's most recent political stance, however, seems to have caught up with the general movement of black consciousness toward the Left; or in any case, it is no longer accurate to speak of him as a liberal:

> We know that a man is not a thing and is not to be placed at the mercy of things. We know that air and water

belong to all mankind and not merely to industrialists.
We know that a baby does not come into the world merely
to be the instrument of someone else's profit. We know
that democracy does not mean the coercion of all into
a deadly—and, finally, wicked—mediocrity but the
liberty for all to aspire to the best that is in him, or that
has ever been.

We know that we, the Blacks, and not only we, the
Blacks, have been, and are, the victims of a system whose
only fuel is greed, whose only god is profit. We know that
the fruits of this system have been ignorance, despair,
and death, and we know that the system is doomed because the world can no longer afford it—if, indeed, it ever
could have. And we know that, for the perpetuation of
this system, we have all been mercilessly brutalized, and
have been told nothing but lies, lies about ourselves
and our kinsmen and our past, and about love, life, and
death, so that both soul and body have been bound in
hell.[4]

Here, and in his latest autobiography, *No Name in the Street*,
Baldwin's tone and viewpoint have been brought into harmony
with his best style, enriching the style with a firmer content and
pushing it to new levels of strength and clarity. He no longer seems
to feel a need to apologize to white intellectuals, pay court to their
biases, or dress himself out for their approval. We can see, comparing his description of the relationship between colonized people
and the colonizing civilization with similar passages in *Notes of a
Native Son*, how far the last seventeen years have taken Baldwin
from the role of loyal dissent. "Old orders" never redeem themselves without bloodshed, "because they have always existed in
relation to a force which they have had to subdue." Their power
is the justification of their history and the guarantor of their
material well-being. But for the millions who have been subjugated, this history "has been nothing but an intolerable yoke, a
stinking prison, a shrieking grave." For them, life itself depends on
the "speediest possible demolition of this history. . . ." And whatever it may have given to the subjugated is of no value, since "they

will never even be able to assess it until they are free to take from it what they need, and to add to history the monumental fact of their presence." Black workers and colonized "natives" have "no honorable access" to the achievements of the West because these achievements "cannot fail to reveal to them that they have been robbed, maligned, and rejected."

> This is why, ultimately, all attempts at dialogue be-
> tween the subdued and subduer, between those placed
> within history and those dispersed outside, break down.
> One may say, indeed, that until this hour such a dialogue
> has scarcely been attempted: the subdued and the sub-
> duer do not speak the same language.... And when such
> a dialogue truly erupts, it cannot avoid the root question
> of the possession of the land, and the exploitation of
> the land's resources. At that point, the cultural preten-
> sions of history are revealed as nothing less than a mask
> for power, and thus it happens that, in order to be rid
> of Shell, Texaco, Coca-Cola, the Sixth Fleet, and the
> friendly American soldier whose mission it is to protect
> these investments, one finally throws Balzac and Shake-
> speare—and Faulkner and Camus—out with them. Later,
> of course, one may welcome them back, but on one's own
> terms, and, absolutely, on one's own land.[5]

In *Notes of a Native Son* Baldwin is introducing himself as a colored human being to the culture which has destroyed his history, asking, since the whites have forcibly taken his labor, for the acceptance of his mind as well. "I am not, really, a stranger any longer for any American alive." Americans should therefore cease treating him like a stranger by separating him from their culture. The experience of whites and blacks in America, when the worst has been said, is "something of an achievement" because it has prepared white civilization to assimilate blacks in good faith, learn from them, welcome them into white churches, universities, neigh-borhoods, occupations, and political institutions, bending to ac-commodate their presence without asking them to sacrifice their dignity. The catch is the question of "good faith," which Baldwin tries to arouse in whites because it is the only way they can live up to their own ideals, the only way they can preserve something worth being assimilated into. If they do not practice good faith, then Baldwin cannot "appropriate these white centuries" without the severest, most painful, deep-rooted, gut-wrenching transformation of his whole attitude toward them; without, in short, committing himself first to smashing the power of their present trustees. In the beginning he wants to appropriate them without rejecting the power. He no longer seems to be under the illusion that this is possible.

What we have in the passage quoted above is an absolutely lucid explanation of why there can be no other viable way for a subject people to deal with an imperialist power except force, and why all talk of the "benefits" of imperialism, such as schools, vaccines, literacy, great poets, restaurants, and highways, is simply an evasion of the basic issue. Baldwin is recognizing that Lenin, Ho Chi Minh, Mao, and Fanon may be right. This is a momentous change for a writer of his stature and a register of how far the collapse of America's cold-war ideology has proceeded.

Yet we can find a direct line of continuity between the new Baldwin and the Baldwin who wrote, "I love America more than any other country in the world." For the early Baldwin usually granted the morality of liberalism so that he could go on to expose how whites were not living up to it. He was one of the few writers in the 1950s to take on the political and racial arrogance of William Faulkner, exposing, in *Nobody Knows My Name,* how the mystique of the South in Faulkner's novels gave covert support to racism. And Baldwin's early style, crippled though it is at times by liberal intellectual jargon, comes out right whenever the content is right; in his role of social critic and enemy of racism, he displays all the distinctive qualities of the black essay since the time of Douglass—expert swordsmanship, polemical finesse, irony, social insight.

> In August of 1955, Governor Hodges, a moderate, went on the air with the suggestion that Negroes segregate themselves voluntarily—for the good, as he put it, of both races. Negroes seeming to be unmoved by this moderate proposal, the Klan reappeared in the counties and was still active there when I left. So, no doubt, are the boys

on the chain gang (Baldwin, *Nobody Knows My Name,* p. 107).

But there is a great difference between being the first white man to be seen by Africans and being the first black man to be seen by whites. The white man takes the astonishment as tribute, for he arrives to conquer and to convert the natives, whose inferiority in relation to himself is not even to be questioned; whereas I, without a thought of conquest, find myself among a people whose culture controls me, has even, in a sense, created me, people who have cost me more in anguish and rage than they will ever know, who yet do not even know of my existence. The astonishment with which I might have greeted them, should they have stumbled into my African village a few hundred years ago, might have rejoiced their hearts. But the astonishment with which they greet me today can only poison mine (Baldwin, *Notes of a Native Son,* p. 139).

Meditating on the ironic use of the words "moderate" and "active" in the first passage, one realizes that they lead toward a kind of intuitive grasp of the class/race power equations of American society, even though the analysis of the system is absent. By linking the Klan and the chain gang with the word "active," Baldwin leads us to consider in what other ways they are linked, how one is responsible for the other, and how both spring from the moderate policies of Governor Hodges and the interests behind him. The same uses of irony are evident in Douglass, when he describes how the church bell rang within hearing of the slave auctioneer's bell.

The irony of the second passage is not only verbal and personal, but historical. The antithesis of the last two sentences, which juxtapose two contradictory meanings of the word "astonishment," condenses with the utmost economy, beauty, and exactness, three centuries of racial dialectic. One type of "astonishment" permits the racist invader to set himself up as a god and make the Africans believe he is superior. The other type is a manifestation of that innocence of the tragic which allows whites to avoid confronting their history while they go on oppressing blacks. It is a brilliant illumination of a complex feeling that radiates backward in time, showing how the weight of the past governs our individual relationships even when we will it otherwise.

Coming back to his Angela Davis letter, we note that, while the content at last indicts the entire system of society in America, assumes a black identity, and commits the writer to a course of political resistance, the language still remembers the Baldwin of *Go Tell It on the Mountain*: "both soul and body have been bound in hell," "wicked mediocrity," "whose only god is profit"; but it also remembers further back, when Christianity was an effective basis for political struggle against slavery. By using Christian overtones in this statement of support for a black Communist, Baldwin implies that the Christian abolitionist tradition, far from being exhausted, may come back to life, may even still have an important place in the movement to abolish the forms of slavery still remaining to us. The concept of "liberty for all to aspire to the best that is in him" is one of the Western ideals which he appropriated from Europe but humanized by its context of antiracism and anticapitalism. The Baldwin of *Nobody Knows My Name* had admired the "maverick" artist who pursued his own path unrestricted by ideas of compulsive unity with his culture. The ideal of the individual's right to pursue his path is still present in Baldwin's hostility to the "coercion of all into a deadly—and, finally, wicked—mediocrity," but it is no longer an obstacle to revolutionary identity or communal spirit.

The parallel clauses and oratorical tone of the letter are familiar features, an extension of the rhetoric of Thompson, Du Bois, and Wright in his summation passages. The four sentences beginning "we know that a man is not a thing" deal with the assumptions of capitalism that corrupt the lives of both white and black. What "we know" are simple, basic human truths, and the repetition of "we know" stresses the fact that they are self-evident, anyone can see them and they should not have to be proved. The second paragraph shifts to Black people in particular, applying the basic, panhuman, self-evident truths to their special condition in North America, with the implied message that what they want is what everyone wants everywhere, and what is in the interest of us all that they should have. While the first paragraph itemizes our human rights, the second itemizes how the system has violated them.

Is this a sharp break with Baldwin's past? The two chapters in *Nobody Knows My Name* which were originally oral addresses carry on the continuing relationship of black autobiography to oratory and political rhetoric. Note how the emphasis on the word "afraid" in this passage broadens the boundaries of the fear until it becomes comprehensive enough to lead us to some sort of grasp of the true depth of racism in the United States:

> If you have been watching television lately, I think this is unendurably clear in the faces of those screaming people in the South, who are quite incapable of telling you what it is they are afraid of. They do not really know what it is they are afraid of, but they know they are afraid of something, and they are so frightened that they are nearly out of their minds. And this same fear obtains on one level or another, to varying degrees, throughout the entire country (Baldwin, *Nobody Knows My Name*, p.134).

The content of the early work also reveals several starting points that will proceed forward to a radical analysis. Baldwin discusses the cultural oppression which white standards of physical attractiveness inflict on black Americans and is very much aware of the connection between black identity at home and the emergence of black nations in Africa. "The American Negro," he says, "can no longer, nor will he ever again, be controlled by white America's image of him. This fact has everything to do with the rise of Africa in world affairs" (ibid., pp. 79–80). It is not far to go from this position to the pan-Africanism of Du Bois and Malcolm X. In fact Baldwin's political instincts were always in favor of a basic transformation of the country, for which all of us must assume responsibility. "Men make their own history," said Marx at the beginning of the *Eighteenth Brumaire*; to which Baldwin, knowingly or unknowingly, adds an "amen";

> Now, this country is going to be transformed. It will not be transformed by an act of God, but by all of us, by you and me. I don't believe any longer that we can afford to say that it is entirely out of our hands. We made the world we're living in and we have to make it over (ibid., p. 154).

Despite his limitations, then, which are a function of his liberal "American" identity, he became a pair of shoulders for others to stand on. *Nobody Knows My Name* has the historical importance of *Up From Slavery* and *The Souls of Black Folk*. It broke new ground, began a new period in the evolution of black autobiography; it is an announcement that black self-awareness, at the beginning of the 1960s, was entering a state of rapid ferment and would no longer be the same.

Chapter 10 *Autobiographies of black women: Ida Wells, Anne Moody and Maya Angelou*

BLACK women did not begin to tell their stories in appreciable number until the third period. There had been pseudonarratives of female slaves, penned by whites, in the nineteenth century, letters by Phillis Wheatley, and biographies of Harriet Tubman and Sojourner Truth. Charlotte Forten, daughter of the wealthy black abolitionist James Forten, wrote a journal in the 1850s, which is a sensitive response of an upper-class Negro girl, becoming a woman, attending an exclusive female seminary, deeply flattered by visits from prominent white abolitionists, sending to Longfellow and Sumner for autographs, unable to sever her mind from the bitter and horrifying reality of the four million poor blacks held in bondage far beyond her elegant livingroom.[1] Going South to nurse and teach black Union troops and freed slaves in 1863, she bestows her highest praise on the black soldiers from Massachusetts who died with their commander during the charge on Fort Wagner, South Carolina. Her journal is important as a description of how a sheltered daughter of the black bourgeoisie travels the long path to support of the slaves and participation in the momentous political events of her time; but its literary value is slight in comparison to the slave narratives themselves. It is only recently that black women, preceded by such figures as Ida Wells, Mary Church Terrell, and Ruby Goodwin, began to rough out a course of high literary interest that is different from the one pursued by the males.

Ida Wells, indeed, is a giant of the form, all the more visible because she wrote and fought during a time when few black women had any hope of being heard outside the home. Her *Crusade for Justice* (1928) is the slave narrative in its purest and truest light, without the sycophantic apology that weakened Booker T. Washington's *Up from Slavery*. Ida Wells apologizes to nobody. She takes the position that slavery still exists; therefore it is still appropriate to combat it with the old abolitionist fervor. But *Crusade for Justice,* unlike the original slave narratives, came on the scene like a literary Rip Van Winkle, long after the abolitionist era was dead and gone, long before the rebirth of militant spirit among the black masses. The book lacks nothing of the power and righteous anger of Frederick Douglass; but the identity must feed on different hopes. There is no mass movement, no companion file of slave narrators traveling by her side. Resistance must be its own reward.

All her life, Ida Wells fulfilled the role of vigilant sentry for the rights of her people, determined not to abandon the post even if she herself were abandoned. At the age of fourteen she lost her parents to a yellow fever epidemic and had to fight the adult community for the custody of her six little brothers and sisters. Getting a job as a country schoolteacher, she supported the family and was soon forced to sue the Chesapeake & Ohio Railroad for the right to ride back and forth to her school in the first-class car. Like Douglass and Sojourner Truth, she did not ignore the virtues of direct action: she bit the conductor on the back of the hand when he tried to drag her out of the seat. The court awarded her damages, but the decision was overturned by a higher state court and she ended up having to pay the costs.

So began a career of more than forty years of struggle for black and women's rights. She fought as a writer, speaker, organizer, and physical combatant, focusing much of her energy against the practice of lynching. Threatened with lynching many times herself, she exposed the facts of white repression in the South to audiences all over Britain and America. She was able to establish that lynching was not a peripheral excess committed only by a handful of fanatics; it was in fact a system of organized terror, supported by the authorities, participated in by the mass of Southern whites, sanctioned by the news media, and ignored or condoned by the federal government. What is more, most of the lynching victims were killed for political reasons that had nothing to do with actual "crime": e.g. attempting to vote Republican, exercising the Constitutional Bill of Rights, etc. The allegation of rape was almost always groundless, and the victim often not even the person charged with the deed. For decades, blacks were tortured and burned alive at the stake, the spectacles being advertised days in advance by the local papers and better attended than a county fair.

The autobiography of Ida Wells is tremendously important as a historical source; for she made it her business to visit the scenes of race riots and atrocities, gather data from eyewitnesses, publish accounts that would correct the racist bias of the white press, and organize relief and defense efforts for the victims. Through her we learn not only the intensity of repression directed at blacks, but the little-known state of grassroots resistance: women's clubs, discussion groups, mutual assistance leagues, black-edited newspapers and pamphlets that did their good work and died.

Her style has the righteous force of a mother protecting her children. The mother is the one person who will not desert you when trouble comes, even if she has to fight alone. This is the identity created by Wells's language—a mother of black freedom: "There was not a single uplifting influence along the whole length of State Street," she wrote of a Negro slum in Chicago, "and I did not think that our Christian forces should leave State Street to the devil" (Wells, p. 303). Threatened with reprisal by a secret service agent for opposing the government's treatment of Negro soldiers in Houston, Texas, during World War I, she replied, "I would consider it an honor to spend whatever years are necessary in prison as the one member of the race who protested, rather than to be with all the 11,999,999 Negroes who didn't have to go to prison because they kept their mouths shut" (ibid., p. 370). On another occasion she told the white employer of an exploited black girl that "since she [the employer] had had the girl's labor for the five years she had been in Chicago, with no remuneration therefor, steps would be taken to see that she got what was due her if it became necessary" (ibid., p. 410). It did not become necessary.

Ida Wells created the identity of mother and protectress; Maya Angelou in *I Know Why the Caged Bird Sings* (1970) inspires the urge to protect. Her identity is birdlike and vulnerable, the terrified daughter winning her way slowly toward the certainty of motherhood.

In many ways, *I Know Why the Caged Bird Sings* resembles Richard Wright's *Black Boy*. The setting is a small segregated town in the rural South; the parents have sent the children to live with relatives, one of whom owns a general store; Maya and her brother are forced to attend church, where they amuse themselves by making fun of the more zealous members of the congregation; the preacher comes to dinner and eats all the chicken; there is constant friction between the blacks and the poor whites; the fact of her oppression gradually intrudes on the writer's consciousness when she observes what happens around her—the hypocritical speeches of the white superintendent in their segregated school, the refusal of a white dentist to fix her teeth after her grandmother had salvaged his business; her brother helps fish a decomposed Negro body out of the pond while whites stand around and tell malicious jokes; the local sheriff gives them casual warnings whenever the Klan is about to go on a rampage; and finally, she migrates to a Northern city. Maya Angelou's complex sense of humor and compassion for other people's defects, however, endow her work with a different quality of radiance; she does not have Wright's mortal seriousness, or his estrangement, and does not take his risks.

Ordinary objects and experiences are rendered with child-like fascination and sensuousness, as though, if they were stones on Jacob's ladder, the reader would be so busy investigating them he would forget to ascend. "The pickle juice made clean streams down his ashy legs, and he jumped with his pockets full of loot and his eyes laughing a 'How about that?' He smelled like a vinegar barrel or a sour angel."[2] Food preparation is described with the loving appreciation of someone to whom good food is a staff of life, and a consummation of meaningful work:

> The missionary ladies of the Christian Methodist Episcopal Church helped Momma prepare the pork for sausage. They squeezed their fat arms elbow deep in the ground meat, mixed it with gray nose-opening sage, pepper, and salt, and made tasty little samples for all obedient children who brought wood for the slick black stove. The men chopped off the larger pieces of meat and laid them in the smoke-house to begin the curing process. They opened the knuckle of the hams with their deadly-looking knives, took out a certain round harmless bone ("it could make the meat go bad") and rubbed salt, coarse brown salt that looked like fine gravel, into the flesh, and the blood popped to the surface. (Angelou, p. 19).

The fact that this is a church-related activity gives their church the earthiness of salt pork and vegetables; "fat arms" pressed into the meat (with a resemblance between the arms and the meat) become almost a form of worship. At the same time, food is the center of the child's consciousness, because it is the economic basis of the family's survival; her grandmother earns their living by weighing and measuring flour, selling canned goods, keeping chickens and hogs; when the stock prospers, they prosper; when the food is moving off the shelves and salted into the curing house, the money is coming into the till, and grace to the family table. Feeding hogs, too, is a humorous memory instead of, as in Douglass, a bitter reminder of how little the black children were fed by comparison.

> Bailey and I sloshed down twilight trails to the pig pens, and standing on the first fence rungs we poured down the unappealing concoctions to our grateful hogs. They mashed their tender pink snouts down into the slop, and rooted and grunted their satisfaction. We always grunted a reply only half in jest. We were also grateful that we had concluded the dirtiest of chores and had only gotten the evil-smelling swill on our shoes, stockings, feet and hands (ibid., pp. 13–14).

Sloshing down the twilight trails to the pig pens re-creates the sound of the pails, the dusky path, and the coming darkness, while chuckling gently at the "romance" of childhood: she follows the twilight trail, not to see the Wizard, but to slop the hogs. Their gratitude, grunts, and tender pink snouts evoke the kind of feelings one might have about spoon-feeding a hungry baby: the kinship with the hog, the recognition of the animal in ourselves (the children grunt a reply), the sticky mess, our adult fastidiousness, and the creature's total, droll, candid indifference to anything but its own needs. Humor like this is not satire, but love for the sounds and sights of being alive.

This loving attachment to objects, which is also a responsibility to them and insistence on their reality, permeates the style itself in the form of solid images, rooted in the basic rituals of our physical presence: eating, excreting, playing in the dirt, and running barefoot. Observing a corpse, Angelou "concluded that she had looked like a mud baby, lying on the white satin of her velvet coffin. A mud baby, molded into form by creative children on a rainy day, soon to run back into the loose earth" (ibid., p. 137). The image in this case is a vivid fact of life, demanding a full and meditative comparison between mud babies and human beings. In the background is a kind of Zen suggestion that life comes and goes like the spontaneous play of a child, that the processes of nature happen without preconceived object and should be experienced by the moment.

Like Redding and Wright, Angelou can also reconstruct the economic skeleton of her environment: what people did for a living, how their work brought them into relation with each other, and how the relative positions of owners and workers affected their behavior and attitudes. She remembers the cotton pickers who came into her grandmother's store in the morning, before work, to buy sardines and cheese. "One man was going to pick two hundred pounds of cotton, and another three hundred. Even the children were promising to bring home fo' bits and six bits." But at the end of the day, "the people dragged, rather than their empty cotton sacks," having transferred their life energies to the ownership of the white employers.

> Brought back to the Store, the pickers would step out of the backs of trucks and fold down, dirt-disappointed, to the ground. No matter how much they had picked, it wasn't enough. . . .
> The sounds of the new morning had been replaced with grumbles about cheating houses, weighted scales, snakes, skimpy cotton and dusty rows. In later years I was to confront the stereotyped picture of gay song-singing cotton pickers with such inordinate rage that I was told even by fellow Blacks that my paranoia was embarrassing. But I had seen the fingers cut by the mean little cotton bolls, and I had witnessed the backs and shoulders and arms and legs resisting any further demands (ibid., pp. 6–7).

As in so many black autobiographies, the reality of the writer's life conflicts with the lies of movies and books, and part of the energy

behind the work goes toward debunking the racist imagery of
white culture.

White domination intrudes on several occasions, charging the
material with political resentment, opening the narrator's eyes all
at once to the fact that she belongs to a subject caste. During her
high school graduation, when she has received a book of poems,
sung the anthems, and begun to feel some pride in her accomplishment, two white men step onto the stage and announce the im-
provements that are in store for the school system: the white school
will receive new microscopes and chemistry equipment, and the
Negro school will get new paving for their athletic field. "Graduation . . . was finished for me before my name was called," she remembers. "The meticulous maps . . . memorizing the whole of *The
Rape of Lucrece*—it was for nothing. . . . Who decided that for
Henry Reed to become a scientist he had to work like George
Washington Carver, as a bootblack, to buy a lousy microscope?"
She wishes that Gabriel Prosser and Nat Turner had killed all
whitefolks "in their beds," and that she could "see us all dead, one
on top of the other."

> A pyramid of flesh with the whitefolks on the bottom, as
> the broad base, then the Indians with their silly toma-
> hawks and teepees and wigwams and treaties, the Negroes
> with their mops and recipes and cotton sacks and spirit-
> uals sticking out of their mouths. The Dutch children
> should all stumble in their wooden shoes and break their
> necks. The French should choke to death on the Louisi-
> ana Purchase (1803) while silk-worms ate all the Chinese
> with their stupid pigtails (ibid., pp. 150–53).

When she is refused a job as conductorette in San Francisco, the
streets become "alien and cold," twisting with "malicious intent."
"Old buildings . . . were then imposing structures viciously joined
to keep me out" (ibid., p. 228). In Douglass, too, slavery makes the
very trees and rivers of America seem cursed with the spirit of
robbery and wrong.

But, unlike *Black Boy* and *The Life and Times*, the subject of
I Know Why the Caged Bird Sings is not really the struggle of
the bird; it is the exploration of the cage, the gradual discovery of

its boundaries, the loosening of certain bars that she can slip through when the keepers' backs are turned. Wright gave his "whole being" over to coping with the atrocities that surrounded him, and Douglass's principal concern was always the abolition of slavery. For Maya Angelou, resentment of the whites, and the necessity to break through their closed walls of hostility, are forced on her from time to time because she must live in relation to their world; she experiences often the humiliation of their scorn without being able to make an honorable response. But her primary reasons for living, her happiness, sorrows, lessons, meanings, self-confidence, seem to come from within her private circle of light. Part of her is always untouched by the oppression, observing and commenting on it from a distance. What makes the difference may be a closer integration with her background: she never had to defend herself with a knife from the assaults of her family; her mother always maintained a degree of independence, aggressiveness, and beauty that gave Maya a belief in her own powers and a person to consult and emulate when something happened to weaken that belief. The women respected and supported each other. Her grandmother's general store gave the family a position of strength in the black section of Stamps, Arkansas, that was available to few other blacks. The most traumatic experience of her childhood, being raped, has no overt racial content; the rape was committed by a black man, avenged by her uncles, and scarcely involved the white authorities at all.

It may be, too, that the self-image, the "manhood," of Wright and Douglass was assaulted more consistently and deliberately by the system of caste, and so required them to build their identities much more in terms of facing down the oppressor. Anne Moody was able to manipulate white men with her looks; Richard Wright was smashed in the teeth with a whiskey bottle, threatened with an iron bar, forced to say "yassir" and "nawsir" to white men who patted his female acquaintances on the behind, and could easily have been lynched and castrated for failing to grin on cue. Maya Angelou recalls the effect on her brother of having to recover the body of a dead Negro. "His voice was ancient with shock. He was literally bug-eyed. . . . He was away in a mystery, locked in the enigma that young Southern Black boys start to unravel, start to *try* to unravel, from seven years old to death" (ibid., p. 168).

The distance in Maya Angelou's work is achieved by her sense of humor. She has the power of joking at herself, of re-creating the past in a comic spirit without belittling the other people involved and of capturing the pathetic and tragic overtones of the laughter without being overwhelmed by them. Frightened of a ghost story about the dead Mrs. Taylor, a woman who had always screamed her orders in the store because she was half deaf, Angelou remarks, "the thought of that voice coming out of the grave and all the way down the hill from the cemetery and hanging over my head was enough to straighten my hair." As in Langston Hughes, the humor is often a way of shattering racist images by using them. She knows that the "superstitious" dread Negroes are supposed to have for graveyards is the butt of racist jokes and has felt the perpetual torture of trying to make her hair conform to white standards of beauty; both experiences are subdued, and controlled, by the comic purpose. It is the fear, and the author's ability to laugh at her insecurities, that we remember most—the caged bird's mastery of her song.

Like Johnson, she gives church services a richly comic treatment. The preacher is chased off the pulpit, mauled, hugged, and beaten by an inspired matron who, seized by the Holy Spirit, keeps yelling "preach it! Preach it!" At a later service, the congregation is prepared; the Reverend increases his volume, and the matron rises from her seat: "I say, preach it!" "Hot dog," says Maya's brother, "she's going to beat his butt." The Reverend, however, slips from the pulpit without ever interrupting the sermon, trailed by the matron and half a dozen others trying to restrain her. "Great God of Mount Nebo," he says, as she hits him on the back of the head with her purse, and his false teeth jump out on the floor, where they lay grinning beside Maya's right shoe.

> But Reverend Thomas shrugged off Sister Monroe's weakening clutch, pulled out an extra-large white handkerchief and spread it over his nasty little teeth. Putting them in his pocket, he gummed, "Naked I came into the world, and naked I shall go out."

Maya "dreaded laughing in church" because if she lost control, "two things were certain to happen. I would surely pee, and just as surely get a whipping." But the laughter "pressed at all my body openings, forcing everything in its path. . . ." Each time she looked at her brother, they "howled louder than before," only able to get out "I say, preach." Later they receive the whipping of their lives.

> Laughter so easily turns to hysteria for imaginative children. I felt for weeks after that I had been very, very sick, and until I completely recovered my strength I stood on laughter's cliff and any funny thing could hurl me off to my death far below.
> Each time Bailey said "Preach it" to me, I hit him as hard as I could and cried (ibid., pp. 35–37).

Nothing is *merely* humorous in this book; behind the laughter is a vision of human frailty, a compassion for people's crippled backs and false teeth, their embarrassment, their attempts to cling to some semblance of dignity in the midst of the ridiculous, and their uncontrollable emotions—Sister Monroe's "preach it! Preach it!" and the child's gas, urine, tears, and hysterical powerlessness to be serious.

We have learned to expect that a black autobiography will probably contain a confrontation scene, where the narrator knocks an overseer into the cow dung, pulls a razor on his tyrannical uncle, or aims a gun at a policeman; this is the point where he becomes a self, a power in his own right, able to exert some control over his world, to construct a life worth writing about. *I Know Why the Caged Bird Sings* contains one of the most unusually subtle, ambiguous, understated confrontation scenes in the history of the form. As Maya's grandmother stands outside her store, three "po' whitetrash" girls, notorious for baiting Negroes, come over the hill and begin to make fun of her. Maya watches from inside, thinking about the "rifle behind the door" and the sawed-off shotgun in Uncle Willie's trunk; but the old woman stands by the door, smiling, humming spirituals, while the children call her insolently by her first name and ape her movements. When this produces no result, they make faces, clown, do hand stands, whisper obscenities, and show off their pubic hair. The grandmother changes her song and never moves. As they leave, they yell in succession, "Bye Annie," and she replies, " 'Bye, Miz Helen, 'bye, Miz Ruth, 'bye, Miz Eloise." Maya is enraged that she calls them

"Miz," but the grandmother's face "was a brown moon that shone on me."

> She was beautiful. Something had happened out there, which I couldn't completely understand, but I could see that she was happy. Then she bent down and touched me as mothers of the church "lay hands on the sick and afflicted" and I quieted.
> "Go wash your face, Sister." And she went behind the candy counter and hummed, "Glory, glory, hallelujah, when I lay my burden down."
> I threw the well water on my face and used the weekday handkerchief to blow my nose. Whatever the contest had been out front, I knew Momma had won (ibid., pp. 24–27).

In a male autobiography, it would have been important to alter the power relationships of such a scene by threatening or fighting; here, the grandmother's refusal to respond brings her own weapons into play. She is an adult, an elderly woman, and need not stoop to their level; she has total mastery of her feelings, even to the point of remaining serene enough to address them as "Miz"; they have diminished themselves, confirmed their childishness and poverty, by asserting skin privilege when they have nothing else to give them status. At the same time she is not really free to respond any other way, for if the children knew they could get on her nerves, they would repeat the scene every afternoon, perhaps going on to break the windows and report her "insolence" to their parents. Knowing this may be the reason why she needs the songs. Her psychological victory is also a consolation prize.

The scene concentrates the tension between white and black into a kind of metaphor; on the one hand, nasty children, who have nothing but their race, treating a black grandmother like another child, practicing the rituals of white power with the full complicity of the adult whites, taunting her with their sex and agility, trying to demolish her self-composure; on the other hand the adult woman choosing the most dignified course, silent endurance; forced to choose it in fact by the sanctions of the caste system which supports the children's behavior, yet refusing to recognize in them anything but white children, refusing even to register their offensiveness, or humanity, by deviating from the normal formulas of respect toward whiteness. She cannot resist their game but does not play it either. Her triumph must be silent, unnoticed by those whom she has vanquished.

Part of Maya Angelou's work overlaps on the themes of the male autobiographies—her attitude toward education, her conscious adoption of pride in blackness as a defense against white condescension—but she also speaks of the special problems encountered by black women and affirms life in a way that no male author could duplicate. The female identity crisis in the book is centered around her appearance; she feels plain and ugly, ashamed of her skinny legs, and yearns to have long, blonde hair and blue eyes. As a child, she allows her stepfather to molest her in return for his affection. She withdraws from everything after the rape, "packing" sounds "down deep" in her ears so "the world would be quiet" around her. She "walked into rooms where people were laughing, their voices hitting the walls like stones," and "simply stood still in the midst of the riot of sound." Silence would soon "rush into the room from its hiding place" because she had "eaten up all the sounds" (ibid., p. 73). This is a form of imprisonment that affects chiefly women: to be trapped between too little sex appeal and too much, perpetually worried over the shape of one's legs, the size of the breasts, the texture of the hair, the proportions of shoulders, waist, and hips; to be condemned for giving in to male demands and ostracized for resisting them; to be used like a rubber doll with a hole in it, made the object, and the victim, of male sexual pathology. Mr. Freeman, the rapist, after ejaculating on the sheets, pours water over them and orders Maya to say she wet the bed, or "I'll have to kill Bailey." Freeman's defense lawyers act as though *she* had raped *him*; and even her uncles, who later kick Freeman to death, make her feel responsible for having killed him. "I could feel the evilness flowing through my body and waiting, pent up, to rush off my tongue if I tried to open my mouth. . . . If it escaped, wouldn't it flood the world and all the innocent people?" (ibid., p. 72) Her shock is analogous to Bailey's, when he discovers the dead Negro in the pond—and, what is worse, the callous, snickering pleasure of the whites, as though they fattened on Negro terror and death like maggots. Bailey's shock derives from seeing what can happen to Negro males under white rule; hers, from experiencing what can happen to females under male rule.

But Maya Angelou does not submit tamely to the cage. She is
repeatedly thrust into situations where she must act on her own
initiative to save herself and thereby learns the strength of self-
confidence. At one point she lives for weeks in a junkyard with other
orphan children. She drives her drunken father home from Mexico
to California without ever having learned how to drive. Determined to discover what sex is all about so she can prove whether
or not she is a lesbian, she walks up to a casual acquaintance on the
street and says, "Hey, would you like to have a sexual intercourse
with me?" The man replies, "You mean, you're going to give me
some trim?" She is puzzled by his imbalance of values, because
she intends, not to give him anything, but to take something from
him (ibid., p. 240). The event, predictably, is a letdown, leaving her
bewildered and pregnant. "What happened to the moonlight-on-
the-prairie feeling?"

White dominance, male dominance, adult obtuseness, sex, love,
passion, sexual identity, pregnancy, all leave her hopelessly confused. The book ends with a symbol. She is afraid to roll over and
crush her three-week-old baby at night. When she falls asleep, the
baby rolls against her side; unconsciously, she bends her right
arm and makes a tent for the baby out of the blanket. "See, you
don't have to think about doing the right thing," says her mother.
"If you're for the right thing, then you do it without thinking."
Continuity is achieved by the contact of mother and child, the sense
of life begetting life that happens automatically in spite of all
confusion—perhaps also because of it. Male autobiographies strive
consciously for this irrepressible spirit, wrest it from tyrants, defend it at the risk of life itself. The experience of the baby connects
the woman to the ages of human birth, death, hope, and wonder
beyond the artificial conventions of race; the man has to sweep the
Veil aside himself and search for his own connections.

Anne Moody, however, battles for her meanings on the field of
political action with a courage and strength equal to any man's.
Raised in a two-room shack in Mississippi, her childhood might
easily have been lived on a plantation in 1855; "Mr. Carter's big
white house" overlooked the Negro cabins, most of whose occupants
were tenant farmers for Mr. Carter.[3] In some ways she was worse
off than the slaves, for when her father deserted the family, the
whites had no obligation whatever even to feed them; her mother

was reduced to clinging desperately for support to a succession of men, each of whom left her with more mouths to feed.

Eating the white family's leftovers makes Anne aware of the class differences between whites and blacks; "It was the best food I had ever eaten. . . . They had all kinds of different food with meat and all. We always had just beans and bread" (Moody, p. 23). Not her poverty, however, but the murder of Emmett Till is what begins to stoke her hatred of Mississippi whites. Hearing the white woman she worked for condone the murder makes her feel like "rotten garbage." It is her first introduction, at the age of fourteen, to "the fear of being killed just because I was black" (ibid., p. 107).

Like most contemporary black writers, she has little use for the old-time religion. She remembers as a child being baptized in a river full of floating cow manure (ibid., p. 63). The sermons, among other functions, taught the exploited, poverty-ridden blacks not to envy their employers' big houses, fine cars, and beautiful clothes (ibid., p. 58); just as, in slavery times, preachers told the slaves to work hard, tell the truth, and eschew stealing the master's chickens. But her disillusionment with religion after she becomes a civil rights worker takes place on a deeper level. "The God my Baptist training taught me about was a merciful and forgiving God, one that said Thou shalt not kill, Thou shalt not commit adultery, Thou shalt not steal. . . ." Yet she had seen whites kill, steal, and commit adultery against Negroes throughout the South and "God didn't seem to be punishing anyone for these acts." Most of the Negroes, on the other hand, were "humble, peace-loving, religious people," but they suffered as though they were responsible for being killed and brutalized (ibid., p. 305).

As the oldest girl in the family, it was up to Anne, when she reached adolescence, to help support the younger children by doing odd jobs for white people—cleaning porches, washing dishes, babysitting, and waiting on table. She is thrust into an aggressive role by the absence of a consistent breadwinner in the house. Later, when she reaches high school, she is hired to tutor white boys in Algebra and falls into their parents' disfavor because one of them begins to pay her a lot of male attention. She has the ambivalent fortune of being pretty. If she resists the attentions of the whites, she is insolent and snobbish; if she does not, she is trying to get out of her place by exploiting them. On the other hand, she never suffers the insecurities of Maya Angelou. Perhaps for this reason, her style lacks Angelou's quality of gentleness and humorous compassion for people's weaknesses. Throughout adolescence, Anne Moody takes a girlish delight in parodying and shocking the conventions meant to control the sexual curiosity of high school students and applied primarily to females. She starts a fad in the eighth grade of wearing tight jeans, and organizes an assembly program of chorus girls so effective in their flirtations that the principal hurries them off the stage. Before "coming of age," the most important event in her life is getting a new gown in which to be high-school queen.

But the birth of the 1960s changes her entire value structure; childish things are put aside. *Coming of Age in Mississippi* could also be included in the chapters dealing with the revolutionary narratives; for, unlike Dick Gregory, she was involved in the civil rights struggle as a foot soldier, living in Mississippi, subject to reprisal month in and month out by Mississippians, under pressure from her family to shut up and go quietly back to school, harassed and threatened by the FBI, expecting to be shot, raped, or bombed by the local rednecks, with no glamour, no publicity, no bank account to redeem her sacrifices, while the better-known movement leaders took the credit for her accomplishments. Under these conditions her zeal shines like the face of Joan of Arc. She worked for CORE, which is not a revolutionary organization; but what she suffered and achieved seems close to the experience of a Black Panther; close, even, to the fate of the black Communist Angelo Herndon. Although she missed going to the penitentiary, one of her best friends was on the chain gang when she bid him farewell.

Registering Negroes to vote, trying to desegregate lunch counters and bus stations, passing out free food and clothing to poor blacks, are the transgressions that bring her into conflict with the whole racist superstructure of Southern society, exposing her to its deepest sicknesses and punishing her with repressions normally reserved only for revolutionaries. In a sense, her position as a foot soldier makes these reformist programs, for her, revolutionary acts; they teach her the interdependence, in the Southern pattern of rule, between breaking a strike of black workers in a chicken factory, electing all-white legislatures, maintaining all-white waiting rooms and restaurants, separating white from black children in

school, exploiting black cotton-pickers, and inculcating in the
whites a hysterical fear of interracial friendship, love, sex, marriage,
or mutual support of any kind. "Communists! Communists! Communists!" shout the white high-school students during her sit-in
at Woolworth's, perceiving instinctively the ease with which attacks
on race oppression lead to attacks on capitalist property, on the
American Myth itself, as they smear catsup in her hair, spatter
her legs with mustard, and throw her off the stool (ibid., pp. 237–
38). They lay bare, for her scrutiny, the madness of reaction, the
stark terror of those for whom all change is a threat to their ego and
will stop at nothing to prevent change. The punishment endured
for winning even the most trivial reform discloses, bit by bit, the
secrets of the institutions that demand her awe and respect. She
opens them like a child peeking into forbidden closets, finding, not
just skeletons, but trunkfuls of bones, mangled bodies hanging
on hooks, with Bluebeard, wearing a gun and a badge, waiting in
the shadows to clutch her and hang her up by the hair.

Episode by episode, she is stripped of her innocence, faith, and,
above all, her obedient trust of white authority. As a maid in a white
woman's kitchen, she learns that several of the important white
men in town cheat on their wives with Negro maids. She learns that
behind every house-burning and lynching there is smug, frightened, silent complicity in the faces of white people she knows and
works for. She learns, sitting in the white waiting room of a bus
station and being jeered and assaulted by bus drivers with families,
that most whites all over the South have the mentality of a mob,
that even riding buses, going to work, and shopping in the stores
they are still a mob, ready to be galvanized by the slightest challenge.
She learns about exploitation in a chicken factory, when she is
brought in to scab on the striking workers, and the processing
line gradually increases speed until the sweat runs down her legs,
the nausea churns her stomach, and her "face, arms, and clothes
were splattered with blood and chicken shit" (ibid., p. 145). She
learns contempt for Negro men who smile "in a white man's face,
addressing him as Mr. So-and-So, saying yessuh and nassuh . . ."
(ibid., p. 110). She learns about the hypocrisy of the federal government, when, after she is arrested, threatened, tossed around and
locked in a paddy wagon with the windows closed and the heater
on, FBI agents investigate *her* instead of the local police. For several

days she is kept in a make-shift concentration camp, destroying
the last of her illusions about "the land of the free and the home
of the brave" (ibid., p. 251).

What identity results from these experiences? Toward the end of
the book, she begins also to sound like a soldier, haunted by scenes
of violence, pathetic cowardice, and useless bravery, stranded on
shores of knowledge that civilians cannot share, doubting the value
of the struggle but not wanting to let her friends down, living and
dead, by abandoning it, and beginning to put her greatest value
on those lulls of rest and horseplay in between assignments, when
the war seems strangely distant and the birds are heard singing for
the first time in months. Her idealism is deflated when the mass of
poor blacks whose rights she defends will not defend her, will
not register to vote, and will not even be seen at the freedom house
except to pick up the free clothes (ibid., pp. 290–91). She bitterly
resents the movement leaders, like a private resenting his distant
generals. She cannot rid herself of the memory of C. O. Chinn, a
local Negro merchant who, for helping the civil rights workers,
lost his business, his standing in the community, his savings, and his
white "friends," receiving finally a sentence on the chain gang.
Hearing the song "We Shall Overcome," she concludes the autobiography: "I wonder. I really wonder." As she rides to Washington
with a busload of friends, there is an atmosphere of impending
doom for the cause of civil rights. They laugh and sing the movement songs, but gathering like clouds on the horizon is the realization of how much may have to be dared, and endured, before
Bluebeard is defeated and his castle returned to the servants.

> As long as I live, I'll never be beaten by a white man again.
> . . . You know something else, God? Nonviolence is out.
> I have a good idea Martin Luther King is talking to you,
> too. If he is, tell him that nonviolence has served its
> purpose. . . . If you don't believe that, then I know you
> must be white, too. And if I ever find out you are white,
> then I'm through with you. And if I find out you are
> black, I'll try my best to kill you when I get to heaven
> (ibid., p. 285).

Chapter 11 *Inside history*
The revolutionary self

THE narrator of *Invisible Man*,[1] when he steps "outside
the groove of history" and into his Harlem basement
full of light bulbs, becomes a metaphor of submerged
identity; he is under the ground, having no official
address to which bills and tax forms can be sent, shut inside the
"tomb of slavery," to use Douglass's language, striking back at the
white system by using his very anonymity to waste its electric
power, to provide a quiet, persistent, perpetual tax on its strength.
White society bleeds like a blind hemophiliac through the tiny
wound of the invisible man's light bulbs. We know that such
atomized resistance, such a little cut, will not bleed the giant to
death, but the drain is always there, a constant reminder of un-
redressed wrong and unresolved guilt.

For the invisible man, the light is also an act of self-definition.
There will be no darkness within his tomb; the drained energy of
the oppressor will illuminate the victim, at least to himself. If he
was unable to become visible in the groove of history, this bath
in a flood of stolen power still has the virtue of joining self-assertion
with defiance. Indeed, one must be defiant to assert the self at all
in a world where the power belongs to the power company.

The problem faced by the autobiographies of the "black revolution" is how to come forth from the tomb. In the case of convict
writers like Cleaver and Jackson, the image applies in a quite
literal sense; locked behind prison walls, whose function is to keep
the invisible man invisible to white society so that its crimes will
not be exposed to the light, how is the self to reach beyond the
bars, to join hands with others in the same tomb and roll away the
stone? And if it is impossible to move the stone immediately, how
can the victim most encumber the oppressor with the burden of
his own deeds and thus hasten the eventual day of liberation? In the
case of a writer from the "black bourgeoisie," such as Leslie
Alexander Lacy, the prison is his own alienation from both the

black and white worlds, his conflict of loyalties between the values
of white liberalism and black revolution. His problem is how to
convert the weaknesses of his position into strengths.

The answers to these problems require, as a precondition, that the
narrator step back "inside history." History, for Ellison, has no
heart, no conscience, and no respect for individuals; it is a blood-
less intellectual abstraction in whose name the "brotherhood"
will shed innocent blood, ignoring what the people really want and
feel. For Cleaver, Seale, Jackson, Lester, Malcolm X, and Rap
Brown, history gives more elbowroom to the self; it is made by the
self struggling to overcome the obstacles to his growth on a higher
level; history is the force of many selves, who have come to the
point in achieving their identities where they realize that further
growth is impossible until they act collectively to break the chains
of white institutions. To be inside history means to pursue one's
selfhood in harmony with a revolutionary movement. To rise from
the tomb, you create values that connect you politically to your
oppressed brothers and sisters.

At the "very bottom" of the American white man's society, in
prison, Malcolm X "found Allah and the religion of Islam and it
completely transformed my life."[2] From this beginning he wins his
way to an identity which is black, human, and revolutionary, each
aspect expressing and depending on the other two. The realization
that white cultural oppression has robbed the black man of
human identity makes the achievement of *black* identity essential
to the act of resistance. "You don't even know who you are," Malcolm's brother had told him. "You don't even know, the white
devil has hidden it from you, that you are of a race of people of
ancient civilizations . . ." (Malcolm X, p. 161). Malcolm distinguishes between "Negro" and "black" in order to highlight the
political content of the latter: a "Negro" is one who identifies
himself on the white man's terms, one who accepts the definition
of himself given to him by white civilization: " 'Negro' is a false
label forced on you by your slavemaster! He has been pushing things
onto you and me and our kind ever since he brought the first slave
shipload of us black people here . . ." (ibid., p. 254). A black man
is one who resists this oppressive definition and is thus able to
develop an ideology independent of the master culture.

By rejecting the corrupt culture of the whites, one becomes part

of the greater human family outside the United States, entering
into cultural alliance with black, brown, and yellow people all over
the earth.

> What makes the black man think of himself as only an
> internal United States issue is just a catch-phrase, two
> words, "civil rights." How is the black man going to get
> "civil rights" before first he wins his *human* rights? If the
> American black man will start thinking about his
> *human* rights, and then start thinking of himself as part
> of one of the world's great peoples, he will see he has a
> case for the United Nations (ibid., p. 179).

When American black people establish "direct brotherhood lines
of communication" with the independent nations of Africa, they
acquire powerful leverage over the white man's government at
home (ibid., p. 347). After his graduation from the Muslims Malcolm X made it clear that the result of such pan-African identity was
not hatred of whites as a racial category, but struggle against
"whiteness" as a cultural element. Primarily, "white man" described attitudes and actions. "In America, 'white man' meant
specific attitudes and actions toward the black man, and toward all
other non-white men" (ibid., p. 333).

> I'm for truth, no matter who tells it. I'm for justice, no
> matter who it is for or against. I'm a human being first and
> foremost, and as such I'm for whoever and whatever
> benefits humanity *as a whole* (ibid., p. 366).

There is no contradiction between human and black identity,
because "black" distinguishes from the concept of "human" propa-
gated by white racist, imperialist ideology. When white imperialism holds up images of "humanity" that are white in culture,
as it does, for example, in the image of the white Christ or the
white Tarzan, then to assert black identity is to redefine the true
human image. The result may also be profoundly valuable to
whites, because it helps them to dissociate themselves from the
attitudes of "whiteness." "In our mutual sincerity we might be able
to show a road to the salvation of America's very soul" (ibid., p.
377).

Eldridge Cleaver, at the start of his prison career, has reached the state of mind where *Invisible Man* ends: atomized resistance, enslaved by hate and love to "whiteness"; only, instead of white light bulbs, the symbol of his need to be visible is white women. Its expression is rape. "I became a law unto myself—my own legislature, my own supreme court, my own executive" (Cleaver, *Soul on Ice*, p. 13). But through this isolated resistance, he forfeits human identity. The task of *Soul on Ice*, like the task of so many black autobiographies, is redemption from the limbo of dehumanization. "That is why I started to write. To save myself" (ibid., p. 15). Writing is a conscious construction of identity on human terms: "human" signifying respect for the right of all human beings to live and grow, effort to keep from becoming like the oppressor in the process of combating him, and sense of unity and brotherhood with other people.

> I had to find out who I am and what I want to be, what type of man I should be, and what I could do to become the best of which I was capable. I understood that what had happened to me had also happened to countless other blacks and it would happen to many, many more (ibid.).

Identity with the Muslims is his first meaningful link with a political movement. Like Malcolm X, Cleaver graduates beyond their narrowness of vision, in which the white man is "the devil," to an anticapitalist, antiimperialist perspective.[3] Like Malcolm X, he demonstrates that the outlook of "Blackness" is a realization of one's own humanity, whereas "whiteness" is the outlook of an oppressive culture.

> When whites are forced to look honestly upon the objective proof of their deeds, the cement of mendacity holding white society together swiftly disintegrates. On the other hand, the core of the black world's vision remains intact, and in fact begins to expand and spread into the psychological territory vacated by the non-viable white lies, i. e. into the minds of young whites (Cleaver, *Soul on Ice*, p. 77).

After his release from prison, Cleaver's class and revolutionary identity finds an outlet in his Panther membership. His gravitation toward the views and passions of men in rebellion makes him a citizen of the Third World—the world of the Chinese, the Vietnamese, the Cubans, the Algerians.

Seize the Time, by Bobby Seale, *Die Nigger Die,* by H. Rap Brown, *Soledad Brother,* by George Jackson, and *Search for the New Land,* by Julius Lester, all construct identities on revolutionary terms. Samuel Ward had said in 1855 that his autobiography was an antislavery history, because he led an "anti-slavery life." Douglass's life was a capsule history of the antislavery struggle. *Seize the Time,* similarly, is not only an autobiography of Seale, but "the story of the Black Panther Party and Huey P. Newton." The book begins with a one-man riot by its author in support of Malcolm X on the day of his assassination. He identifies with the "bad nigger off the block" and African anticolonialism in naming his son "Malik Nkrumah Stagolee Seale." The image of the "bad nigger" is specifically a class category. The book is full of polemics against black "cultural nationalists" who are "jiving in the confines of the ivory walls, the ivory towers of the college,"[4] and who sell out the struggle of the "brother on the block" at the crucial moment. Black identity is important but not sufficient, for the black cultural nationalists "sit in a fucking armchair and try to articulate the revolution while black people are dying in the streets" (Seale, p. 119). Whiteness for Seale, as for Malcolm X and Cleaver, is a matter of culture rather than race:

> I say white not in the context of the color of their skin,
> but white in relation to their puritanical views, to the
> absolutist concepts they were trying to drill into the kids'
> heads. These absolutist concepts are very directly related
> to racism (ibid., p. 106).

Hence, it is possible to ally with whites who have rejected these concepts and are moving on a collision course with the system that gave birth to them. Seale is a black *worker,* a sheet-metal mechanic and carpenter, among other trades. The struggle is not a "race struggle," but a "class struggle against the avaricious businessmen and the small ruling class who exploit us and perpetuate the racism that's rampant in our communities" (ibid., p. 417). Class definitions are somewhat confusing, or perhaps confused, in *Seize the Time* and in the politics of the Black Panther party, for the party claims to represent the "Afro-American lumpen proletarian" at one point rather than the black working class proper (ibid., pp. 179–80); at another point the book includes both groups under the same heading: "When I say working class, I mean those who are employed and unemployed, living below subsistence and at subsistence level" (ibid., p. 262). And apparently the party urges its members not to hold regular jobs (ibid., p. 202); a policy which seems self-defeating in terms of organizing workers. But the narrator's identity nevertheless gives priority to class over race. The black policeman who serves the white power structure is a "nigger pig, a bootlicker pig" (ibid., p. 192) and is no less an enemy than if he were white. The black revolutionary can identify with Chicano and Latino people, Chinese and Indians, because all are exploited in the same neocolonialist fashion; they are a "nation within a nation" not on the basis of color alone, but on the basis of their economic status (ibid., pp. 351–52).

The main object of *Die Nigger Die*, which is subtitled "A Political Autobiography," is to fight "Negroism." When white culture succeeds in eradicating black identity from black people, "negroes have been created." Negroes are the "close allies of whites in trying to eliminate Black resistance to undesirable acculturation."[5] "Black" means to resist being institutionalized, or "assimilated" by the mainstream. It is not a color, but "the way you think" (H. R. Brown, p. 13). Rap Brown's upbringing was working class: his father was a worker for Esso Standard Oil. Working-class identity is not important in *Die Nigger Die* the way it is in *The Big Sea*, for example, but it is assumed throughout. "Blackness" is a class attitude. The emphasis of the concept is on cultural resistance:

> The biggest difference between being known as a Black
> man or a negro is that if you're Black, then you do every-
> thing you can to fight white folks. If you're negro, you do
> everything you can to appease them. If you're Black,
> you're constantly in and out of trouble, because you're
> always messing with "the man." If white folks say it's
> more cultured to whisper, you talk loud. If white folks say
> gray suits are fashionable, you go buy a pink one. If they
> say america is great, you say america ain't shit (ibid., p. 55).

The political danger of this stance is that, if whites said capitalism, imperialism, and colonialism were bad, a Black man would presumably have to say they were good. Rap Brown, therefore, like Seale and Cleaver, considers black identity to be incomplete. One must also have an effective political identity, toward which "Blackness" is only the first step. "We must be prepared to fight to the death to destroy this system known as capitalism, for it is this system that oppresses the majority of mankind" (ibid., p. 129). One can still have neocolonialist exploitation with black faces in the seat of power. "Blackness alone is not revolutionary" (ibid., p. 130).

George Jackson also combines black with Third-World and revolutionary identity. "Just because I want to be my black self, mentally healthy, and because I look anyone who addresses me in the eye, they feel that I may start a riot anytime."[6] Being his "black self," however, does not mean being an enemy of different races who share the same class and politics. "We must build the true internationalism now" (Jackson, p. 204). Identity is discovered in the process of revolting against the modern master-slave relationship. "I don't want to raise any more black slaves. . . . When I revolt, slavery dies with me" (ibid., p. 189). But the "enemy" is a class, and not a racial, enemy.

> The blanket indictment of the white race has done nothing but perplex us, inhibit us. The theory that all whites are the immediate enemy and all blacks our brothers (making them loyal) is silly and indicative of a lazy mind (to be generous, since it could be a fascist plot). It doesn't explain the black pig; there were six on the Hampton-Clark kill. It doesn't explain the black paratroopers (just more pigs) who put down the great Detroit riot, and it doesn't explain the pseudo-bourgeois who can be found almost everywhere in the halls of government working for white supremacy, fascism, and capitalism (ibid., p. 222).

Identity in Julius Lester includes a frank recognition that "Black culture is superior to white culture" because of its roots in tribalism and its role as a defense against oppression, whereas white culture reflects the fragmentation, alienation, racism, and cash nexus of capitalism. Lester is careful to add, "no one said that black people are superior to white people, or that John Coltrane is superior to Bach." The "effeteness of white culture" is apparent from the way whites "have always used black culture as a means of getting out of themselves."[7] But true cultural identity harmonizes different peoples within the process of building a new world; it does not separate them or make them enemies. "In Vietnam," he writes, "I learned what man could be if given the opportunity. Even during a war, the Vietnamese exemplified a humanity I have never known."

> But the "I" which is me is more than my name, an identification tag used for social convenience. When "I" say that "I" am a revolutionary then "I" become You, if you will allow me, and You become "I." God, that's so hard. Most people won't let you inside them. We are educated to keep our "I" exclusive, to protect it and shelter it, but when we're afraid to let somebody else enter our selves, we don't live (Lester, *Search for the New Land*, p. 130).

Black identity has always been a theme common to all black autobiography; but the emphasis on politics and revolution in these works is far greater than in the second period. W. E. B. Du Bois, James Weldon Johnson, Claude McKay, Paul Robeson, and Richard Wright had not so completely dissociated themselves from "white" culture, though Johnson and others had warned that such dissociation would be the result of continued racism in America. Revolutionary identity, cutting across racial lines to ally with a class and political movement, recalls the radical Christian identities of the slave narrators, which also immersed them in what for that time was a revolutionary viewpoint that cut across racial lines.

The black abolitionists did not typically regard Christianity as a "white man's religion" but a system of universal truth that blacks could rescue from the moral despoliation of the white proslavery church. The modern black militants, on the other hand, consider it of crucial importance to develop a system of thought from Third-World cultural roots; hence the importance of Mao, Fanon, and Nkrumah in their canon of heroes. In a sense they are only harvesting the ideas planted by the giants of the second period: Paul Robeson, for example, when he adopted the principles of the Bandung Conference as his platform, was developing a political stand from Third-World roots. But the laws of social dialectics still apply whether a system is composed of one race or many; to champion a Third-World ideology is not, for Robeson or the contemporary militants, to abandon the common ground shared by "workingmen of all countries." Exploited people have a common interest in terminating exploitation. If Fanon or Mao happen to speak more deeply to the experience of many black people than Marx, this is because colonialist exploitation is somewhat different in character from classical Euro-American capitalist exploitation; a difference which can be accounted for (e.g. as in Lenin's *Imperialism the Highest Stage of Capitalism*) by the Marxist method of seeking answers to political questions in the organization of society, not in "human nature" or race identity.

The prison autobiographies, we have seen, are especially hostile to the bourgeois "Negro" who remains loyal to white values. It is quite instructive to compare these books with an account by a former "proper" Negro, who arrived at his new self by painstakingly divesting his mind of all the illusions and make-believe of his background. Leslie Lacy's *The Rise and Fall of a Proper Negro* works more self-consciously at the problem of identity than Seale, Cleaver, and Jackson. Taking nothing on faith, he must question and reject ways of thinking that the proletarian blacks were never encumbered with. He is subject to more conflicting influences because he comes from the Negro upper class: on the one hand, his environment and family separate him from poor blacks and carefully school him to eat with correct manners, talk with a soft-spoken, educated speech, and think with a white, university-trained value system. On the other hand, during a minor auto accident, white people treat him exactly as they treat the poor blacks. But he does not have their internal defenses; nothing has prepared him for the experience of being a "nigger." Wherever he goes, he is outside looking in; at the university, he is the Negro roommate, the Negro member of the class, the Negro date or dance partner; on the white Left, he is told to get over his obsession with being black; on the black Left, he is told to get rid of his white girl friend and cleanse his mind of whiteness. The habit of taking nothing on faith, which does not leave him after he succeeds in rejecting bourgeois ideology, makes it impossible for him to accept the doctrines of the various left-wing parties. In Ghana, he is an Afro-American tourist distrusted by all classes, even the black refugees from South Africa.

The beauty of Lacy's autobiography is the way he has been able to turn the weaknesses of his background into strengths. Self-doubt, excessive introspection, inability to take a firm stand on anything, the tendency to waver and withdraw under the pressure of sharpening class conflict, belief in a world of fantasy, are all *petit bourgeois* characteristics which cast their shadows over Lacy's career; but in him they lead to a manly struggle with internal chaos, a more serious and subtle examination of reality. Since he must reach the right path with his mind, the steps have to satisfy his intelligence as well as his feelings. His deep suspicion of all political doctrine and his unwillingness to make *The Rise and Fall* a movement manifesto, in part simply reflects his belief that we have had too many manifestoes too soon and not enough evaluation of exactly who we are and where we want to go.

To Seale and Jackson, for example, Nkrumah is simply a hero. But Lacy lived under his regime, organized a Marxist Study Forum that was dissolved by Nkrumah's police just when it was beginning to bear fruit, and spoke with peasants whose relatives languished in his jails for minor political infractions. Still emerging from his trip to Ghana with a respect for Nkrumah's accomplishments and an overall sense of commitment to black socialism, Lacy seems more deeply aware of human weakness and complexity, of the ease with which ideals can be betrayed and rhetoric substituted for freedom. He makes his judgments with care, while not allowing the complexity of experience to serve as an excuse for total paralysis.

His revolutionary models are two men from Vietnam who come to Africa to speak about American imperialism. They "looked rather ordinary—suits, ties, clean shaven—" and were also "calm, intelligent, civil, practical, violent, sensitive, secure, modest but certain, possessed by a sense of history, and they showed concern and love for their families, who stood near their sides." In contrast to these figures, American radicals have failed to grasp "the full significance of a revolutionary experience. It is not a one-shot deal, a one-lifetime thing" but requires a "continuing process." We must think of our activity as a foundation for that of our grandchildren. If black people "have the heart to be critical of each other, from a point of commitment and love," then the grandchildren "will have organized a black culture which is disciplined enough to sustain a revolutionary struggle. . . ."[8]

The values of the new works champion many forms of individual and collective resistance. Their distinction from the preceding period is mostly a question of emphasis, political frame of reference, and conscious examination. Fighting back in John Thompson may only involve an individual confrontation with an overseer. In the early Du Bois, in Redding, in Johnson, one sees isolated incidents where arms were used as protection against lynch mobs. In Hughes, there is sympathy with the use of force by the revolutionary Russian and Asian masses, but Hughes is an observer of these events, an outside commentator. In Seale, Jackson, Rap Brown, Cleaver, Lester, and Malcolm X, violence is consciously examined as a revolutionary theory, much as it was in the *Life and Times of Frederick Douglass*. The narrators are inside the mass movement, defending the use of arms from within the revolution as a vital necessity. Armed force as a value is a key means of linking the individual and the mass. In no case, however, does shooting down the enemy become a goal espoused for its own sake, or imply indiscriminate assaults on whites. "I'm not for wanton violence," said Malcolm X, "I'm for justice . . . when the law fails to protect Negroes from whites' attack, then those Negroes should use arms, if necessary, to defend themselves."

> I *am* for violence if non-violence means we continue postponing a solution to the American black man's problem—just to *avoid* violence. I don't go for non-violence if it also means a delayed solution. To me a delayed solution is a non-solution (Malcolm X, pp. 366–67).

According to Rap Brown, "Black people have always been violent, but our violence has always been directed toward each other." Nonviolence should be practiced "in our community and end there. Violence is a necessary part of revolutionary struggle" (H. R. Brown, p. 144). *Soledad Brother* is dedicated to George Jackson's younger brother Jonathan, "who died on August 7, 1970, courage in one hand, assault rifle in the other . . . the *true revolutionary*, the black communist guerrilla in the highest state of development, he died on the trigger, scourge of the unrighteous, soldier of the people;"

> to this terrible manchild and his wonderful mother
> Georgia Bea, to Angela Y. Davis, my tender experience, I
> dedicate this collection of letters; to the destruction of
> their enemies I dedicate my life.

In early Panther theory, individual armed confrontation with the police is an educational tool to teach the people that they can successfully resist the state. "We knew," writes Bobby Seale in *Seize the Time*, "that at first the guns would be more valuable and more meaningful to the brothers on the block, for drawing them into the organization . . ." (Seale, p. 83). But the shooting is not sought by the brothers; it results from the enemy's methods of terror; it is a choice made by the oppressors. If they choose to continue their oppression, then they are compelling the party, and the people, to protect their programs of liberation by force of arms:

> We don't use our guns, we have never used our guns to
> go into the white community to shoot up white people.
> We only defend ourselves against anybody, be they black,
> blue, green, or red, who attacks us unjustly and tries
> to murder us and kill us for implementing our programs
> (ibid., p. 71).

Cultural resistance involves any value made use of by the black writer to preserve his integrity, to maintain goals, ways of thinking, and behavior patterns that are independent of the oppressor's values and cultural definitions. Education and knowledge continue to have the importance that they had in the slave narratives. They are part of the battle. Where education in second-period works tended to alienate the writer from the people, the black revolutionaries solve this dilemma by defining and attacking the education of the oppressive culture and supporting the education that contributes to the revolution. The key stage in the formation of the Black Panther party is when Bobby Seale and Huey Newton sit down together to discuss Fanon's *Wretched of the Earth* (ibid., p. 26). And in his job as supervisor in the Poverty Program, Seale would "get the dudes to do the jobs real quick" so that time would be left to "talk about the history of black people and the experience of black people, and how the system was really against us, and how we had to grow up and be more functional" (ibid., p. 43). The object of education is to fight the "brainwashing" not only of black people, but of "the proletarian masses of America."

> We want to unbrainwash our people by telling them the true history. One must tell the true history in terms of the class struggle, the small minority ruling-class dominating and oppressing the massive, proletarian working-class (ibid., p. 262).

Donald Reeves, a student in New York City, found high school, like prison, to be a concentration of the racism and repression that existed all over America. "The Board of Education created the police state here. The Board of Education pitted the white community against the Black community to justify the necessity of a police state, in a so-called institution of learning. Hundreds of kids in this school were on drugs." Valid education would let the students "leave their classrooms to confront the world they are expected to live in, to become conscious of the real world." During this time, students would be free "to find out 'Who am I?' " The discussions usually reserved for the aftermath of an assassination or a riot "should have been held 365 days of the year."[9]

For Rap Brown, "Education in america has to be viewed as propaganda machinery. . . . It propagandizes against us. It makes us hate ourselves" (H. R. Brown, p. 21). The best education for "young bloods" is "in the street."

> I learned how to talk in the street, not from reading about Dick and Jane going to the zoo and all that simple shit. The teacher would test our vocabulary each week, but we knew the vocabulary we needed. They'd give us arithmetic to exercise our minds. Hell, we exercised our minds by playing the Dozens (ibid., pp. 25–26).

The white man's education, in Rap Brown and Malcolm X, reminds them of the human waste of the great verbal and mathematical talents of ghetto blacks whose only opportunities for expression are hustling, numbers-running, and playing the Dozens. Malcolm X, like the slave narrators, was self-taught, copying words out of the dictionary in prison and reading so voraciously that "months passed without my even thinking about being imprisoned. In fact, up to then, I never had been so truly free in my life (Malcolm X, p. 173). His homemade education gave him, with each additional book that he read, "a little bit more sensitivity to the deafness, dumbness, and blindness that was afflicting the black race in America" (ibid, p. 179). In *Soul on Ice*, education and knowledge make social liberation possible: "The sins of the fathers are visited upon the heads of the children—but only if the children continue in the evil deeds of the fathers" (Cleaver, *Soul on Ice*, p. 83). Knowledge is also a defense of personal integrity: "My mind would be free and no power in the universe could force me to accept something if I didn't want to" (ibid., p. 5).

The prison autobiographies by Cleaver and Jackson give knowledge and integrity a special poignancy, a special power that is duplicated nowhere else except in Douglass and Richard Wright. Because freedom of the mind is the only freedom possible to the convict, it is searched and articulated to a much greater, more passionate degree than in most of the autobiographies of writers who have never been imprisoned. It is interesting to find this depth of insight into the meaning of mental freedom in the *Prison Journals* of Philip Berrigan; it is a common ground of resistance shared by white and black, the nearest approach to that truly *human* identity that we dream will be achieved when the New Land is found. In Cleaver, its highest personal expression is in the love letters to Beverly Axelrod and the final letter, "To All Black Women, from All Black Men."

In George Jackson, integrity and mental freedom are the meaning of his life, the invisible force, the magic of ideas that reach through prison walls to join the life force of people in rebellion everywhere against cash nexus, ignorance, slavery, manipulation, and bureaucracy. Discovering and implementing the right system of ideas is the redemption of suffering, the redemption of ten years spent in "Dachau," as Jackson called his prison, to be followed by a brutal death at the hands of his guards. The value placed on his life by the state of California was the $70.00 which he had allegedly robbed from a gas station and for which he had received the sentence of one year to life—a greater devaluation of his existence than he would have encountered on an auction block in the state of Mississippi in 1860. But Jackson created his own value by study, reading, and thought, using ideas to peck through the shell of commodity relations and come forth with a conscious human identity. "I am given to understand that it is the strong who rule the weak," he wrote his mother, "but, in turn, the wise rule over the strong" (Jackson, p. 83). His letters to his father and friends ask repeatedly for books: "I have made inroads into political economy, geography, forms of government, anthropology, archaeology, and the basics of three languages, and when I can get hold of them some of the works on urban guerrilla warfare" (ibid., p. 85). He advises his brother Jon, in an early letter, to specialize in some branch of knowledge that will "help the war effort," that is, the black war for liberation. Knowledge and integrity provide the things that enable him to be a whole man, a "power on earth," in the words of Douglass. He would like to be released to "develop a few ideas that have occurred" to him, but if

> it is a choice between that and surrendering the things
> that make me a man, the things that allow me to hold my
> head erect and unbowed, then the hill can have my bones.
> Many times in the history of our past—I speak of the
> African here in the U.S.—many times we were presented
> with this choice, too many times, too many of us choose
> to live the crippled existence of the near-man, the half-
> man. Well, I don't care how long I live. Over this I have
> no control, but I do care about what kind of life I live,
> and I can control this. I may not live but another five
> minutes, but it will be five minutes definitely on my
> terms (ibid., p. 84).

Jackson, like Douglass and John Brown, considered that he had found his life by being willing to lose it. When he learns to live this choice, day after day, the relationship between the prisoner and the guard, psychologically, becomes reversed.

There is a vast difference between the mental freedom of black autobiography and the song lyric, "you better free your mind *instead*" in the Beatles' song, "Revolution II." For the Beatles, when they made this song, mental freedom was a complacent withdrawal from political involvement, a solipsistic exercise in which one cultivates a state of "happiness" apart from man's social ex-

istence and reads his own "freedom" into the world of the unhappy
wage slaves beyond the range of the amplifiers. If they do not
appear happy, it is their fault for not "freeing" their minds. But in
Jackson, Cleaver, Douglass, Wright, Malcolm X, there is no
"instead." Mental freedom is achieved by political understanding
and action, and is inconceivable without them; for the only alternative is the ideology of the master culture.

Although education and knowledge are values common to the
entire history of black autobiography in America, there is a definite
pattern of development in its meaning and goals. During the
slavery period, education in white culture meant advancement.
The academic success of one Negro was a rung on the ladder of
achievement for the race. It was proof that black people were not
racially inferior. The task of education was to assimilate as many
Negroes as possible into the mainstream and thus destroy their
special status as a class of slaves. During the early twentieth century,
assimilation has failed to take place; white education leads to the
alienation of the educated black people from the masses, who
continue to remain outside the mainstream culture, a colonialized
subject caste. The need is felt for something more: Du Bois turns
his cultural tools toward the study of the race issue to create a
foundation for a later political movement. J. Saunders Redding,
Langston Hughes, and Claude McKay rediscover the value of
black culture. During the most recent period, "white" education is
a hostile power to be opposed. Individual success in the white
man's world creates "Uncle Toms," Negroes who ally with the
enemy. Assimilation on white terms is attacked because it threatens
black cultural integrity and sweeps away the cultural defenses
blacks have evolved against pressures to submerge and split their
identity. Education and knowledge in the recent books imply the
study of black history and culture, the exposure of the gaps and
falsehoods in white education, and mastery of ideas and skills
that "serve the people." Significantly, the education which is of
most service as a tool of liberation is, in all periods of black literature, wrested by stealth, deceit, and force from white civilization at
great personal risk. White culture is used by the revolutionaries—
the ideals of Tom Paine and Thomas Jefferson, the analyses of
Marx and Marshall McLuhan, the heroic memory of John Brown
—but on their terms, for their aims. They "steal the sacred fire"

without allowing it to burn the black out of their souls.

The demise of Christianity in black identity is an aspect of resistance to the whites. Christian rhetoric and exhortation remain alive, as one can see from the titles of some of the books—*Search for the New Land, Manchild in the Promised Land*—because the rhetoric has been too deeply ingrained in black political tradition to be given up. But the religion is actively opposed, the vacuum left by its demise filled by black culture, the Nation of Islam, or communism. Malcolm X thought that "the black man in North America was spiritually sick because for centuries he had accepted the white man's Christianity." In using the adjective "so-called" to refer to white Christians, Malcolm is still making the abolitionist distinction between "true" and "false" Christianity (Malcolm X, p. 313), but he believed that Islam was the "one religion that erases from its society the race problem" (ibid., p. 340). George Jackson has no use for any religion whatsoever:

> How could there be a *benevolent* superman controlling a world like this. He would have to be malevolent, not benevolent. Look around you, evil rules supreme. God would be my enemy. The theory of a good, just god is a false idea, a thing for imbeciles and old women and, of course, Negroes (Jackson, p. 151).

The work ethic is a traditional value in the new autobiography but has undergone some predictable changes. The abstract idea of the "dignity of labor" has almost disappeared, traces of it surviving perhaps in the Muslim asceticism of Malcolm X. The noblest work is that which builds the revolution. Black people have no obligation to white employers beyond getting the most money for the least effort, since the conditions of labor are a form of economic neoslavery. Bobby Seale used to tell his trainees in the Poverty Program:

> "All right, you've got six hours of work today. You get one hour for lunch. Now if all you cats get together and do this job you can do it in four hours. I know you can do it easily in four hours." Then I'd say, "I'll let you off for the next two hours, and I'll see to it that you still get your pay for the entire six hours" (Seale, p. 36).

H. Rap Brown, on his job for the Department of Agriculture library, was never "too hip on punching time clocks and going through all them kind of changes, so anytime I could get leave—sick leave, bathroom leave, any kind of leave—I'd leave" (H. R. Brown, p. 65). Only in the less militant authors, specifically Claude Brown and Dick Gregory, does work take on the dimensions of an ethic, a pathway to individual success through which the drive to overcome his special handicaps pushes the Negro on to excellence. Malcolm X had this drive until told by a white teacher that he had better aim at being a carpenter because a lawyer was "no realistic goal for a nigger" (Malcolm X, p. 36). After his involvement in the Nation of Islam, he worked more than he ever had in his life, but work lost its meaning as a form of bourgeois achievement reflecting glory on the individual. "All of the credit is due to Allah. Only the mistakes have been mine" (ibid., p. 382).

The loss of bourgeois individualism is the best way to characterize what has happened to the work ethic in black autobiography as a whole. The Protestant ethic emphasizes individual accumulation and advancement. The slave narrators were able to work with this ethic because, for the Negro, individual and racial advancement seemed almost synonymous. When this ceased to be true, the Protestant ethic became one more element in the master culture that had to be resisted, one more obstacle to serving one's people. Individual accumulation was seen to be "individualism" for the few who advanced and self-sacrifice for everyone whose labor advanced them.

The politics of the new autobiographies link the rebirth of black consciousness with the rebirth of feminism. Some of the slave narrators had related abolition to the cause of women's rights, and the early feminists, Lucy Stone and Susan B. Anthony, got their start in the cause of antislavery. Frederick Douglass, among his other eminences, was a great champion of women's liberation. But it is not until the new feminism of the 1960s that the connection between the two issues is given an important place in black writing. Female and black oppression stem from a common source in capitalist private property society. The issue is highly complicated, however, by the fact that "manhood," which is a form of resistance to white power, is also a culturally determined role used to oppress

women. According to Malcolm X, "Islam has very strict laws and
teachings about women . . . the true nature of a man is to be strong,
and a woman's true nature is to be weak . . . he must control her
if he expects to get her respect" (ibid., p. 226). *Manchild in the
Promised Land* is full of chauvinistic references to women as
"bitches." George Jackson's early letters castigate his mother for
blunting the "manhood" of her children, and any woman he has
when he gets out "must let me retrain her mind or no deal" (Jackson, p. 95). But the later letters project an image of woman as equal
to man, if she is a guerrilla liberation fighter and comrade of the
revolution. The exchange of letters between Lester and a woman
in the movement at the end of *Search for the New Land* struggles
to find some common ground of equality for men and women
within the cause. And the last several pages of *Seize the Time*
polemicize against male chauvinism because it interferes with the
functioning of the party.

Cleaver's *Soul on Ice* devotes two full chapters, "Primeval
Mitosis" and "Convalescence," to the link between the two issues
and their common roots in the organization of capitalist society.
Class society, according to Cleaver, "projects a fragmented sexual
image." The owning class, because of its administrative function,
is identified with Mind, and the producing class with Body.
Sexual function as an attribute of Body, in the cultural myth of a
class system, tends to be relegated to the producers; i.e. their sexual
potency is exaggerated and considered superior to the potency
of the administrative elite. The women of the elite must project an
image of Ultrafemininity to contrast with the effeminate Omnipotent Administrator. The domestic component in her nature is
"projected onto the women in the classes beneath her, and the
femininity of the women below is correspondingly decreased"
(Cleaver, *Soul on Ice*, p. 181). In a society where class function tends
to follow roughly along racial lines, the separation of Mind and
Body, Omnipotent Administrator and Supermasculine Menial, is
identified with the separation of white and black. The black man's
effort to acquire administrative power, therefore, appears to the
white supremacist as a sexual threat, a threat to the socially defined
sexual roles—and in the long run it is. The woman of the producing
class, in particular the black woman, is oppressed by being cast
in the role of Aunt Jemima, and the woman of the elite is oppressed

by being made into a feminine toy, denied the right to come down from her pedestal and assert herself.

This theory, developed and explored for several pages, assimilating among other works the "White Negro" by Norman Mailer, allows Cleaver to fit the white "hippie" phenomenon into the overall framework of the black revolution; for young whites combat the division between "Mind" and "Body" by acting out the images that are associated with the "nigger": rhythm, libidinousness, black slang, contempt for American values, wild dress and grooming codes, shattering of sex stereotypes, laziness, thievery, and drug use. It is evident in the theory that complete liberation from racial oppression, at least in America, necessarily implies liberation from the oppressive component in sexual roles. The white man cannot free himself of racism without also freeing himself of his proprietary complex toward the white woman.

Black autobiographers had always known through their experience with the sexual paranoia of white racists that racism was inseparable from the question of sex. "In the core of the heart of the American race problem," said James Weldon Johnson, "the sex factor is rooted" (Johnson, p. 170). "I think the Anglo-Saxon mind becomes morbid when it turns on the sex life of colored people," said Claude McKay (McKay, p. 75). But Cleaver explains the problem as a question of politics, and connects it to a mass historical movement. Friedrich Engels had shown in *The Origin of the Family, Private Property, and the State* that the sex roles as we know them reinforce the division of society into classes; Cleaver has applied this thesis to the American context, reinterpreting it to shed light on the forms taken by the social dialectic in the United States—specifically the clash of black power and white reaction. When the subject class moves for its freedom, the classes whose identity and well-being depend on keeping them down—in America this category may include large strata of middle-income whites —feel the loss of power as a loss of potency. For the lower strata, who had nothing but the illusion of power to begin with, the reaction may be all the more intense; they are thereby forced, without preparation, without warning, to confront their true condition, to admit their life is a lie, and to base their sexuality on something besides, on the one hand, romantic fantasy, and on the other, screwing and being screwed in the market place.

Chapter 12 *The language of black satire*

To get out of the prison of slavery, the revolutionary self must do battle with his jailers. This is a necessity that attends his decision to be a person instead of a thing. The jailers are not about to let him go merely because he thinks and feels like a person and wants to be alive. Those who give orders to the jailers never even see him, don't even know he exists as an individual. The sixty wealthiest families and their corporation executives, generals, attorney generals, judges, governors, legislators, and behavioral engineers are aware of him only as part of a cost structure. Resurrection from such a vast, impersonal, automated morgue requires far more than guns. "Some days," writes Lester, "I have to have the faith that sitting here at this typewriter can be a revolutionary act with an effectiveness equal to that of a gun. At the same time . . . I must know that this act . . . is no substitute for the power that only grows from the barrel of a gun" (Lester, *Search for the New Land*, p. 190).

The most important weapons in the prisoner's arsenal are his ideas; for the right ideas enable him to withstand the pressure of the enemy's values and give him the faith that he will eventually escape. The main object of black revolutionary satire is to keep the ideas ready and right; that is, to attack the jailer's culture, to unravel the web of falsehood that ties his infrastructure together, to thrust his concepts away so they cannot police the self from inside the skull.[1] The autobiography performs these essential tasks with the oppressor's very words, but they must undergo a "sea change" of purification to become useful and beautiful.

We can see why purification is needed, and what it involves, by examining some of the differences between black and white satire. The black works are rooted in a tradition of political activism, realism, and confidence. The white satirists, from Mark Twain to Kurt Vonnegut, have strengths of their own, but it is revealing that most seem to spend a lot of time on the outer fringes of consciousness, the twilight zones of surrealism, despair, and isolation. One thinks of the cartoons of Jules Pfeiffer, with their emaciated, defeated, self-parodying antiheroes; the misfits of *Catch-22*, who can escape the bureaucracy only by attempting to row all the way to Sweden in a rubber raft; or the outcome of *Cat's Cradle*, in which a scientist with the moral sense of a two-year-old invents a formula to convert all the water in the world to ice, and in which God's final message to the human race is "I don't need you anymore. Die." One also thinks of the cartoons of *The East Village Other*, with their absurd distortions of perception in imitation of the effects of psychedelic drugs.

White satire attacks the dominant white culture, but typically it either locks itself into the dead end of self-conscious alienation or borrows heavily from Negro and Indian images, in the manner of rock culture, in order to escape. Black satire rests on an independent subculture formed in the process of struggle against white power. We can find black authors in whom surrealism, madness, and/or despair are the prevailing modes of consciousness (e.g. Fenton Johnson and sometimes Ellison) but these are exceptions. The rule is a tone of assurance which assumes that masses of black people have passed through similar experiences and support the author's vision. The confidence of militant black satire results from the feeling of the authors that their day is coming, that their problems are no longer going to be ignored, that they, as writers and political activists, are "part of the solution." Their realism consists of how they conceive the object of their attacks. The problem is *external* to so-called innate "human nature"; its locus is white culture, the white-controlled system of commodity relations. Their satire exposes the contradictions of this system so that they can be re-solved. The black writers are a kind of literary people's court for the trial of oppressors. White satire tends to assume that everyone is an oppressor, or that there are no oppressors, only victims. Hence it is possible to criticize oppression, but not to imply social solu-tions; for "human nature" itself is oppressive and irrational. We cannot expect much better from the "damned human race," as Mark Twain called us. Whatever solutions exist are individual and subjective.

The difference between black and white satire is especially clear when we examine the way blacks use irony. They have no monopoly on verbal irony, but its political content is a consistent feature of their styles. The black author appropriates the language of the oppressor and makes it ironic by using it in the context of the oppressed. All verbal irony is defined by the fact that a given word meaning superimposes one frame of reference on another, contradictory frame. "Angela, Franklin, and Newton Hoenikker had in their possession seeds of *ice-nine*," writes Vonnegut, "seeds grown from their father's seed—chips, in a manner of speaking, off the old block."[2] In black writing, the two frames most often express opposing class and racial perspectives, and the irony therefore becomes a form of class and racial rebellion against the customary word usages of the whites. These passages from Cleaver illustrate the point:

> Everywhere there are those who want to smash this
> precious toy clock of a system, they want ever so much
> to change it, to rearrange things, to pull the whites down
> off their high horse and make them equal.

> A strange thing happened in Watts, in 1965, August. The
> blacks, who in this land of private property have all
> private and no property, got excited into an uproar be-
> cause they noticed a cop before he had a chance to wash
> the blood off his hands.

> The blacks . . . have no bank accounts, only bills to pay.
> The only way they know of making withdrawals from
> the bank is at the point of a gun (Cleaver, *Soul on Ice*,
> pp. 131, 136).

The word "equal" usually appears in the contexts of "equal opportunity," "created equal," "equal rights," etc. as though the white middle class had all achieved "equality," but a minority of Americans (i.e. blacks) are still "unequal," that is, culturally inferior, and need help rising into the middle class. Attention is focused on the poor as the "unequal," with the implication that we should study them, not society, to find out why they "fell behind." In Cleaver it is the rich whites who are unequal. To solve this inequity, one does not increase the opportunity of the poor to become unequal by rising as individuals into the ranks of the rich; one pulls the rich "down off their high horse." The pun on private property makes the same point: it is a land of property for the rulers, and private for the ruled. The ironic meaning of "private" implies that a con game has been played on the blacks—"heads I win, tails you lose." Moreover, in the context of the phrase, not even the "private" (control of one's person) is secure, because it can be violated almost at will by the police: "they noticed a cop before he had a chance to wash the blood off his hands." The irony of making "withdrawals" from the bank at the point of a gun derives, like the other examples, from class contradiction. "Withdrawal" in its ordinary financial sense is a legal, respected social relation of capitalism. In its ironic sense it is an understatement for assault on capitalist property by black workers, and a jeer at the white banker's definition of legality and respectability.

Julius Lester in *Search for the New Land* uses Lyndon Johnson's speech on the death of Martin Luther King for a similar ironic effect:

> "We can achieve nothing by lawlessness and divisiveness among the American people. It's only by joining to- gether, and only by working together, can we continue to move toward equality and fulfillment for all of our people. I hope that all Americans tonight will search their hearts as they ponder this most tragic incident."

Lester's comment whittles these lies into arrows of truth and shoots them back at the podium:

> King's corpse was not cold before blacks turned night into day. They knew that the bullet had killed a little of each of them. For ten days blacks "joined together" and "worked together" and the smoke from the purifying flames even drifted over the White House in huge, black billows (Lester, *Search for the New Land*, pp. 149–50).

We remember Douglass's definition of himself as a "bad sheep," his determination to live *"upon free land"* as well as "with Free- land," and his inversion of the master's proverb "give a nigger an inch and he will take an ell"; or Rinngold Ward's ironic refer- ence to his mother as his "dam," and William Wells Brown's memories of the "Republican whips" and "Democratic chains" of slavery.

This clash of opposing perspectives occurs also in the confrontation scenes with the "pigs" of the Oakland Police Department in *Seize the Time*. The scenes have the triple purpose of satirizing the "pig" image, demonstrating that police power can be fought, and reinforcing black pride. The ironies are numerous, many of them submerged below the surface of awareness. Both the "pigs" and Huey P. Newton are modeled on the traditional heroes of American folklore. The "pig" is the *reductio ad absurdum* of the old Western marshal, and Newton is a spiritual descendant of Denmark Vesey, Gabriel Prosser, Nat Turner, and Stagolee. In a scene where a "big beefy cop moved forward," unhooked his gun and made threatening gestures, Newton "walked right up to within a few feet of this fat pig" and challenged him to draw. When the cop made no response, Newton "jacked a round off into the chamber of his shotgun" and called him a "cowardly dog." The other five Panthers in the group were "spread out behind Huey." The cop eventually "let out a great big sigh and just hung his head." Another scene features a confrontation between a sheriff and a line of "brothers" holding guns. The sheriff took out his shotgun and "jacked a round off."

> Soon as the pig jacked that round off, Huey jacked a round off. And the brother next to Huey jacked a round off, and another brother jacked a round off, and another. And the only sound the pig heard was, clack-cup, clack-cup, clack-cup, clack-cup, clack-cup, clack-cup, clack-cup, right down the line. The sheriff looked at these Panthers jacking these rounds off, took his shotgun, ejected his round out of the chamber, locked his shotgun back up, got back in his car and drove away. That was the baddest set on the scene (Seale, pp. 128, 144).

The "pigs" of the Seale quotations are parodies of the gun-toting white chauvinist hero. The racism is inherent in their function: to carry out the orders of those in power, to defend "truth, justice, and the American Way" by policing the black and Indian community, to suppress resistance. The "pig" with the itchy finger feels challenged by the mere fact that Panther guns have put him on an equal footing with the blacks. Seale attempts to build Newton into a similar kind of hero, but one with whom black people can identify. The difference between the two images is to be sought in the social background of the confrontation. The white police are servants of an oppressive system, and the black rebels are resisting them. What makes Newton a criminal in the eyes of the "pigs" is precisely what makes him a servant of the people in the eyes of his supporters. It is significant, also, that the members of the black group stand up together, that Newton's action expresses a group solidarity. The policemen who challenge them are isolated at the critical moment. The "beefy cop" has nothing to fight for except "face," and perhaps his job. He retreats before determined adversaries who are fighting for their freedom. If he has to confront them, he would rather do so at a distance, from missile launching pads and air bases, with the National Guard waiting in the wings.

The language of the passage gives the guns a subdued sexual importance, particularly in the repetition of the word "jack off" for putting a shell in the chamber. The scene is freighted with meaning: the visible display of guns is an assertion, on the political level, of white society's failure to emasculate the black man psychologically. At the same time it evokes the myth of superior Negro sexual potency; the shotguns are a phallic taunt at white terror of the Negro male. There is much to be said against "armed confrontation" as a tactic between a young, weak party and the repressive power of the state,[3] but as a form of satire and psychological defense, the narrative of these scenes is a success.

The white sexual fear of the Negro is also an ironic theme in Lester and Rap Brown. As in the work of Seale, the object is not to deny the basis of the fear, but to mock the terrified whites, to rub their noses in their own myth. "Today they're talking about teaching sex in school. But that's white folks for you. They got to be taught to screw. . . . At the age when little white kids were finding out that there was something down there to play with, we knew where it went and what to do with it after it got there" (H. R. Brown, p. 30). Lester is deliberately graphic and colloquial in his language: "if there was anything which drove a cracker over the brink of insanity it was the thought of a big, black dick sliding in and out of a white pussy. (What the white female mind thought of the idea has not been recorded in the annals of history. And the white man is afraid for it to be" [Lester, *Search for the New Land*,

p. 35]). By pushing the myth into consciousness with a picture, Lester insists that white men deal with their "white problem," the nightmare which they try to suppress by their political suppression of blacks. "Is this what you feel threatened by?" says the tone; "then take a good look at it. You deserve to feel threatened."

In *Die Nigger Die* and *Search for the New Land*, there are attempts to experiment with new forms of irony. Rap Brown includes several pages of picture collages. The pictures, taken from national magazines, are arranged to bring out a contradiction of American society: the top of one page is an advertisement for wigs, showing Negro models who conform as closely as possible to the white ideal of feminine beauty. "Enjoy the light side of life. A whole new world has opened up to me." The bottom of the same page shows two older women with gray hair, a younger one with a blonde wig; they are crouching in a heap of rubble; the younger one holds a crying child (H. R. Brown, p. 7). On the inside covers, Lyndon Johnson's head is superimposed on the statue of liberty, Humphrey and Whitney Young are shaking hands and gloating down at a sidewalk full of black corpses, a white housewife is target-practicing with a pistol, and Westmoreland's picture is placed over a line of black girls in white formal gowns. There are also black and white cops in the background.

The "found poems" of Julius Lester are quotations from the news media set up as poetry on the page. In a sense, they are exercises in verbal irony on a grander scale; they take whole anecdotes, lift them out of the ruler's frame of reference, and give them the superimposed meaning of the ruled.

WINNING FRIENDS II

The United States Army
said today
that members of the

Fourth Psychological Operations Group
would soon begin handing out
small packages of
cigarettes,
each imprinted with a
propaganda message.

The 100,000 packages will be
distributed to
prisoners and detainees
during interrogation periods.
Teams will later pass out
the cigarettes
to Vietnamese
in
hamlets and villages.

Each package,
containing four cigarettes,
is imprinted with the Vietnamese-language abbreviations
for
the Republic of Vietnam.
The package wrappings are
red
and
yellow,
the colors of the South Vietnamese
flag.
The packages will be inscribed:
"The Government of Vietnam
cares for
its people."

(*The New York Times*—14 April 1968)

These passages encourage us to read newspapers with a different
attitude; but in the context of Lester's entire book, they are also
motifs in a symphonic score. The idea is to create a whole printed
structure that captures the historical process through selected
images, catalogs, newspaper clippings, essays, personal narrative,
some of the material arranged in parallel columns where the
two sides of the page comment on each other. The section entitled
"History of the World Since 1945" is a list of forty-seven wars. The
"poems" use the sources and statements of the enemy to expose
his weaknesses. "Winning Friends II" is nothing short of a study
in why the American military failed to win the support of the
Vietnamese; or to be more exact, why it was monstrous and hypo-

critical beyond words that they should have expected to win it.
Within the major irony of the Government of South Vietnam
distributing little love-and-kindness messages during interrogation
sessions (the "detainees" also having been bombed off their land
by ARVN helicopters) is the added irony that the gifts are a cancer-
inducing agent.

The satirical passages in *Manchild in the Promised Land* look at
the culture of Harlem from a child's point of view: the observer
is innocent, unable to see the larger significance of the details he
reports. The irony lies in the difference between the two under-
standings of child and adult, and between the conception of slum
life that might be held by a white social worker and the reality of the
black ghetto.

> This was the building where Mr. Lawson had killed a
> man for peeing in the hall. I remembered being afraid to
> go downstairs the morning after Mr. Lawson had busted
> that man's head open with a baseball bat. I could still
> see blood all over the hall. This was the building where
> somebody was always shooting out the windows in the
> hall. They were usually shooting at Johnny D., and they
> usually missed. This was the building that I loved more
> than anyplace else in the world. The thought that I would
> never see this building again scared the hell out of me.[4]

The usual reaction of the white middle class to slum conditions in
the black ghetto is pity, shock, disgust, perhaps fear for the children, or fear for themselves if they have to travel through the slum.[5]
The reaction of the child to the slum tenement is comic because
it is unexpected, but it also points up the vast distance between the
perceptions of middle-class whites and ghetto blacks, and the
powerlessness of liberal reform to solve the problem. If this environment is the child's only enjoyment and stimulation, and if
these are the adult roles he is given to imitate, then any talk of
"rehabilitating" ghetto youth in reform schools and penal institutions, or, for that matter, in new housing projects within the old
system, would probably be wasted breath, even if the schools and
clinics themselves were well run. The arrogance, blindness, and
condescension of the white power apparatus is represented by
the judge who first sent Claude Brown to a training school for boys,

explaining to his mother that "he knew what he was doing and that one day she would be grateful to him for doing it" (C. Brown, p. 16). But the true object of the satire, again, extends beyond the immediate experience of the child. The manchild did not create the Promised Land to which he has been subjected. It is white society that has created and that profits from the colonialized subculture of the black ghetto. The racism is built into the administrative machinery of the system; the black masses have little power to make it work for their benefit.

> When we got to court, the lawyer was already there. He spoke to Dad, and Dad yes-sirred him all over the place, kept looking kind of scared, and tried to make the man think he knew what he was talking about. When the lawyer came over to me and said, "Hello, Claude; how are you?" and shook my hand and smiled, I had the feeling that God had been kicked right out of heaven and the meek were lost. . . .
>
> When we went into the courtroom, the lawyer went up to where the judge was sitting and started talking to him. They seemed to be friends or something. Almost everybody there seemed to be friends—the bus driver, the other lawyer, the people from the bus company. The only ones who didn't seem to be friends with anybody was me and Dad. . . .
>
> While Dad and I were sitting there waiting for something to happen, I kept thinking about the time I saw a big black man take a little pig out of his pen at hog-killing time down South. He took the pig and tied him to a post, patted him on the back a couple of times, then picked up his ax and hit the pig in the head and killed him. The pig died without giving anybody any trouble, and the big black pig killer was happy. In fact, everybody was happy, because we were all friends and part of the family. The only one there who didn't have a friend was the pig (ibid., pp. 96–97).

Not only are the masses powerless to control the machine, but systematic discrimination in education has made it difficult for them even to understand the language of the administrators: "I couldn't understand what the judge and the lawyers were talking about; the words they were using were too big." The method and the beauty of the satire is to expose the social function of the courtroom through exact observation. The simplicity of the observer, who lacks the sophistication of his executioners but is also unencumbered by their values, penetrates straight through the rituals of the legal process to expose its support of corporate domination. This scene invites comparisons with the legal indictment quoted from the narrative of William and Ellen Craft in chapter two. The Crafts use the actual language of the legal process to parody it. Brown concentrates on the physical mannerisms and behavior of the lawyers and the judge. In both cases, the subject is the contradictions of white society. The chief contradiction in the example from Brown is between the friendly behavior of the judge, lawyers, and bus company officials, who are no doubt proud that even penniless Negroes can avail themselves of the trappings of American democracy and citizenship, and the true nature of what they are doing, which is seen and felt in naked aspect only by the victim.

The speaking voice in Cleaver's satire is not that of an innocent or unsophisticated observer, but of an angry, battle-scarred veteran victim of persecution who is aware of the context surrounding his imprisonment:

> I'm perfectly aware that I'm in prison, that I'm a Negro, that I've been a rapist, and that I have a Higher Uneducation. I never know what significance I'm supposed to attach to these factors. But I have a suspicion that, because of these aspects of my character, "free-normal-educated" people rather expect me to be more reserved, penitent, remorseful, and not too quick to shoot off my mouth on certain subjects. But I let them down, disappoint them, make them gape at me in a sort of stupor, as if they're thinking: "You've got your nerve! Don't you realize that you owe a debt to society?" My answer to all such thoughts lurking in their splitlevel heads, crouching behind their squinting bombardier eyes, is that the blood of Vietnamese peasants has paid off all my debts; that the Vietnamese people, afflicted with a

rampant disease called Yankees, through their sufferings
—as opposed to the "frustration" of fat-assed American
geeks safe at home worrying over whether to have bacon,
ham, or sausage with their grade-A eggs in the morning,
while Vietnamese worry each morning whether the
Yankees will gas them, burn them up, or blow away
their humble pads in a hail of bombs—have canceled all
my IOUs (Cleaver, *Soul on Ice*, p. 18).

Human brutality, hypocrisy, and selfishness are attacked here, but
they are manifestations of a class-race ethos rather than perennial
qualities of "human nature." The terms "split-level heads,"
"squinting bombardier eyes," "fat-assed American geeks," etc.,
direct the criticism specifically at social and political behavior. A
split-level head with bombardier eyes would value technical gadgets
and other commodities, that is, split-level ranches, bombers, and
bomb sights more than human life. The eyes squint at Cleaver
as though dropping bombs on him too, lining him up in the cross
hairs of scorn. A "fat-assed American geek" is someone from the
white middle class who is amused or fascinated by the oppressed as
though they were animals in the zoo.[6] What the "geeks" worry
about is juxtaposed with what the Vietnamese worry about to
illustrate the complicity of the former in imperialism. Cleaver is
rebelling against the dominant culture's concept of the prisoner's
"debt to society" by indicting society as a worse and more fundamental criminal. You cannot owe a debt of suffering to a murderer
who defines all resistance to himself as "crime." You can owe the
debt to the innocent human beings you have raped and robbed,
but their innocence is not represented by the authority which gases
and burns up the Vietnamese and bombs their humble pads. The
language represents the object of the satire as a political enemy. To
direct the satire at "the damned human race" would be to blur
the distinction between enemies and friends and thus imply an
altogether different kind of solution, or no solution at all. Cleaver's
course of action is to become rebellious, independent, radical, to
fight back against the white society's prison authorities. If the
problem is "human nature" on the other hand, then the enemy is
yourself, and the solution is the Beatles' "you better free your mind
instead."

> Both police and the armed forces follow orders. Orders.
> Orders flow from the top down. Up there, behind closed
> doors, in antechambers, in conference rooms, gavels
> bang on the tables, the tinkling of silver decanters can
> be heard as icewater is poured by well-fed, conservatively
> dressed men in horn-rimmed glasses, fashionably
> dressed American widows with rejuvenated faces and
> tinted hair, the air permeated with the square humor
> of Bob Hope jokes. Here all the talking is done, all the
> thinking, all the deciding. Gray rabbits of men scurry
> forth from the conference room to spread the decisions
> throughout the city, as News. Carrying out orders is a
> job, a way of meeting the payments on the house, a
> way of providing for one's kiddies. In the armed forces
> it is also a duty, patriotism. Not to do so is treason
> (Cleaver, *Soul on Ice*, p. 130).

Here the method is to look at the actual process of "following orders" through the eyes of one who is completely detached from and opposed to the mythology of "law and order" in a capitalist society. The repetition of "orders" as a single sentence draws attention to the concept. There is also a hint of parody. Orders. They "flow from the top down." Where is the top, and what is it? It is behind closed doors, at the top of the stairs, where the receivers of orders have no place, no access. It is a sterile class ethos of conservative dress, face lifts, hair dye, and square humor; the orders come from those who share a particular life-style, and, by implication, serve the interests of that life-style. The motives of those who follow orders, who are "only doing their job," are ridiculed by the sarcasm of "kiddies" and the context of the paragraph. Orders cause slaughter, massacre, bayonets shoved into bodies, napalm burning children to a crisp. That carrying out such orders could be called "a way of providing for one's kiddies" is an enormity thoroughly deserving of the comparison to Nazi Germany which it so often receives. Men who are only "gray rabbits" go about their methodical, respectable, routine "jobs" which have consequences they cannot even admit, much less comprehend.

Satire in black writing has always borne a close relationship to political speech. *Die Nigger Die* is full of racy anecdotes, humor, fiery invectives against the enemies of black liberation, and political jokes. Lyndon Johnson is a "big-eared, ugly, red-necked cracker" with ears so big if he wiggled them "he could fly." Humphrey is a "little red punk" who looks "madder than a pimp with dogshit on his shoe."

> If "the man" wanted to he could tell Black folks, "Bring me all the rocks you can find, and for every rock you bring, I will give you a million dollars." Bloods would bring rocks for days, little rocks, big rocks, rocks nobody knew existed. And, when the man got all the rocks, he'd tell Black folks, "We're using rocks for money."

> White man'll buy a watch for $5.00 sell it for $49.95 and call the difference, profit. Profit is a nice word for stealing which the society has legitimatized. Catholics go to church every week and gamble, but they call it Bingo. The Pope blesses 'em, so it's all right. The state of Nevada is built on a deck of cards and a roulette wheel, but that's okay, 'cause it's white folks that passed the law saying it was okay. But you let us get over in the corner of the alley with some dice and try to make a little profit and here come the police, the judge, the jailer and the sociology student (H. R. Brown, p. 140, 18).

The language of the passage on Johnson and Humphrey pulls them down off their "high horse" in effigy and makes them equal. It dispels the mystique of office by cutting directly through it with a series of colloquial insults; the images expose the politicians' real attitudes, just as Claude Brown's metaphor of the pig and the pig-killer takes the legalistic mask away from the courtroom proceedings. The paragraph also resembles the black folk custom of "playing the Dozens" as explained by Rap Brown elsewhere in his book (ibid., p. 26): "The Dozens is a mean game because what you try to do is totally destroy somebody else with words. . . . If you fell all over each other laughing, then you knew you'd scored. . . . America, however, has Black folk in a serious game of the Dozens." To actually play the Dozens with the politicians, therefore, is simply to name America's game, to toss aside the pretences and bring it out into the open.

The humor involves the application of some familiar ghetto experience or idiom to describe the respectable, highly serious, exalted
and ritualistic processes of robbery, murder, and arrogance in
the white world. By using the folk illustration ("a pimp with
dogshit on his shoe," "we're using rocks for money," "let us get over
in the corner of the alley with some dice") the writer is demonstrating that the complexities of the system are perfectly intelligible
to the ghetto "folk," even though the words used by the judges,
lawyers, and politicians may be "too big." To include the sociology
student in an itemization of the usual repressive apparatus of the
state provokes laughter because it is seemingly incongruous, an
unexpected insight, an exposure of the political bias behind
knowledge-gathering in this society. In large part, the humor is
exultation at seeing through a fraud, at not being fooled. The joke
is on the frauds.

But in political satire, laughter is always with a tight mouth, and
humor shifts quickly to furious anger; for discrimination, starvation, lying, murder, and robbery are not funny. The joke is in
the twists and turns which the profit-mongers go through to avoid
confronting their deeds and in that shared moment when everyone
realizes that the emperor has no clothes. But when the subject
changes to the deeds themselves, then ridicule is apt to change—
appropriately—to brooding epithet. In the letters of George Jackson, every epithet aimed at the ruling class seems charged with
regret that it was not a softnose .45 caliber bullet.

He calls the white boss a "colonizer, a usurer, the original thief,
a murderer for personal gain, a kidnapper-slaver, a maker of can-
non, bombs, and poison gas, an egocentric parasite, the original
fork tongue," a "fat rat," a "flea" who richly deserves to die for
his crimes (Jackson, pp. 96, 35, 176, 203).

The emotion behind these statements is frank hatred. But it is
given form and purpose, made useful, controlled by intelligence. A
man with a lifetime of reasons to feel hate, he was able to direct
it where it belonged and where it would be most likely to change
something. "I would permit no man, no matter what his colour
might be," said Booker T. Washington, "to narrow and degrade
my soul by making me hate him" (Washington, p. 165). But it
is hard to feel that hate did anything more degrading to Jackson's
soul than purge it of the colonizer. He could have helped the

prison authorities to heal his wounded spirit by breaking it, in which case he might have renounced hate, rebellion, integrity, and independence, "won the victory over himself," to quote Orwell; and his parole board would have seen, in the fact that he could not look them in the eye, that he was "rehabilitated" and it was time to let him out.

When black satire trains its guns on other black people, the result is usually different from the self-agonizing and breast-beating of *Mother Night, God Bless You, Mr. Rosewater,* and *The Mysterious Stranger.* As a rule, there is no assumption that all human beings are corrupt and everything we do to change society ends in tyranny, absurdity, and pathetic defeat. The satirist perceives corrupt blacks as agents or dupes of white society, obstacles to the struggle, traitors to black unity. They are doing what the white man wants them to do. They have an alternative in the black movement. In Twain and Vonnegut, on the other hand, there is no alternative except the tenuously bracing and alienated medicine of laughter. As Malcolm X writes:

> I'd guess that eight out of ten of the Hill Negroes of Roxbury, despite the impressive-sounding job titles they affected, actually worked as menials and servants. "He's in banking," or "He's in securities." It sounded as though they were discussing a Rockefeller or a Mellon—and not some gray-headed, dignity-posturing bank janitor, or bond-house messenger. "I'm with an old family" was the euphemism used to dignify the professions of white folks' cooks and maids who talked so affectedly among their own kind in Roxbury that you couldn't even understand them. I don't know how many forty- and fifty-year-old errand boys went down the Hill dressed like ambassadors in black suits and white collars, to down-town jobs "in government," "in finance," or "in law."
>
> ... I was measured, and the young salesman picked off a rack a zoot suit that was just wild: sky-blue pants thirty inches in the knee and angle-narrowed down to twelve inches at the bottom, and a long coat that pinched my waist and flared out below my knees.
>
> As a gift, the salesman said, the store would give me a

narrow leather belt with my initial "L" on it. Then he said
I ought to also buy a hat, and I did—blue, with a feather
in the four-inch brim. Then the store gave me another
present: a long, thick-linked, gold-plated chain that
swung down lower than my coat hem. I was sold forever
on credit (Malcolm X, pp. 41, 52).

These passages are focused on black characters, but their real
object is white values and exploitation. The black maids, cooks,
janitors, and messengers unconsciously parody the white image of
success by attempting to apply it to their own lives, where it has
no reality. The hollowness of the image is underscored by its total
irrelevance to the needs of the people who emulate it and depends
for its realization on the exploitation and self-deception of the
black servants, who then manifest its social function all the more
clearly by acting out the success myth in relation to other Negroes.

The passage in which Malcolm buys his first zoot suit is somewhat more indirect. The last sentence, "I was sold forever on credit,"
makes the description of the suit ironic as well as ridiculous; for,
besides being oppressed culturally by "fashions" styled by white
merchants for sale in the black ghettoes, the narrator, paying for the
privilege at inflated prices and interest, considers himself lucky
to have the chance. There is also a verbal irony in the word "sold,"
with its heavy connotations of fraud. Why did Malcolm submit
to being sold? He was not born stupid, but "brainwashed." "I had
joined that multitude of Negro men and women in America who
are brainwashed into believing that the black people are 'inferior'—
and white people 'superior'—that they will even violate and muti-
late their God-created bodies to try to look 'pretty' by white
standards" (ibid., p. 54). He is an innocent victim of capitalism.
Like traders carrying beads, trinkets, and gaily colored cloth as a
cover for stealing the land and labor of Africa, the white stores
deliberately sell him a racist image as a status symbol and will then
use his appearance to justify and reinforce the colonialized position
of his people.

The style is also a proud rejection of this self-deceptive posturing,
a sign that the "brain-washing" can be neutralized and the trader
driven out if the victims will only open their eyes to his game,
take pride in the identity God has given them.

Claude Brown is much less explicit in his projection of alternatives than Malcolm X, but when he satirizes blacks, the blame for their vices leads back to the white system. The language of heroin users in this passage functions to deceive them into complying with their own destruction; the slang places a social value on the drug. The ultimate source of the traffic, however, is not the ghetto. The outside suppliers exploit the ignorance and powerlessness of the users for money.

> I think everybody up there had the feeling it was time to
> move on. It was time to stop smoking reefers and stop
> drinking wine; it was time to start getting high. They
> were snorting this horse, and this horse was making them
> bend; it was making them itch and nod and talk in
> heavier voices. It made you sound like a real gangster
> or like a real old cat. And everybody wanted to sound
> old (C. Brown, p. 104).

But while they build the idea that heroin is "cool," the terms "horse," "snort," "bend," "itch," "nod," "old," tell the literal truth of what it does; and so the "cool" atmosphere surrounding drug usage is made sinister and threatening by the same terms that seem to make it attractive. It is a plague in disguise, a white plague from beyond the ghetto walls.

All satire has the general purpose of exposing, and if possible, correcting human follies. In addition, it serves to carve out an island of dignity for the satirist, where he can sweep away the chatter of the market place and build a sane, harmonious life. What black satire adds to this purpose is a clear vision of the human follies peculiar to North American history. Stranded in a hostile continent where two standards of morality prevail, one for whites and another for blacks, the black writer cannot carve an island of dignity without support from his brothers and sisters. To live on it alone is unthinkable. He cannot correct human follies without attacking the hostile standard for virtue. And he cannot do this without taking sides in a class-race conflict. He thus becomes an instrument for the prisoners to make their way out of the tomb.

Chapter 13 *History as subjective experience*

T is one thing to be "inside history," and another to live history inside the self, to pump blood and oxygen through its facts across the placenta of your personal concerns. The past is the womb that contains us; the future is the history we contain in the seeds of our individuality, the embryo that we must bring to birth with our actions. Full consciousness of both is necessary if the truer and better self is to awaken, and another world be born. The language of modern black autobiography is a heroic effort to make the individual a meeting place for the past and future. When the meeting succeeds, the result, expressed concisely by the subtitle of Lester's *Search for the New Land*, is "history as subjective experience."

The long shadow of the slave narrative still falls across this meeting place. Whenever the terrain resembles the wilderness of slavery, the achievements of the narrative are on hand like special equipment for wilderness travel, which the writer may take out and refurbish according to his needs. The *Autobiography of Malcolm X* uses approximately the same form. The progression of events is familiar: the gradual realization of the limitations imposed on the narrator by the white world, the accumulated resentment and hostility toward white condescension and racism, the desire for economic independence, the flight to a Northern city, the discovery of a system of ideas that gives him a vision of the road to freedom, and the active participation in organizations that fight for the interests of black people. The slave narrative tradition adopts a particular stance toward this pattern in which the author's life is treated as an object lesson, and his role in the book is to use himself as the text of a sermon; he is a minister or teacher, demonstrating how the moral and political obstacles he faced can be overcome by others in the same circumstance. "I have given to this book so much of whatever time I have because I feel, and I hope, that if I honestly and fully tell my life's account, read objectively it might prove to be a testimony of some social value" (Malcolm X, p. 378).

In keeping with his objective, Malcolm X tells his story as though it were a moral parable. Each separate incident has a message for the reader; the first part of the paragraph, commonly, presents the incident, and the second part draws the lesson:

> He had on a big Army overcoat. He took that off, and I kept laughing and said he still had on too many. I was able to keep that cracker stripping off clothes until he stood there drunk with nothing on from his pants up, and the whole car was laughing at him, and some other soldiers got him out of the way. I went on. I never would forget that—that I couldn't have whipped that white man as badly with a club as I had with my mind.

> I heard the usual hustler fates of so many others. Bullets, knives, prison, dope, diseases, insanity, alcoholism. I imagine it was about in that order. . . . I was thankful to Allah that I had become a Muslim and escaped their fate (ibid., pp. 77, 216).

There are dozens of examples of how Malcolm's role as a "messenger of Allah" informs the structure and direction of the book, in the same way that Pennington and Ward designed their autobiographies to teach the gospel of antislavery as messengers of the true Christ. Malcolm's message is as unsparing of himself as of white society. As an adolescent, he had seduced and abandoned a girl named Laura, who later became a "wreck of a woman," a drunkard, prostitute, and lesbian; Malcolm blamed himself for this, offering only the excuse that "like so many of my black brothers today, I was just deaf, dumb, and blind" (ibid., p. 68). But the chief object of the message is the white man, because he is the one who needs it most: "It was right there in prison that I made up my mind to devote the rest of my life to telling the white man about himself—or die" (ibid., p. 185).

The Christian religious rhetoric of the slave narrative is echoed sometimes in Malcolm's Muslim imagery: Mr. Muhammad is a "little humble lamb of a man," whose teachings cut back and forth like a "two-edged sword" from his mouth "to free the black man's mind from the white man" (ibid., p. 211). Even fainter Christian echoes are heard in Lester, when he sits "among the graves" and weeps "for those who saw the Promised Land and did not know that even the birds cannot fly there" (Lester, *Search for the New Land*, p. 190). And the final chapter of *Soul on Ice*, after the most abstract excursions into political and psychological theory, returns to Biblical and Promised-Land allusions; a completely appropriate ending, because it is at this point that Cleaver's new identity steps forth, cleansed of his mental enslavement to the "white witch." The language enlarges that identity by placing him inside the traditions stemming from the slave narratives.

But the slave rhetoric that proved the hardiest plant, that contemporary black writers have found most useful to their own needs, is the rhetoric of the American Revolution and the Declaration of Independence. Dick Gregory's recording, *The Light Side, the Dark Side*, refers to the Declaration as the document that America forgot to label "white only"; he advises young people to turn off the sound when TV newsreels of black riots are shown, and read the Declaration aloud to their parents. In *Seize the Time*, the legal and ideological basis of the Panther gun patrols is the Constitution. The Black Panther ten-point program incorporates part of the Declaration into its statement of objectives. The same rhetoric merges unobtrusively with the personal voice in this passionate letter of Jackson to his father, in which he is defending his revolutionary convictions:

> At each phase of this long train of tyrannies, we have conducted ourselves in a very meek and civilized manner, with only polite pleas for justice and moderation, all to no avail. We have shown a noble indisposition to react with the passion that each new oppression engenders. But any fool should be able to see that this cannot be allowed to continue. Any fool should be able to see that nature allows no such imbalances as this to exist for long. We have petitioned for judicial redress. We have remonstrated, supplicated, demonstrated, and prostrated ourselves before the feet of our self-appointed administrators. We have done all that we can do to circumvent the

eruption that now comes on apace. The point of no
return in our relationship has long been passed (Jackson,
pp. 62–63).

Here the Declaration impels the mode of expression as well as the
ideological content. The fact that this is a private letter rather than
a public manifesto indicates that the narrator defines his rebellion
to himself in these terms; the rhetoric has been assimilated into
his way of thinking about who and what he is.

Like the slave narratives, the contemporary works must take on
the job of articulating black thought, life, and feeling to a general
public. The descriptions of black life in the recent books closely
resemble the descriptions of slave life in the old ones: what it
feels like to rot in a jail cell, what happens in the normal prison
routine, what ghetto existence is like on the day-to-day level, what
"police brutality" means, are subjects which parallel what it was
like to pick cotton, fix railings, take a whipping, wear chains, and
get sold on the auction block. They serve to show how little has
changed in the basic quality of the black man's experience with
white society. Cleaver, for example, tells us that "each cell has a
small sink with a cold-water tap, a bed, a locker, a shelf or two along
the wall, and a commode"; his cell door "is a solid slab of steel
with fifty-eight holes in it about the size of a half dollar, and a slot
in the center . . . (Cleaver, *Soul on Ice*, p. 41). Jackson gives detailed
accounts of what happens when the guards raid the prisoners'
cells in search of contraband. Bobby Seale's description of the
court's attempt to gag him during the trial of the Chicago 8 should
be juxtaposed with William Wells Brown's account of the taming
of Randall in chapter two of this book. The guards held Seale's
nose, "set the wad of rags right up against my lips and began to
press real hard. . . ." He could feel the blood "seeping out of my
gums" and "the inside of my lips busting, because . . . I was holding
out as hard as I could" (Seale, p. 344).

Seale, Cleaver, and Jackson, the writers who have known first-
hand the terror of the American prison system, use a language that
fits their experience like a skin. Nouns of punishment, force,
fighting, and command, strong, simple verbs that refer to clubbing
and maiming the human body, stand out like clenched fists in a
matrix of low-keyed analytical sentences:

You must begin with directors, assistant directors, adult authority boards, roving boards, supervisors, wardens, captains, and guards. You have to examine these people from director down to guard before you can logically examine their product. Add to this some concrete and steel, barbed wire, rifles, pistols, clubs, the tear gas that killed Brother Billingslea in San Quentin in February 1970 while he was locked in his cell, and the pick handles of Folsom, San Quentin, and Soledad.

He came to visit me when I was in San Quentin. He was in his forties then too, an age in men when they have grown full. I had decided to reach for my father, to force him with my revolutionary dialectic to question some of the mental barricades he'd thrown up to protect his body from what to him was an undefinable and omnipresent enemy. An enemy that would starve his body, expose it to the elements, chain his body, jail it, club it, rip it, hang it, electrify it, and poison-gas it. I would have him understand that although he had saved his body he had done so at a terrible cost to his mind. I felt that if I could superimpose the explosive doctrine of self-determination through people's government and revolutionary culture upon what remained of his mind, draw him out into the real world, isolate and identify his real enemies, if I could hurl him through Fanon's revolutionary catharsis, I would be serving him, the people, the historical obligation (Jackson, pp. 23–24, 181).

The second passage of Jackson is a beautiful synthesis of narrative, polemic, love, terror, power, and gentleness. The ideological metaphors purge his love for his father of unexamined sentimentality: "force him . . . to question some of the mental barricades . . . draw him out into the real world, isolate and identify his real enemies, if I could hurl him through Fanon's revolutionary catharsis. . . ." Words like "hurl," "starve," "chain," "reach," "hang," transmit their energy to "self-determination," "superimpose," "revolutionary culture," "historical obligation." The maiming words reflect real events and immediate threats at the same time that the political abstractions interpret their long-range context.

A moment of intimacy is placed on the crossroads of past and future, as was Wright's final meeting with his father in *Black Boy*. Jackson tries to make that moment mean something beyond an affectionate impulse; he transforms it into a reality where serving the individual and "serving the people" do not exclude each other, where the personal redemption of his father will be a step in the historical redemption of the wretched of the earth. The language reinterprets the sentiment of love, giving it a social and political range quite beyond popular Western culture, in which "love" is most often fantasized as a withdrawal from society, a loyalty excluding the rest of humanity, or an island of infantile gratification combined with self-abasing service to a single individual.

In describing a guard raid on the prisoners' cells, Jackson links the police function at home with the military function in Vietnam; the prison by implication becomes a field of common interest between the prisoners and the Viet Cong.

> San Quentin was in the riot season. It was early January 1967. The pigs had for the last three months been on a search-and-destroy foray into our cells. All times of the day or night our cells were being invaded by the goon squad: you wake up, take your licks, get skin-searched, and wait on the tier naked while they mangle your few personal effects (ibid., p. 181).

The term "search-and-destroy" builds the bridge between Vietnam and San Quentin, together with the actual resemblance of what the "goon squad" is doing to what American troops do when they raid suspected Viet Cong villages or interrogate "detainees."

Seize the Time is most forceful in its images of the people's resistance to the power of the police. Besides the verbs of physical struggle, such as "grab," "push," "kick," "shove," there is a preoccupation with the sound and feel of weapons. The slave narratives set a precedent for this characteristic in their accounts of various whips, belts, chains, and clubs and how they were handled for the maximum terrorizing effect on the slave.

> At the same time I was pulling the shotgun away from him, Huey grabbed this pig by the collar, pushed his head back up against the roof of the car, then shifted around

and got his foot and kicked him in the belly, shoving
him all the way out of the car. The pig fell backwards
about ten feet from the car but as he was going out, no
sooner had Huey finished putting his foot in this pig's
belly, kicking and pushing him out of the car—and the
pig was being propelled and off balance, away from the
car—than Huey was grabbing hold of the barrel of the
shotgun. No sooner did brother Huey's feet hit the
ground, but he was jacking a round off into the chamber,
"Clack upp," and taking three quick steps (Seale, p. 95).

This scene contains no conscious appeal to history, but it bears the
handwriting of the past as clearly as a child might preserve the
shape of his grandfather's nose. The bad sheep stands up to the
master with liberty or death in his hand: "At last I caught hold of
the stick," John Thompson had written of a battle with his overseer, "wrenched it from his hands, struck him over the head, and
knocked him down, after which I choked him until he was as
black as I am."

Cleaver's language reminds us that words of political analysis can
get up and walk across the page:

The police department and the armed forces are the two
arms of the power structure, the muscles of control and
enforcement. They have deadly weapons with which to
inflict pain on the human body. They know how to bring
about horrible deaths. They have clubs with which to
beat the body and the head. They have bullets and guns
with which to tear holes in the flesh, to smash bones, to
disable and kill. They use force, to make you do what
the deciders have decided you must do (Cleaver, *Soul on
Ice*, p. 128).

In the process of charging the paragraph with active verbs like
"inflict," "beat," "tear," "smash," "disable," "kill," he transfuses
unexpected life into the standby word "do." Ordinarily a mere
auxiliary, "do" in this context takes on some of the energy of the
verbs that precede it. "Do" means specifically the act to which you
are driven by the threat of beating, tearing, smashing, and dis-
abling. The language also strips the pretensions away from the

function of the police. Compare the above passage to this typical statement of the objectives of a college "criminal justice" curriculum:

> The programs in Criminal Justice are designed to educate men and women to work thoughtfully and effectively in various law enforcement, correctional and crime prevention or control programs in the State of Vermont, or elsewhere as they may choose, or upon graduation seek some other role in society fortified with a broader understanding and deeper appreciation of the legislative constraints under which they may live.[1]

Language concentrates politics here by providing the primary form for class values; the wording is a social relation and a vehicle of class identity. It is clear which author views things from the receiving end of "correctional and crime prevention or control programs" and which author views them from the administering end. The statement of curriculum objectives does not contain a single word that refers to a concrete fact. Its purpose, indeed, is to disguise and rationalize facts; the language is emotionally neutral, innocuous, academic, and therefore hypocritical as a statement of objectives, because there is nothing neutral about the reality behind it; whereas Cleaver's purpose, and his contribution, is to reveal facts. The brutality of the deed is to find a corresponding brutality in the word. The thing is named for what it is. "I think all of us, the entire nation, will be better off if we bring it all out front" (Cleaver, *Soul on Ice*, p. 17).

Colloquial language, ghetto idioms, and brutal candor are also means of rebellion against the language of social scientists, social workers, counselors, and corporate bureaucrats. The fact that white administrators can refer to a convict as a "resident," and a prison as a "crime prevention and control program," indicates what black writers object to in white definitions, and why they consider the mainstream culture to be effete and sterile. The use of ghetto idioms is an effort to renew English, to discover an English which has not been totally corrupted by lies, and thus redeem political discourse from meaninglessness and obscenity. The meaning of "telling it like it is," before this phrase, too, became obscene by constant hypocritical usage in white media, was not only to uncover the bitter truth, but to transmute language through the mouths and pens of the only people who can afford, *as a group*, to speak the truth: the oppressed, the enslaved, the sufferers, the propertyless, the convicts.

Emerson and Thoreau, too, had wanted to regenerate the word by making it one with the thing and invite the muddy boots of street talk into literature's drawing rooms. To accomplish this, they knew that they had to listen to railroad workers, blacksmiths, raftsmen, and lumberjacks. Black polemicists may be clearing the ground in a similar manner for a new period of literary greatness. But whether or not it has a permanent effect on literature, ghetto language here and elsewhere gives a solid backbone of experience to the political ideas of the narrators. It emphasizes how those ideas are forced on them by their living conditions; they are tools in the fight for survival.

The language is also one of the means by which the narrator constructs a black identity in his autobiography. "To be Black in this country is to be a nigger," Rap Brown said, in distinguishing between Black and Negro. "To be a nigger is to resist both white and negro death. It is to be free in spirit, if not body." Ghetto idioms therefore function as a sign of membership in the black community, in the brotherhood of those who resist. "It's no secret that in America the blacks are in total rebellion against the System. They want to get their nuts out of the sand" (Cleaver, p. 134).

Malcolm X seems to adjust his colloquialisms according to which stage of his life he is relating. In the early part of the *Autobiography*, ghetto slang is used to create a gestalt of his career as a hustler and to display his moral authority as a regenerated sinner offering leadership to others like him:

> Shorty would take me to groovy, frantic scenes in different chicks' and cats' pads, where with the lights and juke down mellow, everybody blew gage and juiced back and jumped. I met chicks who were fine as May wine, and cats who were hip to all happenings.
> That paragraph is deliberate, of course; it's just to display a bit more of the slang that was used by everyone I respected as "hip" in those days.

Later the language shifts to Muslim rhetoric, shaped by Malcolm's personal eloquence and magnetism.

As they had in the slave narratives, the political speech, the sermon, and the oration animate the contemporary styles—old spirits drawn to the new voices by the urgency of the occasion.

> It's a crime, the lie that has been told to generations of black men and white men both. Little innocent black children, born of parents who believed that their race had no history. Little black children seeing, before they could talk, that their parents considered themselves inferior. Innocent black children growing up, living out their lives, dying of old age—and all of their lives ashamed of being black. But the truth is pouring out of the bag now.

> "*Think* of it—think of that black slave man filled with fear and dread, hearing the screams of his wife, his mother, his daughter being *taken*—in the barn, the kitchen, in the bushes! *Think* of it, my dear brothers and sisters! *Think* of hearing wives, mothers, daughters, being *raped*! And you were too filled with *fear* of the rapist to do anything about it! And his vicious, animal attacks' offspring, this white man named things like 'mulatto' and 'quadroon' and 'octoroon' and all those other things that he called us—you and me—when he is not calling us 'nigger'!"

> "The Honorable Elijah Muhammad teaches us that since Western society is deteriorating, it has become overrun with immorality, and God is going to judge it, and destroy it. And the only way the black people caught up in this society can be saved is not to *integrate* into this corrupt society, but to *separate* from it, to a land of our *own*, where we can reform ourselves, lift up our moral standards, and try to be godly. The Western world's most learned diplomats have failed to solve this grave race problem. Her learned legal experts have failed. Her sociologists have failed. Her civil leaders have failed. Her fraternal leaders have failed. Since all of these have

failed to solve this race problem, it is time for us to sit
down and *reason*! I am certain that we will be forced to
agree that it takes *God Himself* to solve this grave racial
dilemma" (Malcolm X, pp. 181, 202, 246).

The first passage, taken from Malcolm's text, differs very little in
tone and style from the second two, which are quoted from his
speeches. In keeping with his objective to make the truth pour out
of the bag, the main effort of passages one and two is to re-create
for his listeners the visible impact of the indignities they have been
made to suffer. Referring to Thomas Merton, a Trappist monk
and social critic, Cleaver wrote that he had only to read Merton's
essay on the racist oppression of Harlem "to become once more a
rigid flame of indignation" (Cleaver, *Soul on Ice*, p. 35). The
intention of Malcolm X's rhetoric is to produce that reaction in the
audience; to flush the racism of the whites out to the surface, and
steel the determination of the blacks to resist. "Malcolm talked
shit, and talking shit is the iron in a young nigger's blood. Malcolm
mastered language and used it as a sword to slash his way through
the veil of lies that for four hundred years gave the white man the
power of the word."[2]

The methods of Malcolm's language were also used by Ward,
Thompson, and Douglass. In the sequence of clauses beginning
"little innocent black children," the three sentences elaborate on
each of the three adjectives modifying "children." In the first
sentence, the indignity centers around being black: it is because
they are black that their history has been concealed. In the second,
the indignity is centered around being little, because they are too
young to protect themselves from the belief of their parents
that they are inferior. In the third, the locus of the bitterness is
the word "innocent," which connotes both ignorance and guiltless-
ness: all their lives the children, through no fault of their own,
are ignorant of the truth that could free them. The parallelism
enables the clauses to resonate backward and forward. The word
"black" is repeated each time, stressing the reason for all the
indignities—racism.

Passages two and three achieve emphasis by suggesting in print
the tone of the spoken voice. In the third, the repeated italicized
words, "think," "taken," "raped," "fear," "nigger," contain the

main idea of the speech. The parallel clauses proceed by elaborating and extending that idea, adding extra detail with each repetition and providing variety within a set rhythmic pattern. The stressed words in the fourth example do the same thing: "integrate," "separate," "own," "failed," "reason," "God Himself" are the anchors of the paragraph. Besides emphasizing the main idea, they also carry the tone of the voice, modulating between reason and anger, urgent talk and shouting. Short, parallel repetitive sentences again elaborate the central theme; "The Western world's most learned diplomats have failed. . . . Her learned legal experts have failed. Her sociologists have failed. Her civil leaders have failed. Her fraternal leaders have failed. Since all of these have *failed* to solve this race problem. . . ." The advantage of parallel structures and repetition in an oral speech, besides holding the attention of the audience and insuring that they respond to the point, is that the speaker need not be at a loss for words. Extemporaneous speech and extemporaneous music (blues and jazz, for example) both have in common the technique of variation on a single basic pattern. Instead of having to lapse into silence while he gropes for a new pattern, the speaker or musician can extend, invert, or punctuate the old one, increasing or decreasing its tempo and volume. The word "failed" is the basic pattern in the preceding series; in the first five sentences, the subjects would be stressed, and the voice would drop slightly on the verb, thus highlighting the list of personages. In the final sentence, the voice would rise, putting stress on the verb as the conclusion of the list.

Malcolm's rhetoric is thus fairly typical of black expression. We have noted the resemblance between the syntax of Langston Hughes and the black music that he admired and imitated. Dick Gregory's recording, "The Light Side, The Dark Side," carries along certain refrains, such as "you youngsters got a big job," "we tired of these white insults," that his jokes and anecdotes illuminate. This excerpt from a Stokely Carmichael speech exemplifies the technique of refrain and repetition varied by the voice:

> Now you've got to be crystal clear on how you think and
> where you move. You've got to explain to people. I didn't
> go to Mississippi to fight anybody to sit next to them. I
> was fighting to get them off my back. That's what my fight

is. That's what my fight is. I don't fight anybody to sit
next to him. I don't want to sit next to them. I just
want them to get the barriers out of my way. Because I
don't want to sit next to Jim Clark, Eastland, Johnson,
Humphrey, or none of the others. I just want them to get
off my back. Get off my back.[3]

In Malcolm X, the modulations of his speaking voice also impel
his writing voice. The tone is the same; "isn't" and "victims" are
italicized; the key idea is repeated within parallel and inverted
forms.

Cleaver's writing bears the mark of the same oral tradition:

In America everything is owned. Everything is held as
private property. Someone has a brand on everything.
There is nothing left over. Until recently, the blacks themselves were counted as part of somebody's private
property, along with the chickens and goats. The blacks
have not forgotten this, principally because they are
still treated as if they are part of someone's inventory of
assets—or perhaps, in this day of rage against the costs of
welfare, blacks are listed among the nation's liabilities.
On any account, however, blacks are in no position to
respect or help maintain the institution of private property. What they want is to figure out a way to get some
of that property for themselves, to divert it to their own
needs. This is what it is all about, and this is the real
brutality involved. This is the source of all brutality
(Cleaver, *Soul on Ice*, p. 134).

And Rap Brown's:

America's a bitch. Being Black in this country is like
somebody asking you to play white Russian roulette and
giving you a gun with bullets in all the chambers. Any way
you go, jim, that's your ass. America says you got to have
money to live and to get money you got to have a job. To
get a job, you got to have an education. So along comes
a Black man and he gets a worse than inferior education
so he can't qualify for a job he couldn't get because he was
Black to begin with and still he's supposed to eat, keep his

family together, pay the rent and buy an Oldsmobile. And white folks wonder why niggers steal and gamble. I only wish we would stop this petty stealing and take care of Chase Manhattan Bank, Fort Knox or some armories (H. R. Brown, p. 19).

And Seale's:

I cussed Colonel King out for what he was. I cussed him all the way down the streets. I had a whole big crowd of cats jiving and watching me cuss him out while they were taking me down in front of the barracks and all the way back across the lawn in front of the squadron head-quarters. They put me in a truck and I was still cussing him. I cussed him all the way across. Then I blotted them all out. I just forgot about them. And they put me in jail (Seale, p. 11).

And Jackson's:

This camp brings out the very best in brothers or destroys them entirely. But none are unaffected. None who leave here are normal. If I leave here alive, I'll leave nothing behind. They'll never count me among the broken men, but I can't say that I am normal either. I've been hungry too long. I've gotten angry too often. I've been lied to and insulted too many times. They've pushed me over the line from which there can be no retreat. I *know* that they will not be satisfied until they've pushed me out of this existence altogether. I've been the victim of so many racist attacks that I could never relax again. My reflexes will never be normal again. I'm like a dog that has gone through the K-9 process (Jackson, p. 32).

And Lester's:

So the first time some cracker let you know that he thought you were a low-down dirty good-for-nothing no-count black-ass nigger, you were ready and just lay back and waited and one night, one of them hot-ass mutha-fucking nights when if cactus grew in the ghetto it would get up and go look for shade, one of them kind of nights

> when you knew the devil had turned on the air condition-
> ing, one of them nights when you bounced a ball on
> the sidewalk and it didn't bounce back but just lay there
> and melted, one of them nights when a cop stopped some
> black man for doing something and somebody, nobody
> ever knows who the hero is, says, "Man, I'm sick and tired
> of this shit!" and the cop, who had arrested five hundred
> niggers single-handed the week before and nothing had
> happened, looked up and saw a brick coming down on
> him that looked like it was as big as the moon and as
> he ducked, his prisoner jerked away and ran down the
> street and just as the cop reached for his gun, his motion
> was halted by the delicious sound of a big plate-glass
> window breaking and that was it! The shit had hit the
> fan and those who had been without were about to get.
> The sound of windows breaking doesn't carry around the
> world, but it travels mighty fast throughout the ghetto
> and following the religious commandment of BLESSED IS
> HE WHO TAKES WHAT HE WANTS AND DON'T FORGET TO
> DUCK, the people go shopping (Lester, *Search for the New
> Land*, p. 119).

Repetition, parallelism, loose sentences with dramatic pauses that
build toward a climax, and variations of a single pattern are all
there, generated from the political speech, the sense of talking
directly to an audience which the speakers are trying to arouse. But
each sample still has the ring of an individual voice; they are like
different members of the same family, all of whom give back the
general impression of their parents' features but combine them
differently in each case for a unique result.

The indignation of Malcolm X has a strong moral and intellectual slant; he chooses the pejorative word "crime," for example,
to describe the children's ignorance of black history; he emphasizes
the white man's sexual degeneracy, recalling the scenes from slavery
that inspire the most vivid moral and psychological horror; the
chief focus of his criticism is the white man's *historical* treatment
of black people, which must be evoked vicariously through the
images of rape, whereas the focus of the Panthers is more likely
to be the immediate experience of police brutality and suppression.

Malcolm's tone is highly serious and didactic, even prophetic, when he speaks of the doom God has planned for white civilization; he assumes the role of a Jeremiah. In listing the various experts of the West who have failed to solve the racist problem, he is addressing himself as a leader to a world community of leaders, condemning their ignorance and offering advice to correct their mistakes. His attitude toward the "sincere" whites is similar; he is a teacher with a lesson, demanding that his pupils change before it is too late. His voice is individualized by the stress patterns, which give the impression of inspired fervor, as of a minister with a message.

The focus of Cleaver's attack is not moral, but political and economic (the difference being a question of emphasis). The source of brutality is to be found in the institution of private property. He justifies assaults on property on the grounds that blacks have always been excluded from this institution; and, by implication, he identifies with the black so-called "criminal" who would walk into a bank with a gun and clean out the vault. Like Proudhon, he believes that property is theft. Malcolm X, on the other hand, tended to assume that the "racist problem," as he correctly designated it, stems in the first instance from white moral corruption and ignorance, and that the propertyless condition of blacks was a moral question. Cleaver's tone balances between anger and humor. The anger is serious, but the tone mocks and parodies the idea of property as a social value by repeating it in different contexts. He pauses to explore the satiric possibilities in the metaphor of inventory and cost. Each of the short sentences at the beginning, by repeating the idea of ownership, asks the reader to meditate on its ironies. What kind of order can be expected of a society where "someone has a brand on everything?" If there is "nothing left over," how and where are black people going to get "some of that property for themselves" except by taking it? The high moral plane of Malcolm's voice called attention to how far behind he had left his old pre-Muslim identity: he was in effect looking both ways —at his "brainwashed brothers and sisters" and at the guilty leaders of white society, both of whom he was urging to change. Cleaver's voice still includes himself within the viewpoint of the convict; the language places him on the bottom, looking up at the colossus of General Motors, figuring what was wrong with the strategy of his previous rebellion and how to make it more effective. In terms of behavior he had, as he said, left his old life behind, but in terms of perspective, he continues to speak as a "lumpen proletarian."

Rap Brown shares Cleaver's political focus, but the style is more hurried, closer to the tone of conversation (as opposed to public address). Cleaver is measuring the irony of each short sentence, developing the point at the end with the deliberate method of the essayist. Rap Brown's method is no less deliberate, but the language is street talk, somewhat like "signifying." As he explains it elsewhere, "signifying was . . . a way of expressing your own feelings. . . . Signifying at its best can be heard when brothers are exchanging tales." One of his examples is a complaint: "Man, I can't win for losing. / If it wasn't for bad luck, I wouldn't have no luck at all. / Can't kill nothing and won't nothing die. / I'm living on welfare and things is stormy / they borrowing their shit from the Salvation Army" (H. R. Brown, pp. 29–30). Terms like "America's a bitch," "jim," "that's your ass," and the rushed, colloquial syntax of the sentence beginning "so along comes a Black man," tie the narrative voice to the street culture. Among the autobiographies, this syntax is peculiar to Rap Brown.

Julius Lester's passage most resembles it, particularly in the use of run-on sentences and comic images to depict the heat; but one feels a distinction between the narrator's identity and the colloquial idioms. Rap Brown's voice *is* the "brother on the corner." Lester's voice *echoes* the brother, enters into and represents his viewpoint with conscious literary method. The object in Lester is to suggest with language the atmosphere surrounding the start of a riot; he is practicing the literary art of mimesis, whereas Rap Brown's passage is a folk polemic. Lester also gives his description a historical frame with the allusion to the Emersonian shot heard round the world. He handles language with the sensitivity of a poet: "the cop . . . looked up and saw a brick coming down on him that looked like it was as big as the moon and as he ducked, his prisoner jerked away and ran down the street and just as the cop reached for his gun, his motion was halted by the delicious sound of a big plate-glass window breaking and that was it!" The image of the moon coming down on the cop's head is apocalyptic; the run-on clauses relate all the events together as a simultaneous explosion; there are the ominous silence, the sinister heat, the brick, the subliminal suggestion of blood on the moon, the turning cop reaching for his gun, the running prisoner, and the sound of broken glass; sound and silence, stillness and motion alternate, our sense of each intensified by its opposite. Like a film, the writing records the process of the present moment, the significantly, suddenly changing relations of kinetic objects in space. The scene proceeds from a literary intelligence, concerned with the techniques and methods of written language as a medium. A sentence like "one of them hot-ass muthafucking nights" could have been written by Rap Brown, but "his motion was halted," "delicious sound," "following the religious commandment," "his prisoner jerked away" come from a different level of diction. "Right now," Lester wrote earlier, "my past and my present are a sketch in chiaroscuro; I was a slave and now I am free. But chiaroscuro omits the gradations, the modulations from one key to another, the transition from slave to freedman" (Lester, *Search for the New Land*, p. 69). This is Lester's individual voice, brooding, meditative, full of selves that fight with one another, exploring the intricate, complex relationship between art, history, and identity. The tone of his indignation is quiet and implacable. Rap Brown seems loud and extroverted by contrast.

Jackson's voice resembles Richard Wright's. It does not contain slang, like the "jive," "cuss," and "cat" of the Seale passage, or a deliberately run-on syntax. It is utterly faithful to the thought, however; honest and serious, neither literary nor colloquial; the diction is held in common by all sections of the population. Bobby Seale's paragraph contains a touch of "signifying," playing the role of the defiant "blood" who remains mentally impervious to his enemies even though they have temporary power over his body. Jackson admits his internal damage, like Wright, at the same time that he resists it. His letter is perhaps the least conscious of style as such, deriving its authenticity from the content alone.

The demands of politics influence the language of these autobiographies in several ways. The folk idioms and images, the verbs of terror and force, as we have noted, reject the abstraction, meaninglessness, and hypocrisy in the political language of the white apologists for racist institutions. Many passages are derived from the rhetoric of sermon and speech. Like the slave narratives, the third-period books are didactic; they draw moral and political lessons and echo, often ironically, the Declaration of Independence. They also resemble the slave narratives in their use of political essay and polemic and in the relation of personal narrative and historical matrix. The writers who are adept at black colloquial style, in particular Cleaver, Lester, and Rap Brown, shift where appropriate to the complex, abstract language of theory. For the convict writers, to employ the language of social and political analysis is to lay claim to "mind," to fight back against the ruling-class media image of the convict as a mindless animal who rapes, murders, and castrates his innocent victims.

Cleaver wrote that in American myth, "black" and "white" corresponded to "body" and "mind," and that the reason Muhammad Ali disturbed white America so much was that he represented the mythic black gorilla claiming the power of the brain and thus refusing to be led around on a string. Cleaver's own style, shifting as it does between colloquial satire and abstruse theory, breaks down the divisions of the myth. The idioms create and maintain his black identity at the same time the abstractions steal the power of analysis from the Omnipotent Administrator and use it to strike off his mental chains.

> Each social structure projects onto the screen of possibility the images of the highest type of male and female sexual identities realizable within the limits of that society. The people within that society are motivated and driven, by the perennial quest for Apocalyptic Fusion, to achieve this highest identity, or as close as they can come to the perfection of the Unitary Sexual Image. All impediments to realization of this image become sources of alienation, obstacles in the way of the Self seeking to realize its ultimate identity (Cleaver, *Soul on Ice*, p. 178).

The strongest books, the books that encompass the most psychological territory and, for different reasons, have the deepest and most lasting effect on the reader's sensibility, the books with the greatest control of language and variety of style, with the largest passion and compassion, the books that most successfully assimilate and unify personal narrative and political message, are probably *Soul on Ice*, *Search for the New Land*, and *Soledad Brother*.

The themes of Cleaver's book, on the personal level, are his

journey from the mental enslavement of pathological love/hate for
the white woman to the mental freedom of love for the black
woman; from petty criminal to political activist; and from brainwashed convict to intellectual innovator. On the historical level,
his theme is the osmosis of values between the Supermasculine
Menial and the Omnipotent Administrator, the breakdown of
cultural segregation between the Mind and the Body, paralleled in
the gradations of his own style from the colloquial to the analytical,
and, at the end, the religious and mystical. The arrangement of his
essays and letters carries through this basic progression, the love/
hate antagonism between black and white, its projection as myth
into the realm of sex and politics, and the hope for a general
movement toward unification. His personal unification is achieved
in the ending, while the work as a whole suggests that the currents
of change in society are sweeping toward the same object, the
"apocalyptic fusion." He is especially strong as a satirist, where his
tone blends goodwill with justified bitterness, and his ironies
redeem such political issues as "law and order," "civil rights,"
"youth in rebellion" and "sexual revolution" from the empty rattle
of Presidential speeches and *Reader's Digest* articles.

Lester's work opens many doors in terms of form and structure.
It is an extension of the black tradition in autobiography: the
"found" poems extend the method of verbal irony; the parallel
columns of personal narrative and current events extend the idea of
linking mass and individual history; the juxtapositions are fresh
modes of satire; the "search for the new land" is also a search for
revolutionary human identity. But there is greater awareness of the
"book" as a medium. The "implacable facts" which were presented
through personal experience in *Black Boy* occur in Lester as
documents. The "book" is printed matter, it communicates as a
symbol sequence in a field of continuously related symbols on all
sides of where the eye falls. To reflect the dynamics of the time
therefore, we are given a collection of printed matter from several
sources, a kind of miniature "documentary history"; but the context breaks down and blends together our ordinary expectations
of what is "document," "history," "poetry," and "autobiography."
The forms are really social relations: a document in one social
setting is a poem in another. Previous autobiographies had mingled
personal narrative, essay, and history in their content, while re-

maining within a form that was relatively fixed. But in Lester, the form itself is liquefied. *Search for the New Land* brings the entire worldwide awakening of the last ten years within the compass of a single perception, implying relationships between events without fully articulating them; the impression of the book rests quietly inside as one gets up from the desk, walks around the neighborhood, and begins to notice how billboards, car fashions, cracked highways, X-rated movies, and articles in the local newspaper are held together in the subtle, tenuous fabric we call "historical consciousness"—our sense of the totality of a social process. A description of "well-dressed, respectable-looking men" thumbing through sex magazines is followed much later by a quotation from *Newsweek* on the horrors of the 1968 Democratic Convention. A vast amount of material intervenes between the two, but one leads through a labyrinth of essay, poetry, news, letters, riots and wars unerringly to the other. You can begin anywhere, actually, reading forward or backward, and all the threads seem to interconnect; everything is a footnote to everything else. The style helps create this impression by the frequent use of parentheses; the text will begin with a historical event, and the parentheses will lead off into a personal experience that illustrates it, perhaps continuing for two or three pages before circling around to a parallel event.

> Being. To Be. In America one was taught TO DO. (The kitchen. That's where I always had the most serious talks with my mother. While she was cooking. "I think I want to be a monk," I told her one afternoon. "A monk?" she exclaimed with horror. "Why?" "Well, that's the only way I could devote all my time to God." "But, Julius, Monks don't do anything.") But what one did affected one's Be-ing and to correct that, Western society evolved Freud, and countless other systems of psychiatry that adjust one's Being so that you can continue the Doing (Lester, *Search for the New Land*, p. 32).

Lester is also a master of the continuous sentence and the paragraph where topics are mixed and the unity is not intellectual but subjective.

Those who were not in the streets, on the corners, back
in the alleys, at the drive-ins, were in their rooms, watching, waiting, looking, knowing that when they could
see a way out of the homes where the sounds from the TV
smashed all possibility of thought and feeling, when
they could get the slightest intimation vibration adumbration of an alternative to following in Dad's footsteps
out the back door and into the garage every morning at
7:30, they would take it. All roads lead to a time clock,
the teachers, preachers, parents said, with know-it-all
smiles. The children said nothing, but late at night, in the
quiet of their rooms, when the television sets were silent,
they prepared themselves. For what, they didn't know.
But when it came, they would recognize it, as a Mississippi
farmer recognizes which rain of spring is the last one,
and the cotton seeds can be planted without fear of their
being washed away. (There was a day, a hot Nashville
summer day. I was seventeen, riding on the bus, the back
of the bus. In my hand was the second issue of *Evergreen
Review* . . . [ibid., p. 27]).

The theme is amplified, not so much by exposition as by subordinated catalogs of prepositional phrases, multiple subjects, and
examples: "in the streets, on the corners, back in the alleys, at the
drive-ins"; "intimation vibration adumbration"; "teachers,
preachers, parents said," etc. This method has a precedent elsewhere in black literature. Langston Hughes's character, Simple,
talked in multiple verb clauses: "I have been caught in the rain,
caught in jails, caught short with my rent, and caught with the
wrong woman—but I am still here!" But in Lester it has a different
tonal quality; the images, diction, and emotion together with the
content of the personal narrative, present a deep poetic, mystical
sensibility ("But when it came, they would recognize it, as a
Mississippi farmer recognizes which rain of spring is the last one.
. . ."); the parenthetic interruptions seem like inward conversation,
so that when the streams of modifiers and subjects accumulate
and the sentences run into each other, the impression is of the swift
release of turbulent feeling, as though water suddenly began to

boil before anyone had noticed it was hot. And as the feelings of
the narrator come to a boil, so do the forces of change in society.
They express and contribute to each other.

The most unusual autobiography in this group is *Soledad
Brother*, partly because, as Jean Genet's introduction points out, it
is an *unwilled* book; Jackson became a writer without meaning
to do anything except keep alive his integrity, talk to his relatives
and friends, and pull together the ideas that enabled him to explain
and cope with the atrocities of prison.

The relationship of Jackson to Douglass and Wright is very
close. Compare Douglass's appendix on the contradictions between
slavery and Christianity with this list of the contradictions of
capitalism:

> We shook hands and the dialectic began. He listened
> while I scorned the diabolical dog—capitalism. Didn't
> it raise pigs and murder Vietnamese? Didn't it glut some
> and starve most of us? Didn't it build housing projects
> that resemble prisons and luxury hotels and apartments
> that resemble the Hanging Gardens on the same street?
> Didn't it build a hospital and then a bomb? Didn't it
> erect a school and then open a whorehouse? Build an
> airplane to sell a tranquilizer tablet? For every church
> didn't it construct a prison? For each new medical
> discovery didn't it produce as a by-product ten new
> biological warfare agents? Didn't it aggrandize men like
> Hunt and Hughes and dwarf him? (Jackson, p. 182).

In the next paragraph, we hear the "strangely tender and cruel,
violent and peaceful" voice of Wright's summation passages, with
their "enthralling sense of wonder and awe in the face of the drama
of human feeling which is hidden by the external drama of life."
Like Wright's father standing in the field holding a hoe in his
gnarled hands, Jackson's father is rendered as a symbol of a defeated generation, "a thousand dreams deferred, broken promises,
forgotten ambitions," his mind going "into a total regression,"
back through shattered hopes "to a time when he was young roam-
ing the Louisiana countryside for something to eat." During this
visit, he called George "by his brother's name twice. I was so
shocked I could only sit and blink." But just behind the father's

veneer of "workaday, never-complain, cool, smooth colored gentleman" lies an abyss of "awesome, vindictive black madness." He is
a product of Depression times, when "Blacks were beaten and
killed for jobs like porter, bellboy, stoker, pearl driver, and bootblack." George writes that he will "forgive them for casting us
naked into a grim and deleterious world" if they will only "stop
their collaboration with the fascist enemy" and "support our
revolution with just a nod" (ibid., pp. 182–83).

The strength and beauty of Jackson's letters derive almost wholly
from a perception of their social context. We must go back to that
context repeatedly to understand what we are reading. Take the
following economic analysis:

> Depression is an economic condition. It is a part of the
> capitalist business cycle, a necessary concomitant of cap-
> italism. Its colonies—secondary markets—will always be
> depressed areas, because the steadily decreasing labor
> force, decreasing and growing more skilled under the
> advances of automation, casts the unskilled colonial
> subject into economic roles that preclude economic
> mobility. Learning the new skills, even if we were al-
> lowed, wouldn't help. It wouldn't help the masses even
> if they learned them. It wouldn't help because there is a
> fixed ceiling on the labor force. This ceiling gets lower
> with every advance in the arts of production. Learning
> the newer skills would merely put us into a competition
> with established labor that we could not win. One that we
> don't want. There are absolutely no vacuums for us to
> fill in the business world. We don't want to capitalize
> on people anyway. Capitalism is the enemy. It must be
> destroyed. There is no other recourse (ibid., p. 184).

The values are clear and sound but contain nothing that would not
appear in a well-written article for a socialist newspaper. As an
article, the language would direct attention only to the politics.
As a Jackson letter, it is surrounded by an atmosphere of suffering,
passion, struggle, courage, tragedy, and redemption; the injustice
of his imprisonment, his racist suppression behind bars, his decade-
long fight with parole and prison authorities, the outrage of his
indictment for the murder of a white guard after guards had shot

down several black prisoners for being involved in a brawl with whites, his anger and tenderness toward his parents, his hunger for love in the letters to Angela Davis, and his assassination, are all facts which cannot be separated from the economic rhetoric. Let us look at it again. "Depression is an economic condition . . . a necessary concomitant of capitalism." It is not built into the structure of the universe, a plan of God, or else frontal lobotomy would be a divine gift. As an economic condition, it can be fathomed and fought, and what remains of your sanity has a use value beyond being able to see the hot iron of life imprisonment for no rational purpose coming toward your enlightened and educated eyes. "Learning the new skills, even if we were allowed, wouldn't help. It wouldn't help the masses even if they learned them. It wouldn't help because there is a fixed ceiling on the labor force." "Economic roles that preclude mobility." Here are the final limits of the prison walls. The hand runs over them, stone by stone, with relief, and a certain wonder. Short sentences pause to consider them, the voice subdued. Because under the surface is the "awesome, vindictive black madness"—guards stripping the prisoners naked, shoving fingers up their anuses, hosing them in locked cells, mowing them down from helicopters and bullet-proof towers. It is necessary to insist on rejecting false comfort. Things that will not help must be pushed away, quietly, firmly, even gently. "There are absolutely no vacuums for us to fill in the business world. We don't want to capitalize on people anyway." Capitalism means to capitalize. (A cousin of decapitate.) "Capitalism is the enemy. It must be destroyed." Pearls of truth shining serenely at the bottom of the madness, stirred to and fro by the calm diction of political analysis. "There is no other recourse."

> Slavery is an economic condition. The classical chattel
> and today's neoslavery must be defined in terms of
> economics. The chattel is a property, one man exercising
> the property rights of his established economic order,
> the other man as that property. The owner can move
> that property or hold it in one square yard of the earth's
> surface; he can let it breed other slaves or make it breed
> other slaves; he can sell it, beat it, work it, maim it, fuck
> it, kill it . . . (ibid., p. 190).

To read the letters *only* as personal statement, without recognizing the validity of their political answers, could lead to drowning Jackson in the same sea of crocodile tears that *Newsweek*, according to Baldwin, dumped all over Angela Davis.[4] But the politics demand consideration as a search for meaning within the pain of imprisonment. The language itself is a claim on freedom. Surrounded by the most brutal and implacable of social facts, he stares them full in the face to arm himself with a theoretical understanding of his condition. He can then see what his choices are, which way the current is flowing and where he is positioned in it. The enumeration of the details of chattel slavery verges on bitter fury ("sell it, beat it, work it, maim it, fuck it, kill it"), but the passion is subordinated to the intellectual purpose of comparing the economics of slave labor and wage labor. The economic language removes the writer from the subject, supplying enough distance to maintain the rule of his mind.

It also tells us that one black prisoner withstood totalitarian suppression with his mind intact; that he accomplished his goal, stated elsewhere, of being more concerned with *how* he lived than *how long* he lived; that he lived on his own terms, comprehending far more about the meaning of his suffering than his captors, feeling the "narrow limits" of their lives, understanding their motives and historical roles better than they understood the social forces behind their very orders. The language tells us that, by taking away his freedom of movement, the oppressor gave Jackson the power of the word. "I add five words to my vocabulary each day, five new ones, right after breakfast each morning when I have forty-five minutes to kill," he wrote his brother (Jackson, p. 142). The language demonstrates that, by driving him into acquiring that theoretical grasp of his relationship to their system, to "the whole rotten hunk," the oppressors were handing him the shovels with which to dig their graves. What we are looking at is the only redemption of suffering that operates in this world, the humanist's version of the faith that out of evil shall come good. And so it is possible, reading Jackson, to find in a geography lesson the self-transcendent, contemplative spirit of Pennington and Woolman:

> In the savanna area south of the Sahara Desert and all the
> way south to the Cape, you find the most fertile farmland

> in the world. Uganda, Kenya, and Tanzania are all just
> like a big park. The temperature never fluctuates more
> than five degrees the whole year around. Every evening
> during the winter months there is a light rain to settle the
> dust. Eighty to eighty-five the whole year. The five oldest
> cities in the world are located in Africa. The oldest lan-
> guage is one spoken in Africa: Mande. The oldest relic of
> man's prehistoric existence was found in Africa, 25 mil-
> lion years old (ibid., p. 126).

Culture, knowledge, learning, continue in spite of, even because of
the worst that man can inflict on his fellow man. Africa is also
important to Jackson for another reason: its antiquity (where man
is concerned, one could say timelessness) gives him a connection
to the root of life, a past, a mother, to lift him out of the cell of
spiritual isolation. His description of Africa is like a pastoral
memory of the lost Eden, the golden age which may return to us
someday if we live our lives aright—"just like a big park . . . eighty
to eighty-five the whole year . . . the most fertile farmland in the
world." We remember that elsewhere in Jackson's letters, and in
history, it is the white man who corrupts this Eden for profit,
exploiting its resources, enslaving the inhabitants, tempting them
to eat of the forbidden fruit and setting them to the cultivation of
the poison tree.

The total absence of black colloquial rhetoric in most of Jackson's letters is a kind of refusal to reflect in style the purely racial
politics that dominated his prison environment, where friends
and enemies are determined primarily by skin color. He remains
outside the limits of his captors even in his tone; rather than bend
or avoid the enemy's language, he will master and command it;
his mind will control their tools while their prisons control his
body. There is a faithfulness to a humanity deeper than race in
this, without denying or resisting racial identity—indeed, while
affirming it. The language of the heavily colloquial writers, such as
Rap Brown, sometimes implies that "Blackness" is the only road
to becoming a revolutionary; whites are chastised and then invited
out of the book, unless they wish to be "used in the struggle."[5]
The message of Jackson's language is that a common ideology and
dedication transcends, without obviating, racial and cultural

differences. He invites readers in and out of his cell on the basis
of politics, compassion, class loyalty, and range of empathy with the
oppressed.

The epistolary form in Jackson is a greenhouse for the seeds of
the new world he dreamed of. The fact that we are dealing with
real personal letters makes everything a record of subjective experience. The essays in Douglass, Du Bois, and Cleaver *come* from
their experience but direct attention elsewhere. But in Jackson
every essay and political message functions as part of the author's
personal life through its very mode of existence as a personal
letter. The inner and outer worlds are indissolubly joined by the
form. Yet the form would be impossible to duplicate, unless you
were subjected to the same brutalities as Jackson, and had to write
letters for the same reasons. You could not sit down and deliberately
produce a book like this. It is not "seminal," useful to other
writers, as is *Search for the New Land*; but it does germinate a new
concept of the writer, perhaps the concept that will reach full
maturity after the husk of the old order splits and falls to the ground
—a human being who writes to understand his world, connect himself to the lives of other human beings, give structure to their
best selves (as a single baby gives structure to the human form in
the chromosomes of millions), and nourish his own dreams; who
may find "writing" convenient for these ends, and may not; but
who would never consider being a "major figure," a "name,"
making a "career" out of a temporary necessity, and claiming personal glory for an act as natural as conversation. If writing is judged
by its organic, flesh-and-bone relationship to the author's gestating
selfhood, and its projection of a worthy model of selfhood that
sings in the winds of the historical process, sings the song of the
wind, indicates its direction, and adds to its speed, then perhaps
Huey P. Newton was not wrong to call Jackson "the greatest writer
of us all." In any case, to praise as a "great writer" a man who had
no such grandiose pretensions is to stand the Renaissance ego on
its head. The last shall be first.

Conclusion

To find the heart of autobiography in American literature, we must turn to the work of black writers. This is the form that seems to give the fullest scope to their literary visions; black poetry and fiction, indeed, are drawn into the orbit of autobiography and vividly marked by its personal tone.

From earliest times, black narratives have possessed great political insight into the contradictions of American society; moreover, the politics have been felt and tested as subjective experience. Both white and black literature in the United States began with autobiographical accounts, but the black accounts had something that was not present in the early colonial journals of William Bradford, Cotton Mather, and Jonathan Edwards: they were instruments of struggle against a hostile class power. This fact affects the whole tradition of black literature; identity has been created in resistance to a powerful foe, and therefore lived at a high pitch of intensity. Every writer must struggle to discover who and what he is; but if you are never able to take who you are for granted, and the social order around you seems deliberately designed to rub you out, stuff your head with little cartoon symbols of what it wants or fears you to be, and mock you with parodies of your highest hopes, then discovering who you really are takes on the dimensions of an epic battle with the social order. Autobiography then becomes both an arsenal and a battle ground.

What makes it an especially attractive form to the black writer is that it lives in the two worlds of history and literature. Black writers also live in two worlds: American and Black, public mask and private face. They have two equally important perspectives which must somehow be brought together into a single field of vision: the subjective awareness and the political message, the unfolding sense of self and the absolute need to gain control over their history. Autobiography affords the greatest opportunities to combine the two perspectives because it develops like a village on the crossroads between the author's subjective life and his social-historical life.

The problem in welding literature and politics is to integrate their goals: literature's primary goal is to deal with the impact of experience on subjective awareness, whereas the goals of political writing are to teach, to exhort, to change opinion and behavior, and to organize. The political novel may too easily lock itself within the limits of allegory, developing characters and situations solely for didactic reasons. Since the reader knows by the very assumptions of fiction that the situations are invented or reconstructed, the message tends to lose its power. On the other hand, if the characters and situations are dominated by the didactic purpose, they become stunted and unconvincing as reflections of experience. In the novel, the two goals may thus interfere with each other. *The Grapes of Wrath* and *Native Son* solve this dilemma only by setting aside special chapters for theoretical interpretation, so that in effect the books develop along two vectors—essay and drama.

The purpose of autobiography, however, is by definition to express and create subjective awareness. Yet it can never be considered apart from its context. It shapes and interprets material but does not invent situation or character. The author and the speaking subject are one and the same. The main character, who is the source of perception inside the book, also has an objective existence outside of it. Whatever he says and does, therefore, has an authenticity rarely possible to duplicate in a fictional construct. The "message" of necessity is simply an extension of his subjective awareness. Message becomes part of the impact of experience on the author. But because the experience is real, it still exists as a message. It is stated as what the author has chosen to do with his allotted time on this planet. Aesthetic appreciation of autobiography, and of poetry and fiction which adopts the autobiographical stance, requires us to go to the author's background, beyond the printed page. In a fictional construct, going outside the work to appreciate it always runs the risk of applying "non-literary" criteria to its evaluation. It is impossible to run this risk with autobiography, because the nature of the form breaks down the distinction between the book's world and the author's world. Message and narrative may still fail to mesh, but the problems of joining them are simplified.

Making language fit the content of an autobiography is essentially a problem of realizing a social form within which to nourish the true self, to examine the miraculous fact of your life. Black writers must work with social forms that are antiself, that symbolize, stereotype, ridicule, ignore, and suppress them; they must renew or invert the forms to make them habitable, point the daggers outward and file the sharp edges off the tool handles. They are brought into rebellion, therefore, against the social forces which perpetually erode the capacity of language to express clear, honest thoughts and complex feelings: racism, lying, hypocrisy, jargon, abstraction as a means of avoiding facts, and the desire to manipulate others for private profit. A black writer may lie, use jargon, and intellectualize to avoid facing facts, but the quest for the true self brings black writing as a whole on a collision course with what passes for "truth" in the American vision of the world. Black identity leads in an antiracist, antiimperialist, panhuman direction. "Panhuman" means what Malcolm X had in mind when he used the phrase "human rights" to replace "civil rights," and stated "I'm a human being first and foremost . . . I'm for whatever benefits humanity as a whole." The autobiographies which move in this direction have enriched beyond measure both the concept of selfhood and the language of political discourse.

A future problem for black autobiography to solve may be how to confront human existence without the shadow of the white man—without relying on him, as *diabolus ex machina*, to condition, by negative example, the meaning of a life well lived. Although some works turn aside from overt politics, the presence of the white man is the single most pervasive influence in every book. It might be that this problem can only be taken up after the historical questions have been resolved—for any attempt to define the meaning of black life in apolitical terms must appear as a failure to deal with white power, as long as that power's control over history remains intact.

The white working class, on the other hand, must learn what "political" identity means; apolitical definitions on their part are a failure to recognize the effect of white-power indoctrination on themselves. For "white power" has never included them and has never meant more than the power of a small group of whites to exploit humanity. However much workers may have shared the ideology of white power, they have not shared its material benefits. It is a truism that in areas of the country where white supremacy is strongest, the condition of all workers is the worst—they are the most divided and poorly paid, the most politically ignorant, and the most vulnerable to rapacious attacks from big business. White workers and their allies must learn from blacks how to create deeply felt connections with the radical currents of their own history, their traditions as abolitionists, Homestead and Pullman strikers, I. W. W., Socialist, and Communist party activists, peace marchers, militant unionists. White power has, in many ways, robbed whites of their history even more effectively than it has robbed blacks. Whites have been made accessories to the crime, apparent beneficiaries of the poison fruit; they are not only robbed, their skin gives them a reason in their own minds to identify with the robbers. When progressive whites discover that they are so identified by the black victims, they have no easy way to enlist on the right side; they feel innocent because they did not personally commit the crimes ("*I* didn't enslave you, *I* never lynched anyone, *I* don't have investments in South Africa"), yet they also feel guilty for being white, for paying taxes, voting, making money, obeying the laws of a white system, and living better than the blacks. They must avoid the self-righteous assertion of their innocence, which results in the irrelevant charges of "black racism" and "discrimination in reverse" whenever the blacks gain a victory; and they must avoid being paralyzed by guilt, which results in nihilism, slavish imitation of black culture, and symbolic protest. Between this Scylla and Charybdis is where they may chart their course toward the new land.

But there is more day to dawn. The revolutionary self is but a morning star.

Notes

Notes to chapter one

1. For a treatment of the slave narratives as historical experience, see Charles Nichols, *Many Thousand Gone* (Netherlands, 1963) and Julius Lester, *To Be a Slave* (New York: Dial Press, 1968). Literary scholarship on the narratives has been sparse. Among the few works which discuss them as literature are Marion Wilson Starling, "The Slave Narrative: Its Place in American Literary History," Diss. New York University 1946, and Benjamin Quarles, "Narrative of the Life of Frederick Douglass," in *Landmarks of American Writing*, ed. Hennig Cohen (New York: Basic Books, 1969).

Although the historical authenticity of the narratives is not at issue in the present work, the arguments in favor of their picture of slavery receive support in Norman R. Yetman's *Life Under the 'Peculiar Institution': Selections from the Slave Narrative Collection* (New York: Holt, Rinehart & Winston, 1970). These selections, a series of interviews with ex-slaves compiled by the Federal Writers' Project during the years 1936–38, confirm the worst that had been said by the blacks in the antislavery struggle and give much added insight into how those slaves survived who were not able to run away.

2. *Narrative of the Life of Rev. Noah Davis* (Baltimore, 1859), pp. 14–15.

3. *Father Henson's Story of His Own Life* (New York: Corinth Books, 1962), p. 19.

4. *Autobiography of a Fugitive Negro* (1855; rpt. New York: Arno Press & The New York Times, 1968), p. 100.

5. *Narrative of the Life of Moses Grandy* (Boston: Oliver Johnson, 1844), p. 19.

6. *Narrative of the Life of Frederick Douglass* (New York: Signet, 1968), pp. 99–104.

7. *Narrative of the Life and Adventures of Henry Bibb* (New York, 1850; rpt. Westport, Conn.: Negro Universities Press, 1969), pp. 23–24.

8. J. W. C. Pennington, *The Fugitive Blacksmith* (London, 1849), pp. 22–24.

9. William Craft and Ellen Craft, *Running a Thousand Miles for Freedom*, 1860, in *Great Slave Narratives* (Boston: Beacon Press, 1969), p. 304.

10. *Narrative of William Wells Brown* (Boston, 1847), p. 54.

11. Solomon Northup, *Twelve Years a Slave* (Auburn, Buffalo, & London, 1853), p. 76.

12. *Black Boy* (1937; rpt. New York: Perennial, 1966), p. 45.

13. *The Life of John Thompson, a Fugitive Slave* (1856; rpt. Westport,

Conn.: Negro Universities Press, 1968), pp. 35–36.

14. Frederick Douglass, for example, mentions that he could get no employment as a calker in New Bedford because of "prejudice against color" (*Narrative*, p. 117), and Lerone Bennett, Jr., in *Before the Mayflower* (Chicago, 1962; rpt. Baltimore: Penguin, 1966) describes how the incoming Irish "fought Negroes for elbow room in the slums and working space in kitchens and on the docks," quoting a Douglass editorial on the subject (see pp. 152–3). But Douglass also tells us that two Irish dock-workers in Baltimore were "deeply affected" by his statement that he was a slave for life and advised him to run away to the North, where he would find friends and freedom (*Narrative* pp. 56–57).

15. *Life and Times of Frederick Douglass* (London: Collier Books, 1962), p. 52.

16. This fact is important as a counter to the resurgence of current myths about slavery in particular and rebellion in general; William Styron's novel *The Confessions of Nat Turner*, for example, disregards the historical evidence of most other slave narratives, as well as the account of Thomas Grey, when he has Nat being taught literacy by a kind master. We are thereby given an image of Nat as biting the hand that fed him. Resistance by force is thus eviscerated from a creative act to an unnecessary tragedy if the slave was shedding blood for what the "enlightened" masters were trying to give anyway; and, contrary to known facts, the slaves are also

judged incapable of maintaining their own clandestine traditions of literacy, in defiance of the master's law.

17. Walker's *Appeal in Four Articles* (Boston, 1830; rpt. Arno Press & The New York Times, 1969), p. 37.

Notes to chapter two

1. Jacob Stroyer, *My Life in the South* (Salem, Mass.: Newcomb & Gauss, 1898), p. 10.

2. *Life of James Mars, a Slave* (Hartford, Conn., 1872), pp. 8, 11.

3. *Moby Dick* (New York: Modern Library, 1950), p. 281.

4. Although if he had read Swift, perhaps the greatest irony would be Ward's attitude toward the starving Irish tenants who provided Swift with his subject.

Notes to chapter three

1. The pattern is described in Robert E. Spiller et al., eds., *Literary History of the United States*, rev. ed. (New York: Macmillan, 1963), pp. 83–84.

2. Douglass, *Narrative*, p. 90. Douglass apparently attached no special importance to the number 39, for in the *Life and Times* he changed it to forty.

3. Thomas Gray, *Confessions of Nat Turner*; rpt. Herbert Aptheker, *Nat Turner's Slave Rebellion* (New York: Humanities Press, 1966), pp. 137–38.

4. Sidney Kaplan, "Lewis Temple and the Hunting of the Whale," *New England Quarterly* (March, 1953), p. 78.

5. I am indebted for this information to Sidney Kaplan, "Towards Pip and Daggoo: Footnote on Melville's Youth," *Phylon* 29 (Fall 1968), 291–302.

6. Ibid. n. 7, p. 292.

7. Lincoln's exact wording was "we are like whalers who have been on a long chase. We have at last got the harpoon into the monster, but we must now look how we steer, or with one flop of his tail he will send us all into eternity." The same metaphor perhaps casts a shadow over Walt Whitman's famous poem, "O Captain, My Captain."

8. One of the tensions of Poe's story is of course that the removal can never be more than apparent; for its method, characters, and themes, even the author's effort to remove it, all tell us something about its historical context.

9. Claude M. Fuess, *Daniel Webster*, vol. 1 (New York: Da Capo Press, 1968), pp. 292–93.

10. *American Renaissance* (London: Oxford University Press, 1941), pp. 18–23.

11. " 'Yam . . . Majah Riblees he lib dar, ap yonnah road ap yonnah. . . . Yam, me tek'ee dar, missy, me tek'ee dar.' " The reference, however, is not to Simms, Knott, Robb, or Poe, but to William Styron in *Confessions of Nat Turner* (New York: Random House, 1967), p. 262. Compare this "blue-gum country-nigger talk . . . with a wet gulping sound of Africa" to the dialect of a "shrewd son of African

parents" from the Carolina seacoast quoted by William Craft: " 'What!' he exclaimed with astonishment, 'to Philumadelphy? . . . By squash! I wish I was going wid you! I hears um say dat dare's no slaves way over in dem parts; is um so? . . . Well,' continued he, as he threw down the boot and brush, and, placing his hands in his pockets, strutted across the floor with an air of independence—'Gorra Mighty, dem is de parts for Pompey; and I hope when you get dare you will stay, and nebber follow dat buckra back to dis hot quarter no more, let him be eber so good.' " See p 300.

Notes to chapter four

1. *My Bondage and My Freedom* (New York: Miller, Orton, & Mulligan, 1855), pp. 396–98.

2. *Narrative of Sojourner Truth* (Boston, 1875) pp. 184–87.

3. *Liberator* 27, no. 3 (15 Jan. 1847): 10.

4. "Speech on the Reception of Abolition Petitions," *Speeches of John C. Calhoun* (New York: Harper & Bros., 1843), pp. 222–23.

5. "Brown was the son of a mother who, like her own mother, had died insane. Three of his mother's sisters and two of her brothers were also intermittently insane. So were one of Brown's brothers, his sister, and her daughter. So, too, were Brown's first wife and one of his sons. If he was not himself mad, he was at least a monomaniac about religion and slavery, a psychopathic individual—not merely

a madman—who revealed the symptoms of paranoia and, by his deeds, provoked those symptoms in others."

The quotation is from p. 316 of *The National Experience* (New York: Harcourt, Brace & World, 1963), a popular college American history text which includes, among its authors, such famous names as John Blum, Bruce Catton, Arthur M. Schlesinger, Jr., and C. Van Woodward.

The writer goes on to misrepresent Brown's original plan as a scheme to "seize some stronghold in the Southern mounains . . . touch off a general slave uprising," and thereby bring about the "collapse" of the peculiar institution. "A few bewildered slaves were induced or compelled to join him," continues the text, confusing Brown's guerrilla plan with his Harper's Ferry raid, and totally ignoring Sheridan Leary, Shields Green, and John Copeland, three of the five black members who participated in the planning of the raid and who fought at Brown's side. Leary died fighting; Green and Copeland joined Brown on the scaffold.

The case for Brown's alleged insanity, and his plans and achievements within the abolitionist movement, are treated at length in Stephen Oates's *To Purge This Land with Blood.*

6. One reason that entitles Samuel Johnson to an echo in a criticism of Douglass is that he once drank a toast, at a company of Oxford dons, "to the next insurrection of the negroes in the West Indies." See Boswell's *Life of*

Samuel Johnson (New York: Modern Library, n.d.), p. 747.

7. Starling, *The Slave Narrative,* p. 428.

Notes to chapter five

1. *Dusk of Dawn: An Essay Toward an Autobiography of a Race Concept* (New York: Harcourt, Brace & Co., 1940), p. 221.

2. *The Souls of Black Folk* (Chicago, 1903; rpt. Millwood, New York: Kraus-Thomson Organization, 1973 [facsimile of the 1953 edition]), p. 4.

3. *Darkwater: Voices from Within the Veil* (New York: Schocken Books, 1969), p. 29.

4. *No Day of Triumph* (New York: Harper & Bros., 1942), p. 43.

5. *The Big Sea* (New York: Alfred A. Knopf, 1940), p. 206.

6. *I Wonder as I Wander* (New York: Hill & Wang, 1956; New York: Hill & Wang, American Century, 1964), p. 59.

7. *A Long Way from Home* (New York: Lee Furman, 1937), p. 115.

8. James Weldon Johnson, *Along This Way* (New York: Viking Press, 1933), p. 159.

9. *Up from Slavery* (New York: Doubleday, Page & Co., 1901), p. 40.

10. *Autobiography of W. E. B. Du Bois* (New York: International, 1968), pp. 136, 339.

11. *It's Good to Be Black* (New York: Doubleday & Co., 1953), pp. 48–49.

12. *Here I Stand* (Boston: Beacon Press, 1958), p. 15.

13. Du Bois talks about the reception of Washington's *Up from*

Slavery in *Dusk of Dawn*, p. 76. The intentions of the white "philanthropy" behind Washington are sufficiently clear from his testimony. Washington himself opposed the labor movement, advertising in the famous Atlanta Exposition Address that Negroes work "without strikes and labour wars."

14. *Crusade for Justice: The Autobiography of Ida B. Wells* (Chicago: University of Chicago Press, 1970), pp. 4–5.

Notes to chapter six

1. Angelo Herndon, *Let Me Live* (New York: Random House, 1937), p. 8.

2. Perhaps the reason for this attitude lay in Du Bois's early intellectual and upper-class bias, or his support, at this time, of basic American political institutions and the general approach to the race question advocated by the NAACP. Herndon does not elaborate. See *Let Me Live*, p. 82.

3. Hosea Hudson, *Black Worker in the Deep South* (New York: International, 1972), pp. 112–13.

4. The most notable exceptions are in white autobiographies that have never been included in our established literary heritage, such as *The Autobiography of Big Bill Haywood* and Woody Guthrie's *Bound for Glory*. Haywood, a labor militant, socialist, and founding member of the Industrial Workers of the World, discovered his ties to humanity through the

labor and communist movements. Guthrie seems joyfully immersed in working-class life wherever he wanders.

5. Benjamin J. Davis, *Communist Councilman from Harlem* (New York: International, 1969), p. 103.

6. See William Z. Foster, *History of the Communist Party of the United States* (New York: Greenwood Press, 1968), pp. 266–67: "Whereas, the Marxists in the United States had traditionally considered the Negro question as that of a persecuted racial minority of workers and as basically a simple trade union matter, the Party now characterized the Negro people as an oppressed nation entitled to the right of self-determination.

". . . The practical consequences, in policy, of the Communist Party's new position on the Negro question were that, in addition to pressing as before for full economic, political and social equality in all their ramifications for the Negro people, the Party also raised the slogan that the Negro people should have the right of self-determination in the 'Black Belt' of the South on the basis of the break-up of the plantation system and the redistribution of the land to the Negro farmers. The demand for self-determination did not mean, however, that the Party advocated the setting up of a "Negro republic" in the South, as its enemies asserted. But it did mean that the Party, henceforth, would insist that the Negro nation should have the right of self-determination, to be exercised by it whenever and however it saw fit to use this right."

See also James S. Allen, *Negro*

Liberation (New York, 1938), p. 21.
Another work on the subject is
Wilson Record, *The Negro and the
American Communist Party*.

7. See *The Prisoner of Sex* (New
York: Signet, 1971), pp. 90, 95, 108.

Notes to chapter seven

1. Elsewhere Du Bois seems more
Pre-Raphaelite, but here the closest
analogue is the Wordsworth of
"Michael."

2. Du Bois quotes from Swinburne
on p. 207.

3. This is not to deny anything
of Hemingway's value as a writer,
or to assert that he should have
written like Hughes. On the contrary, we can ask no more of a
writer than to tell the truth about
his culture.

Notes to chapter nine

1. *Notes of a Native Son* (Boston:
Beacon Press, 1955; rpt. New York:
Bantam, 1968), pp. 19, 20.

2. *Soul on Ice* (New York:
McGraw-Hill, 1968), p. 99.

3. *Nobody Knows My Name* (New
York: Dial Press, 1961), pp. 75 &
xiii resp.

4. "An Open Letter to My Sister
Angela Davis," *If They Come in
the Morning*, ed. Angela Y. Davis
& Bettina Aptheker (New York:
Third Press, 1971), p. 17.

5. *No Name in the Street* (New
York: Dial Press, 1972), pp. 46–48.

Notes to chapter ten

1. *Journal of Charlotte L. Forten*,
ed. R. Allen Billington (New York:
Dryden Press, 1953).

2. *I Know Why the Caged Bird
Sings* (New York: Random House,
1970; rpt. New York: Bantam,
1971), p. 18.

3. *Coming of Age in Mississippi*
(New York: Dial Press, 1968), p. 1.

Notes to chapter eleven

1. Ralph Ellison, *Invisible Man*
(New York: Signet Books, 1968).

2. *The Autobiography of Malcolm
X* (New York: Grove Press, 1964), p.
150.

3. *Muhammad Speaks* 2, no. 9, p.
16, the Nation of Islam newspaper,
carries articles with an antiimperialist viewpoint; but the organization
itself is not anticapitalist. Besides
their chains of restaurants, farms,
and other business ventures,
Muslims adjure their followers to
refrain from "envying" the material
wealth of the Leader; for "whatever Messenger Muhammad has it
Came from Allah."

4. Bobby Seale, *Seize the Time*
(New York: Random House, 1970;
rpt. New York: Vintage Books,
1970), p. 34.

5. H. Rap Brown, *Die Nigger Die*
(New York: Dial Press, 1969), p. i.

6. *Soledad Brother: The Prison
Letters of George Jackson* (New
York: Coward, McCann, 1970; rpt.
New York: Bantam, 1970), p. 139.

7. Julius Lester, *Search for the
New Land* (New York: Dial Press,

1969; rpt. New York: Dell, 1970), p. 57.

8. Leslie Alexander Lacy, *The Rise and Fall of a Proper Negro* (New York: Macmillan, 1970; rpt. New York: Pocket Books, 1971), pp. 223–24.

9. Donald Reeves, *Notes of a Processed Brother* (New York: Pantheon Books, 1971), pp. 238–39, 268–69 resp.

Notes to chapter twelve

1. When the concepts are thrust away, one possible future recourse for the frustrated behavioral engineer may be the Crime Deterrent Transponder System developed by Joseph Meyer, a computer specialist of the National Security Agency. Instead of concepts, the "criminal" would carry an electronic device in his skull as a condition of bail or parole. The device would monitor the subject's every move and send warning signals to a computer whenever he violated a prescribed routine. The plan is explained by Meyer in *Transactions on Aerospace and Electronic Systems* for January, 1971.

2. *Cat's Cradle* (New York: Holt, Rinehart & Winston, 1963; rpt. Dell, 1970), p. 43.

3. For example, the open display of weapons telegraphs to the rulers in advance the plans of the ruled, thus resulting in the avoidable deaths of good people; the theory of "making the news" as an organizing tactic relies on the capitalist media and legal system to spread the party message and defend members instead of on the people themselves; to trust the legal system to defend one's right to bear arms while trying to overthrow the system is to assume that it will not be serious about maintaining itself and will not act to remove a threat.

4. Claude Brown, *Manchild in the Promised Land* (New York: Macmillan, 1965; rpt. Signet Books, 1966), p. 12.

5. A sample of 27 white state college students in Vermont, who had travelled through a big-city ghetto, was asked by this author in 1971 how they felt during the experience. A few responded with straight-laced contempt for the blacks—"they could do better than this if they tried." Most wrote "scared," "sick," "curious," "disgusted," "helpless," "fascinated," "ashamed to be white."

6. "Geek" also has this meaning in Seale, pp. 183 ff.

Notes to chapter thirteen

1. "Curriculum Recommendations" of the Social Sciences Department, Castleton State College, Castleton, Vt. (October 18, 1971). One could also add to this example the insistence of some Vermont "correctional personnel" that prison inmates be referred to officially as "residents."

2. Cleaver, *Post-Prison Writings and Speeches* (New York: Vintage, 1967), p. 38.

3. *Blackamerican Literature*, ed.

Ruth Miller (Beverly Hills: Glencoe Press, 1971), p. 692.

4. *If They Come in the Morning,* ed. Angela Davis and Bettina Aptheker, p. 13.

5. Cf. *Die Nigger Die,* p. 125: "Our job is not to convert whites. If whites are dedicated to revolution then they can be used in the struggle."

Bibliography

Aptheker, Bettina, ed. See Davis, Angela Y.

Aptheker, Herbert. *Nat Turner's Slave Rebellion*. New York: Humanities Press, 1966.

Angelou, Maya. *I Know Why the Caged Bird Sings*. New York: Random House, 1970; rpt. New York: Bantam, 1971.

Baldwin, James. *Nobody Knows My Name*. New York: Dial Press, 1961.

————. *No Name in the Street*. New York: Dial Press, 1972.

————. *Notes of a Native Son*. Boston: Beacon Press, 1955; rpt. New York: Bantam, 1968.

————. "Open Letter to my Sister Angela Davis." *If They Come in the Morning*. Ed. Angela Y. Davis & Bettina Aptheker. New York: Third Press, 1971.

Bennett, Lerone Jr. *Before the Mayflower*. Chicago, 1962; rpt. Baltimore: Penguin, 1966.

Bibb, Henry. *Narrative of the Life and Adventures of Henry Bibb*. New York, 1850; rpt. Westport, Conn.: Negro Universities Press, 1969.

Blum, John, et. al. *The National Experience*. New York: Harcourt, Brace & World, 1963.

Boswell, James. *The Life of Samuel Johnson*. New York: Modern Library, n.d.

Brown, Claude. *Manchild in the Promised Land*. New York: MacMillan, 1965; rpt. New York: Signet Books, 1966.

Brown, H. Rap. *Die Nigger Die*. New York: Dial Press, 1969.

Brown, William Wells. *Narrative of William Wells Brown*. Boston, 1847.

Calhoun, John C. *Speeches of John C. Calhoun*. New York: Harper & Bros., 1843.

Cleaver, Eldridge. *Post-Prison Writings and Speeches*. New York: Vintage, 1967.

————. *Soul on Ice*. New York: McGraw-Hill, 1968.

Craft, William & Ellen. *Running a Thousand Miles for Freedom*. 1860; in *Great Slave Narratives*. Boston: Beacon Press, 1969.

"Curriculum Recommendations." Social Sciences Dept., Castleton State College, Castleton, Vt. Oct. 18, 1971.

Davis, Angela Y. & Aptheker, Bettina, eds. *If They Come in the Morning*. New York: Third Press, 1971.

Davis, Benjamin J. *Communist Councilman from Harlem*. New York: International Publishers, 1969.

Davis, Noah. *Narrative of the Life of Rev. Noah Davis.* Baltimore, 1859.

Douglass, Frederick. *The Life and Times of Frederick Douglass.* 1892; rpt. London: Collier Books, 1962.

————. *My Bondage and My Freedom.* New York: Miller, Orton, and Mulligan, 1855.

————. *Narrative of the Life of Frederick Douglass.* 1845; rpt. New York: Signet, 1968.

Du Bois, W. E. B. *Autobiography of W. E. B. Du Bois* (ed. by H. Aptheker). New York: International, 1968.

————. *Darkwater: Voices from Within the Veil.* New York: Schocken Books, 1969.

————. *Dusk of Dawn: An Essay Toward an Autobiography of a Race Concept.* New York: Harcourt, Brace & Co., 1940.

————. *The Souls of Black Folk.* 1903; rpt. Millwood, New York: Kraus-Thomson Organization, 1973.

Ellison, Ralph. *Invisible Man.* 1947; rpt. New York: Signet Books, 1968.

Forten, Charlotte. *The Journal of Charlotte L. Forten.* Ed. R. Allen Billington. New York: Dryden Press, 1953.

Foster, William Z. *History of the Communist Party of the United States.* New York: Greenwood Press, 1968.

Fuess, Claude M. *Daniel Webster*, Vol. I. New York: Da Capo Press, 1968.

Garrison, William Lloyd. *Liberator*, XVII (15 Jan. 1847), 10.

Goodwin, Ruby Berkley. *It's Good to Be Black.* New York: Doubleday & Co., 1953.

Grandy, Moses. *Narrative of the Life of Moses Grandy.* Boston: Oliver Johnson, 1844.

Gray, Thomas. *Confessions of Nat Turner.* 1831; in Herbert Aptheker, *Nat Turner's Slave Rebellion.*

Henson, Josiah. *Father Henson's Story of His Own Life.* New York: Corinth Books, 1962.

Herndon, Angelo. *Let Me Live.* New York: Random House, 1937.

Hudson, Hosea. *Black Worker in the Deep South.* New York: International Publishers, 1972.

Hughes, Langston. *The Big Sea.* New York: Alfred A. Knopf, 1940.

————. *I Wonder As I Wander.* New York: Hill & Wang, 1956; rpt. New York: Hill & Wang, American Century, 1964.

Jackson, George. *Soledad Brother: The Prison Letters of George Jackson.* New York: Coward, McCann, 1970; rpt. New York: Bantam, 1970.

Johnson, James Weldon. *Along This Way.* New York: Viking Press, 1933.

Kaplan, Sidney. "Lewis Temple and the Hunting of the Whale." *New England Quarterly*, March, 1953, pp. 78ff.

————. "Towards Pip and Dagoo: Footnote on Melville's Youth." *Phylon*, 29 (Fall 1968), 291–302.

Lacy, Leslie Alexander. *The Rise and Fall of a Proper Negro.* New York: Macmillan, 1970; rpt. New York: Pocket Books, 1971.

Lester, Julius. *Look Out, Whitey! Black Power's Gonna Get Your Mama.* New York: Dial Press, 1968.

———. *Search for the New Land.* New York: Dial Press, 1969; rpt. New York: Dell, 1970.

———. *To Be A Slave.* New York: Dial Press, 1968.

Mailer, Norman. *The Prisoner of Sex.* New York: Signet, 1971.

Malcolm X. *The Autobiography of Malcolm X.* New York: Grove Press, 1964.

Mars, James. *The Life of James Mars, a Slave.* Hartford, Conn., 1872.

Matthiessen, F. O. *American Renaissance.* London: Oxford University Press, 1941.

McKay, Claude. *A Long Way from Home.* New York: Lee Furman, 1937.

Melville, Herman. *Moby Dick.* New York: Modern Library, 1950.

Miller, Ruth, ed. *Blackamerican Literature.* Beverly Hills: Glencoe Press, 1971.

Moody, Anne. *Coming of Age in Mississippi.* New York: Dial Press, 1968.

Nichols, Charles. *Many Thousand Gone.* Netherlands, 1963.

Northup, Solomon. *Twelve Years a Slave.* Auburn, Buffalo, & London, 1853.

Pennington, J. W. C. *The Fugitive Blacksmith.* London, 1849.

Quarles, Benjamin. "Narrative of the Life of Frederick Douglass." *Landmarks of American Writing.* Ed. Hennig Cohen. New York: Basic Books, 1969. 90–100.

Reeves, Donald. *Notes of a Processed Brother.* New York: Pantheon Books, 1971.

Redding, J. Saunders. *No Day of Triumph.* New York: Harper & Bros., 1942.

Robeson, Paul. *Here I Stand.* Boston: Beacon Press, 1958.

Seale, Bobby. *Seize the Time.* New York: Random House, 1970; rpt. New York: Vintage, 1970.

Spiller, Robert E., et. al. *Literary History of the United States.* 3rd ed. New York: Macmillan, 1963.

Starling, Marion Wilson. "The Slave Narrative: Its Place in American Literary History." Diss. New York University, 1946.

Stroyer, Jacob. *My Life in the South.* Salem, Mass.: Newcomb & Gauss, 1898.

Styron, William. *The Confessions of Nat Turner.* New York: Random House, 1967.

Thompson, John. *The Life of John Thompson, a Fugitive Slave.* 1856; rpt. Westport, Conn.: Negro Universities Press, 1968.

Truth, Sojourner. *Narrative of Sojourner Truth.* Boston, 1875.

Turner, Nat. *The Confessions of Nat Turner.* See Gray, Thomas.

Vonnegut, Kurt, Jr. *Cat's Cradle.* New York: Holt, Rinehart & Winston, 1963; rpt. New York: Dell, 1970.

Walker, David. *Appeal in Four Articles.* 2nd ed. Boston, 1830; rpt. New York: Arno Press & The New York Times, 1969.

Ward, Samuel. *Autobiography of a Fugitive Negro.* 1855; rpt. New York: Arno Press & The New York Times, 1968.

Washington, Booker T. *Up from Slavery*. New York: Doubleday, Page & Co., 1901.

Wells, Ida. *Crusade for Justice: The Autobiography of Ida B. Wells*. Chicago: University of Chicago Press, 1970.

Wright, Richard. *Black Boy*. 1937; rpt. New York: Perennial, 1966.

————. *Native Son*. 1940; rpt. New York: Perennial, 1966.

Yetman, Norman R. *Life Under the 'Peculiar Institution': Selections from the Slave Narrative Collection*. New York: Holt, Rinehart & Winston, 1970.

Index